GEMSTONES

Symbols of Beauty and Power

Eduard Gübelin, Lucerne
Franz-Xaver Erni, Baden

With photographic contributions by

Erica and Harold Van Pelt, Los Angeles

GEMSTONES

Symbols of Beauty and Power

GEOSCIENCE PRESS, Inc.

Tucson, Arizona

A production of
EMB-Service for Publishers,
Lucerne

© 1999 EMB-Service for
Publishers, Lucerne

English Edition

© 2000 Geoscience Press, Inc., Tucson, Arizona

Library of Congress Control Number: 00-130956

ISBN 0–945005–36–9

Design and concept:
Franz Gisler, Lucerne

Editing:
Eduard Gübelin, Lucerne

Typesetting:
SatzWeise, Föhren, Germany

Photolithos:
Job Color srl, Gorle (Bergamo)

Printing:
Milanostampa S.p.A., Farigliano

Printed in Italy

Page 2: The use of blue benitoites, which are only found in one place on Earth, elevates this necklace to a position of unparalleled rarity.
Fifty-two brilliant-cut benitoites with a total weight of 33 carats (the largest weighs 2.84 carats) and accompanied by seventy-five small diamonds, set in yellow gold.
Designed by McDonald's Jewelry, Fresno, California (USA). Collection: Michael M. Scott, San José, California. Photo: Erica and Harold Van Pelt, Los Angeles.

Right: Unusual intergrowth of bi-color tourmaline crystals from William Larson's Stuart Mine in the Pala Mountains, California (USA).
Next to it, a step-cut, red-green colored tourmaline of 21.50 carats from the same location.
Photo: Erica and Harold Van Pelt, Los Angeles.

7 Flowers of the mineral kingdom

8 Gemstones: their characteristics and their origin
Eduard Gübelin

8 The exquisite rarity

16 The causes of color variety

20 A commitment to eternity

24 Gemstones: their extraction and processing
Eduard Gübelin

24 The extraction of gemstones

32 The cutting of diamonds

34 The cutting of color gemstones

36 Polishing agate

37 Glyptography

40 Portraits of the gemstones
Eduard Gübelin

42 The beauty of color gems

44 The beauty of the phenomenon gems

46 Diamond: king of gemstones

56 Corundum: the colorful palette

60 Ruby: divine crystal spark

66 Sapphire: symbol of the firmament

72 Beryl: the palette of pastel colors

76 Emerald: glittering like leaves in may

82 Chrysoberyls: an exquisite trio

86 Feldspars: a major company

90 Garnets: a courtly household of noble vassals

94 Opal: hummingbird and firebird

100 Peridot: green-golden ray of sunshine

104 Quartz: bustling globetrotter

108 Spinel: the corundum's disguised twin

112 Spodumene: phoenix from the ashes

114 Tanzanite: blue patrician from black africa

118 Topaz: chalice of golden crystal

122 Tourmaline: alpha and omega

126 Zircon: dizzying quick-change artist

130 Portraits of ornamental gems
Eduard Gübelin

132 The beauty of ornamental gems

134 Agate: fire and flames

136 Charoite: reed pipes from the russian karst

138 Jade: metaphor for luck

142 Lapis lazuli: incarnation of the starry firmament

144 Malachite: master of the green shades

146 Rhodochrosite and rhodonite

148 Sugilite: budding mallow spur

150 Turquoise: morning fresh bloom of heaven

152 Gemstones: symbols of authority and power
Franz-Xaver Erni

174 Exquisite treasures

180 Noble gems for the word of god

188 Votive and consecration crowns

194 Beauty, magic, and medicine
Franz-Xaver Erni

194 Famous jewels and their histories

202 Of seals, amultes, and talismans

208 Stones of the month – birthstones

214 Gemstone medicine

218 The fascination of internal life
Eduard Gübelin

222 A passion for collecting
Eduard Gübelin

226 Natural or not?
Synthetics, composites, imitations
Eduard Gübelin

230 Glossary

233 Bibliography

234 Picture credits

240 Index

The colors shown here are not the actual colors of the Boulder opal but a play of color, which is dependent on incident light and caused by diffraction, changing constantly when the stone is moved. The ideal behavior of the color interplay (small picture) consists in the changing color flashes of all the spectral colors of violet, blue, green, yellow, orange and red.
Collection: Eduard Gübelin, Lucerne.
Photos: James G. Perret, Lucerne.

"Look at the gemstone, how firmly enclosed within itself,
how impenetrable, cast in one piece!
It does not keep foreign influence at bay,
its impenetrability is penetrated by heat and light.
And its own color that it has absorbed
In its way, change comes easy.
One minute it sparkles with fire, the next it languishes in matt effect
And iridesces according to how it is viewed.
A lightweight cloud swimming in its lightness
Even changes place which makes you marvel.
Do not marvel but learn a lesson
From the gemstone when you are like it at celebrations.
No heart can enclose itself in itself so rigidly
That no sympathy for the world flows through it.
If you are as hard as it is, then also be as pure
And decorate God's world only as a gemstone."

Friederich Rückert

Driven by an eternal thirst for knowledge, humans have largely robbed nature of its secrets. Gemstones are one exception to this proposition. Despite the most advanced classification methods and the use of modern instrumentation, gemstones still remain in many respects a book with seven seals.

As we enter the twenty-first century, gemstones have lost none of the fascination that they hold for humans. In ancient times, colorful pebbles polished by the ocean waves were collected as "gemstones." The earliest seal cylinders and gems have come down to us from the ancient cultures of the Sumerians, Babylonians, and Egyptians. Instead of adorning themselves with massive lions' manes, men in prehistoric times decked themselves with precious jewels to gain the favor of women. However, Eve's daughters did not begin to adorn themselves with jewelry until much later. In ancient times, gemstones were also in demand as offerings to the gods. But it was not until the fifteenth century that Saint Hieronymous – who already appreciated the value of these sparkling rarities – devoted his attention to the relationship between the twelve gemstones that decorated the breastplate of the high priest in Jerusalem, the twelve months of the year, and the twelve signs of the zodiac. It appears that the assignment of gemstones to the individual zodiac signs started in Poland after the twelfth century when they were designated as birthstones. Since then the composition of the birthstones or month stones has changed many times, the last time being in the mid-twentieth century. In the Middle Ages – before the art of gem cutting was understood – these flowers of the mineral kingdom became the objects of ambiguous symbolism in crowns and scepters. No attempt was made to cut the matte and rather unappealing pebbles until the Renaissance: what radiant luminosity! Such artistic fireworks bursting forth with a wealth of powerful colors! Nowadays, due to a viewpoint largely liberated of any emotion and enveloped in scientific modernity, gemstones are rightfully considered to be the best and most compact way of preserving capital. In contrast to earlier times, however, elevation to the "royal status of gemstone" is limited to those minerals that possess the three ennobling virtues: beauty, rarity, and durability. These alone bestow dignity and value.

The purpose of this book is to guide the layperson with illustrations and text into one of nature's most fascinating puzzles without any need for a specialist's knowledge. Descriptions of the complex physical properties of gemstones have been omitted since the focus is on introducing readers to the beauty of a product of nature. If some additional knowledge about the natural forces at work together in the earth's core can be conveyed, the aim of this volume has been more than met. The next visit to a jewelry store will be made under different conditions, and handling items of jewelry already owned will be marked by a greater appreciation of their value and beauty. While the topic will naturally appeal to the fairer sex in particular, the "Lords of creation" are, apparently, no less interested in an in-depth look at gemstones. Their roles are not only as buyers but also as wearers of jewelry.

INTRODUCTION
FLOWERS
OF THE MINERAL
KINGDOM

GEMSTONES

THEIR CHARACTERISTICS AND THEIR ORIGIN

Above: The octahedral diamond crystal sits on an ultramafic garnet-lherzolite. It came out of the volcanic kimberlite to an area of the Earth's crust where it was accessible to humsns after crystallizing as an accessory product of a lherzolite metamorphism at a depth of around 150 kilometers and under pressures of approximately 40,000 to 60,000 kbar and temperatures of around 1,250°C. Collection: Houston Museum, Houston, Texas (USA). Photo: Erica and Harold Van Pelt, Los Angeles.

Opposite: Magnificent, euhedral crystals, emerald crystal on calcite and quartz from the hydrothermal deposits of the Muzo Mine, Colombia. Collection: Mineralogical Institute of the University of Zurich, Switzerland. Photo: James G. Perret, Lucerne.

THE EXQUISITE RARITY

Knowledge of the rarity and high value of gemstones also raises questions about their origins and formation. The answers can be compared to a voyage of discovery into the past. This voyage takes us to the earth's core, directly to the birthplace of gemstones. There, in the deepest depths, the formation process starts with the most commonplace matter that the earth contains: carbon (C); clay (alumina, Al_2O_3); silica (silicon dioxide, SiO_2); lime (calcium carbonate, $CaCO_3$); magnesia (MgO); alkalis (sodium oxide, Na_2O and potassium oxide, K_2O); and many others. These substances are by no means rare and can be found practically everywhere in the world. Nevertheless, gemstones are of exceptional rarity. For gemstones to be formed, however, another condition comes into play: the harmonization of place and time. The crystallization properties of the basic material, the presence of a colorant, as well as external conditions such as pressure, temperature, and the composition of the nutrient solutions are also necessary. If all the conditions for the development of a rare mineral of simple composition are present, an extremely rare colorant might be responsible for the formation of a gemstone (e. g., chromium in the case of alexandrite, ruby, and emerald; without this colorant, these gemstones would only be colorless chrysoberyl, corundum, and beryl). The color can, however, be attributable to rare crystal lattice distortions (e.g., green diamonds). In other gemstones of more complex structures, rarity depends on an important yet scarce component, such as fluorine in topaz and boron in tourmaline. In a third group, the mineral crystallization is truly unique: The chemical elements involved in formation were only present at one time and in one single location on earth (as in the case of the benitoite, red beryl, blue tanzanite, green tsavolite, and many others).

The vast majority of gemstones are formed as crystals. Their growth is determined by strict rules that can be explained with the help of a few models. One model dictates the structural elements – two atoms in close proximity – one is always positively charged and the other negatively charged. These inversely charged atoms, called ions, attract each other. This power of attraction is called cohesion and influences the consistency of the crystals. In favorable conditions, inversely charged ions combine by melting, in solutions and gases, and form rows, join up to form flat planes, and develop into voluminous crystal lattices arranged according to a specific order. The inner stacking is expressed in well-ordered, multi-surface architecture – crystals that look as if sculptured by a chisel. In this way, a three-dimensional, symmetrical structure of the atoms of complex design is created. The various types of atomic bonds lead to differing degrees of hardness in the gemstones – one of their additional, essential virtues.

How are the birthplaces of gemstones distinguished from ordinary earth? The processes that the earth's crust has undergone during its different developmental stages have led to the creation of a wide variety of mineral deposits. These processes are controlled by two closely con-

GEOLOGICAL FORMATIONS AND ROCKS

1 Red
Early magmatic phase, for example, gabbro (chromite, pyrrhotite, titanomagnetite)
2 Purple
Main liquid magmatic crystallization, for example, plutonite (euclase, cassiterite, topaz, etc.)
3 Red-purple
Phase of residual crystallization (accumulation of volatile elements)
4 Rose red
Pegmatites (beryls, chrysoberyls, feldspars, garnets, topazes, tourmalines, etc.)
5 Light blue
Pneumatolytic formations (euclase, cassiterite, scheelite, topaz, etc.)
6 Lilac
Hot solutions along fissure systems (hydrothermal phase) barite, beryls, fluorite, quartzes, tourmaline, precious metals)
7 Fracture system (faults)
Metamorphic-metasomatic phase, for example, crystalline schist, marbles, skarns, and so forth (alexandrite, jasper, ruby, sapphire, emerald, spinel, etc.)
8 Yellow wavy
Sedimentary deposits and transformations (rivers, lakes, seas) (azurite, malachite, turquoise, chrysocolla, etc.)
9 Lilac blue
Hydrothermal boiling. Chaotic, fast sprouting of gemstones in vein systems (fluorapatite, fluorite, quartz, topaz, etc.)
10 Olive green
Contact metamorphism (low pressure, high temperatures); (enstatite, olivine, emerald, etc.)
11 Orange
Regional metamorphism (high pressure, medium to high temperatures); (corundum, e.g. ruby in gneiss, spinel, etc.)
12 Dull red
Basement rock, high-quality metamorphites (andalusite, sapphirine, etc.)
13 Bright red
Extrusive volcanism, basalts (peridot in lava, e.g., Hawaii), sapphires in Australia, Cambodia, Thailand, and Vietnam
14 Glowing red
Diamond-bearing volcanic pipes erupt (e.g., kimberlite as a diamond-bearing rock transporter). Diamonds formed at depths of approximately 150–200 kilometers.

White
Formation places for gemstones

Black
Fractures with hydrothermal systems

nected events. Under the earth's crust and deep in the earth's interior, there is first a zone of firm rock stratum (continental or oceanic crust) that follows the rigid zone of the earth's upper mantle. From a chemical standpoint, the rock stratum in this zone is of a completely different composition to that of the earth's crust: this is peridotite (rich in magnesium [Mg], relatively poor in silicon [Si], aluminum [Al] and chromium [Cr]). To some extent, molten rock material (magma, from the Greek *magis* [kneaded mass]) can already be present in these upper

zones that go down to less than roughly 100-150 kilometers into the earth (e.g., kimberlite pipes with diamond deposits). Beneath these, there are further zones in the earth's mantle and core down to a depth of around 6,370 kilometers. Today, it is known that the formation of gemstones took place mainly in the outer layers of the earth, that is, in the earth's crust (down to a depth of around 40 km) and in the earth's upper mantle (beneath the earth's crust). Diamonds come from the highest area of the earth's mantle, arriving at the surface by means of pipes that have broken through. The pyrope may also have the same origins. Some portion of the Indochinese and Australian sapphires and rubies and some zircons reached the earth's surface in a similar way, that is to say with basalt lava flows. However, the majority of gemstone formation processes took place within the earth's crust. They were caused by mountain-forming processes and the corresponding layering of a wide variety of rocks, the earth's crust, and the earth's mantle and the sinking of these into the depths, resulting in a complete or partial melting of the rocks. These mountain-forming cycles happened billions of years ago. Mountains of this age, with the encapsulation of a wide variety of rock types, are only preserved within the old areas of the continents (shield areas), often in truncated mountains, that is, mountains that have been almost completely eroded (e.g., the Urals with deposits of emeralds and alexandrite). Over the course of many hundreds of millions of years, this process not only eroded the mountains but also a major section of the upper continental crust. Hence, it is possible to view the lowest layers in the earth's crust that originally lay 40 to 70 kilometers deep in the earth but now outcrop on the earth's surface. The areas of the continental subcrust, as it is known, are particularly informative for an understanding of the processes that led to the formation of primary gemstone deposits.

To simplify things, a differentiation can be made between the two distinct processes responsible for gemstone formation: liquid-magmatic-hydrothermal formation and the formation of metamorphic gemstone deposits. To gain a better understanding of the gemstone formation processes, the following four phases can be defined within the liquid magmatic cycle: an older liquid magmatic phase (1,300°C to 700°C), followed by the pegmatite phase (700°C to 550°C), the pneumatolytic (550°C to 450°C), and the hydrothermal phase (450°C to 100°C).

Some examples of igneous rocks of this type are granite, diorite, and gabbro. Depending on magma composition, the most important rock-forming minerals such as mica, feldspar, quartz and olivine are deposited in strict order. The gemstone labradorite, with its variety spectrolite, as well as peridot and some of the zircons also originate from this oldest rock-forming phase. Apatite, beryl, spinel, tourmaline, and so forth were present as accessory minerals but only in microscopically small sizes.

Within the liquid-magmatic cycle, the magmas went through different stages in their crystallization. Pegmatites (from the Greek *pegma* [something joined together]), which can only be formed after a series of different rocks have been crystallized out during the liquid magmatic phase, are final rock types that are important for the formation of gemstones in this cycle. Specific elements that are difficult to incorporate in minerals are enriched in pegmatites. These enriched elements are the rare earths as well as fluorine, boron, phosphorus, sulfur, uranium, zirconium, and so forth, and precious and heavy metals. The molten mass, rich in liquid and formed by heat and high pressure, remaining after the crystallization phases encountered conditions that were beneficial for growth, particularly when they could interact with adjacent rock. Corresponding to the special conditions under which the crystallization of the pegmatites took place, the crystals achieved the required purity and size necessary to become gemstones. The cavities that exist in many of the pegmatite regions are well known as sources of exceptionally beautiful crystals. The largest crystals are frequently found in the area of pegmatitic gemstone formation; it is simultaneously the most important formation site for gemstones. For example, this is the source of apatite, beryl (aquamarine), chrysoberyl, euclase, kunzite, moonstone, sapphire, topaz, tourmaline, again some of the zircons, as well as a lot of other, less significant gemstones.

Top: Two bi-color tourmaline crystals intergrown with orange morganite and white quartz from the pegmatite of Queen Mine, San Diego County, California (USA). Collection: William Larson, Fallbrook, California (USA). Photo: Erica and Harold Van Pelt, Los Angeles.

Center: Light blue aquamarine crystal embedded between white pegmatitic rock and dark muscovite mica. Found at Dusso near Skardu, Pakistan. Collection: Eduard Gübelin. Photo: Erich Offermann, Arlesheim.

Bottom: With obliquely angled incident light, the cleavage surface of the spectrolite radiates intense and lively spectral colors, to which this ornamental gem owes its name. It comes from a mine near Ylämaa, Finland. Museum a. d. Felsenkirche, Idar-Oberstein.

Top: The red beryl crystal on white rhyolite rock is of pneumatolytic origin and comes from the Wah-Wah Mountains, Utah (USA). Collection: Eduard Gübelin, Lucerne. Photo: James G. Perret, Lucerne.

Center: These sapphires from the snow-white skarn rock near Andranondambo, Madagascar, are the characteristic products of metasomatic processes. Collection and photo: A. Peretti, Adligenswil.

Bottom: Rock crystals accompanied by pink fluorite from Alpine hydrothermal mineral fissures in the Swiss Alps are highly prized by all mineral collectors. Collection: Eduard Gübelin, Lucerne. Photo: James G. Perret, Lucerne.

In the subsequent cooling-down phase, that is, in the postmagmatic residual molten rock, the volatile components were mostly enriched more strongly. In the meantime, they can be highly complex in composition (e.g., solutions rich in salt and methane as well as containing acids or gas and aqueous solutions). The pneumatolytic deposits (Greek *pneuma* [breath or wind], *lyein* [to dissolve]) were formed from these. Even more intense than the pegmatitic mineral solutions, the highly reactive pneumatolytic mineral solutions penetrated into the cracks and crevices of limestone, dolomites, peridotites, and argillite, to name just a few examples of rock. Since these fluids are derived from the magmatic cycle, they are generally not compatible with such types of rock and an intense chemical reaction takes place. A lively exchange of substances is initiated that leads to transformations in the neighboring rocks or metasomatism, as it is called (e.g., emerald formation in Brazil, Russia, and Africa or sapphire formation on Madagascar). The gemstones originating from these deposits have become world famous as a result of their diverse mineral groupings (paragenesis, from the Greek *para* [alongside] and *genesis* [formation]) and their superbly shaped crystals, such as those on Sri Lanka and at Mogok in Myanmar (formerly Burma). The outcome of a complicated combination of other processes with a metasomatic phase includes rubies and sapphires (North Vietnam, Myanmar, and Sri Lanka), emeralds in schist (Zambia, Tanzania, and Transvaal), together with alexandrite in biotite schist (Urals) as well as lapis lazuli in limestone (Afghanistan and Chile).

The most recent and relatively cooled consolidation of the magmatic formation cycle is formed by the hydrothermal phase (Greek *hydor* [water] and *thermos* [hot]). During this phase, hot and differently composed solutions with specific salt, water, carbon dioxide, methane, sulfur, or nitrogen content rose from the depths and were forced into the cracks and fissures of the surrounding rocks. The components of these hydrothermal solutions were primarily silica and a multitude of dissolved elements such as aluminum, magnesium, calcium, alkalis, and scant quantities of elements such as uranium, rare earths, and heavy metals. Dissolved particles were able to crystallize as a result of processes such as cooling, a decrease in pressure, and a reaction from the surrounding rocks. Fluorite originates in this hydrothermal phase as do varieties of the quartz group: amethyst, rock crystal, smoky quartz, and citrine, as well as the precious tourmaline and, to some extent, too, topaz. The emerald from the argillaceous limestone schists of Colombia (Muzo, Chivor) is also of hydrothermal origin. In addition, hydrothermal parageneses are of major economic importance: They are the most important suppliers of gold, silver, copper, lead, zinc, uranium, and other heavy metals.

The metamorphic cycle is an important stage in the formative process of gemstones. It comprises the large group of gneiss rocks, crystalline schists, marbles, and other rocks. Originally resulting from existing magmatic or sedimentary rocks, these rocks underwent recrystallization (metamorphism) under the influence of pressure, heat, and circulating solutions. Metamorphism is generally linked with the rise of magmatic molten masses or with rock-formation processes; unilateral pressure will frequently create a subsequent rock with a schistlike structure. Gneiss and the mica schists, serpentines, and marbles are better known crystalline schists. In the case of these metamorphic rocks, a completely new mineral developed from a group of them without the chemistry of the rocks having been changed in any significant way. In the case of rocks that have sunk to a great depth within the earth, this process largely takes place where they reach zones with relatively high temperatures and pressures. In the wide variety of rocks in those zones, metamorphic gemstones are formed, such as peridot in serpentinites, emeralds in amphibole and mica schists, jadeite in metamorphic gneiss, as well as ruby, sapphire, and spinel in metamorphic carbonates. Some examples of jadeite metamorphic gemstones are found in Myanmar and spinel, sapphire, and ruby gemstones are found in Myanmar and Sri Lanka.

The cycle of weathering processes prior to the final rock-formation tends to be rather poor for gemstones. There are only five weathered products among the select circle of gemstones: turquoise, chrysoprase, opal, malachite, and azurite. Turquoise is a superb random product that is formed by the weathering of acidic, magmatic rock types in combination with the decomposition of neighboring copper ores. Hot water (meteoric water) circulated freely in the decomposing rock and reacted with feldspar and apatite in the magmatic rock, supplying important components for the formation of turquoise. The copper colorant was incorporated into the rock by sprinkles of the copper mineral in the rock. Chrysoprase is the end product of a long chain of unique transformation and enrichment processes with the involvement of alkaline rocks containing nickel. It was formed in the fissures and hollow spaces of the weathering mass as a new formation in the shape of a finely fibrous quartz. The influence of the nickel content in the rock led to the development of a green color. Opals were formed during the course of steady, undisturbed thermal and chemical changes in basalt or sandstones. Green malachite and blue azurite were formed by the superficial weathering of copper ores under the influence of water and other dissolved components.

These primary birthplaces of gemstones, as they are called, are also the present-day location of the deposits. An understanding of these fantastic aspects of the existence, the rarity, and the preciousness of gemstones is sure to grow with the turbulent story of their formation. The secondary deposits, however, also merit our attention.

The final, rock-forming sedimentary cycle is of subordinate or of no importance at all for the actual formation of gemstones; in contrast, however, it is of major importance as their source. Most gemstones are obtained from sedimentary deposits. The gemstones lie well preserved in weathering debris that built up during the decomposition of the rock. They are discovered by washing out. These types of deposits are referred to as "alluvial placers." Due to the effect of water and air, soil acids, temperature fluctuations, and the influence of glaciers, gravel, sands, and clay are created from the weathering boulders that, in turn, form new rocks, such as conglomerates, sandstones, and argillite. Mechanical weathering is supported by a simultaneous chemical weather-

Top: The three brothers in phanerocrystalline quartz: rock crystal, amethyst, and citrine are mostly the product of hydrothermal solutions. The group shown is a cluster of citrines rarely encountered in Nature.

Center: These properly developed octahedral spinel crystals have grown on metamorphic marble in the Hunza valley, Pakistan. Collection: Eduard Gübelin, Lucerne. Photo: Max Weibel, Pfaffhausen.

Bottom: The rubies in the dolomitic marbles near Mogok, Myanmar, in the Hunza valley, Pakistan, Luc Yen, Vietnam, Jagdalek, Afghanistan, and several other places also owe their existence to metamorphic processes. They grew as the last generation after the magnesium became exhausted. Collection: Eduard Gübelin, Lucerne. Photo: Erich Offermann, Arlesheim.

Top: Broad veins of chrysoprase permeate a limonited, nickel-containing serpentinite in the Haneti hills, Tanzania, in which they were formed as a secondary mineral after several transformations. Collection and photo: Eduard Gübelin, Lucerne.

Center: Sawed jadeite blocks in the inventory of a jade dealer in Mogaung, Myanmar. Photo: Eduard Gübelin, Lucerne.

Bottom: Hand-size piece of volcanic trachyte that has an irregular coating of turquoise and was the result of the weathering of its host rock. Found near Madan in the Kuh-i-Binalud mountains near Nishapur, eastern Iran. Collection and photo: Eduard Gübelin, Lucerne.

Opposite: The paragenetic deposition of rose red rhodochrosite and rock crystal in a mineral fissure in the Peruvian Cordilleras is of hydrothermal origin. Collection: Smithsonian Institution, Washington, D.C. (USA). Photo: Erica and Harold Van Pelt, Los Angeles.

ing. The latter also creates new rock products, for example, limestone layers in a wide variety of shapes such as those seen in stalactite caves.

As gemstones are swept away by the water, they intermingle with the weathering sediments in beds and deposits. At this stage, they are sorted according to specific criteria: density, size, resistance, and quality (e.g., large gemstones with cracks rarely survive water transportation undamaged). Sorting according to density, for example, works like this: Heavy gemstones sink faster and therefore collect in hollows or "pockets," as they are called. Specialists call this process "natural selection." For this reason, these secondary deposits are also frequently called placer deposits or alluvial placers. Placers are to be found in today's riverbeds and valley bottoms as well as in older river terraces and hills along the banks at higher elevations, where rivers no longer exist. The jadeite deposits in the conglomerate hills along the Uyu River in northern Myanmar are one example of this process. The secondary deposits are an exquisite gift to humans by nature. The deposits in the placers have not only created a natural selection of top quality stones but are also fairly inexpensive to extract. One interesting example of a gemstone that is to be found both in primary and secondary deposits is the zircon. It is particularly resistant, surviving not only the sedimentary cycle but also the mountain-forming process. Embedded in alluvial sediments, zircons can be repeatedly plunged into the depths of the earth during the course of the earth's history where they are melted down again into magmatic rock or become embedded in rock layers of intense metamorphism. The zircons survive all these processes in barely changed or in slightly rounded form and are later even in a position to grow further. Zircons therefore occasionally have a zonary structure: Old cores billions of years old are surrounded by rims that are only a few hundred million years old. As a unique example, zircon can have been included in almost all the formation processes of gemstone deposits described here. Minerals of this type are called renegade minerals.

A look at the existence of gemstone deposits on a global scale indicates the increased presence of gemstones in one specific region: in rock formations that are over 200 million years old. Frequently, these rock formations are composed of highly metamorphic rocks that can be found deep under young, as yet uneroded mountains. In these depths of the earth, rocks are also formed in a liquid magmatic and hydrothermal cycle. These gemstone-bearing lower regions of the Earth's crust are only exposed after hundreds of millions of years of continuous erosion (e.g., in South Africa, Brazil, Myanmar, India, Sri Lanka, and Madagascar). These gemstone deposits are found either in former riverbeds within sedimentary placers or, more rarely, as primary deposits. These are frequently rocks from the ancient mountain chains that were once united on the original continent – the legendary Gondwanaland. This region is particularly old and has undergone intense and penetrating erosion as it continues doing today in the tropics, the former Gondwanaland, around the Equator. Gondwanaland covered today's continents of South America, Africa, and Australia together with the Indian subcontinent and the islands of Madagascar and Sri Lanka.

THE CAUSES OF COLOR VARIETY

The most eye-catching feature of gemstones is undoubtedly their wealth of colors. In an array that spans the two extremes of infinite delicacy and exuberant power, the stones bewitch and dazzle the eyes of their beholders deep into the subconscious. Research into gemstone colors is one of the most exciting aspects of gemology. Optics and chemistry, as

A delight to behold – crystallized colors kissed to life by the light! Collection: Michael M. Scott. Photo: Erica and Harold Van Pelt, Los Angeles.

well as the science of the construction and the powers of atoms combine – remote from the limitations of space and time – in these crystalline miracles.

The far-reaching influence that light undergoes as it passes through a gemstone and the colors it creates nowadays can largely be explained in terms of a chemical-physical reaction. Color is created by a change in the nature and the behavior of light as it enters and passes through the gemstone. Gemology accordingly makes a distinction between the three main causes of color creation: chemical, physical, and optical.

1. Colors Created Chemically

In the case of chemically created colors, electromagnetic energy (i.e., wavelengths = colors) is extracted from the light. The wavelengths that are not absorbed, that is, the remaining color components of the incident white light, radiate from the gemstone to the amazement of the observer. Transition elements as they are known (titanium, vanadium, chromium, manganese, iron, cobalt, nickel, and copper) and, occasionally, the rare

Idiochromatic coloration
A gemstone is self-colored if an effective coloring element is simultaneously a constituting component of its chemical composition, for example, iron (Fe) in peridot [(Mg, Fe)$_2$SiO$_4$] and in almandine [Fe$_3$Al$_2$(SiO$_4$)$_3$] or copper (Cu) in malachite [Cu$_2$(CO$_3$)(OH)].

Peridot

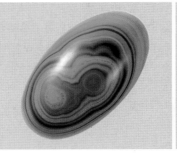

Malachite

Almandine

Red coloration caused by chromium oxide
In allochromatic gemstones, an alien ion that is not part of the gemstone's chemical composition is responsible for the color, for example, chromium oxide in the red gemstones ruby, pyrope garnet, and spinel.

Ruby

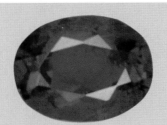

Pyrope

Spinel

Green coloration caused by chromium oxide
Some chromium oxide is similarly responsible for the green color of the gemstones demantoid, emerald, and tsavolite (in the case of tsavolite garnet, in combination with vanadium).

Demantoid

Emerald

Tsavolite

Different colors due to iron oxide
Depending on the valence of the colorant ion, the varieties of a gemstone species have different colors: bivalent iron (Fe^{2+}) colors a beryl blue (aquamarine), trivalent iron (Fe^{3+}) creates a gold beryl, and the mixture of both iron valences results in a green beryl.

Aquamarine

Green beryl

Gold beryl

Quartz colors have different causes
Chromophores factors are completely lacking in the colorless rock crystal.
Amethyst owes its violet color to the admixture of iron in the lattices of the silica in the quartz structure. As a consequence a color center ensues. When heated to over 400°C, the amethyst's color centers change and a yellow to yellow to brown citrine results.

Rock crystal

Amethyst

Citrine

Color caused by irradiation (smoky quartz)

Color caused by diffraction (opal)

Color caused by interference (labradorite)

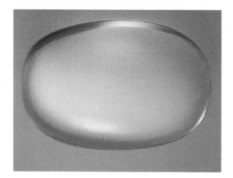

Color caused by scattering (moonstone)

earths of the periodic system are the reason for this occurrence. If these are the main constituent elements in the chemical composition of a gemstone, this is called idiochromatic coloration, for example, iron in almandine garnet and peridot, and manganese in rhodochrosite and rhodonite. These types of gemstones occur in one single color and are fairly constant in their coloration. There are no colorless gemstones in this group of idiochromatic (self-colored) minerals.

Allochromatic coloration is caused by the integration of one or several of these transition elements (there are only ever traces of them and, for this reason, they are also called trace elements) into the structural crystal lattice. This occurs either substitially on the latticework of an important chemical constituent, for example, chromium instead of aluminum in ruby or emerald, or interstitially, that is, somewhere between the constitutional elements; one example of this is nitrogen in yellow, brown, and green diamonds. Without the integration of these foreign elements, the large group of allochromatic (foreign-colored) gemstones would be entirely colorless, as are such gemstones as diamonds, beryls, corundums, topazes, and tourmalines.

Depending on the chemical composition of a specific pigment and its emplacement in the crystal lattice, it can create totally different colors, for example, chromium gives ruby and spinel their red colors, whereas emerald and demantoid turn green. These chromophoric (colorant) foreign elements entered the host mineral as ultrafine metallic vapor in the loosest form of dispersion that can only be demonstrated spectroscopically. Generally speaking, their proportion accounts for barely more than 1 to 5 weight percent, a ludicrously small amount responsible for the transformation of a low-grade stone into a precious gemstone. The majority of the gemstones with which we are familiar have been "infiltrated" in this way.

2. Physical Coloration

Color creation in each individual gemstone is also dictated by its interaction with light, its life element. These phenomena, which are called structural colors, have a variety of causes:
1. Interference colors are produced by the superimposition of sets of light waves on thin films as a result of phase shifts, as they are known. In the shift of an entire phase, the spectral colors are either extinguished or increased. In the case of less or more than one phase, they interfere with each other and form parallel spectral bands. This is how the miraculous color of the twinning and cleavage planes in labradorite (spectrolites) and, along inner cracks, the iridescence of iris quartz is caused.
2. Scattered colors are created by the reflection and dissipation of light on internal structural inhomogeneities, for example, on the structural unevenness in moonstone caused by exsolution, which is called adularescence. Scattered colors also can be produced by a particular angle of the crown facets by means of dispersion. If light falls on a transparent gemstone, it is separated into its spectral color components and is reflected as so-called "fire," for example, in the case of diamonds and

with slightly more intensity in the case of zircon, sphalerite, and sphene. The interaction of reflection and scattering on straight fibers and the finest tubules is expressed in the light phenomena of asterism (star formation) and the cat's-eye effect (chatoyancy).

3. Colors caused by diffraction occur in opal. On periodic latticework, there is a sharp deflection of the penetrating light, for example, in the spaces between the opal globules arranged in a lattice pattern. A similar effect is induced when viewing a bright streetlight from under an open umbrella.

4. Structurally based colors can be effectuated in two different ways. First, color centers can be the result of structural flaws. These could be, for example, voids in the crystal lattice. On their own or in combination with foreign elements, these structural flaws can generate colors, for example, in the pink diamond alone or with the interaction of iron in the case of amethyst. In addition, irradiation colors can occur in nature or can be produced in a laboratory through human intervention. Natural irradiation occurs, for example, as a result of radioactive elements (thorium, uranium), whereas artificial irradiation can be obtained by bombarding the elementary particles of the atom (protons, neutrons, electrons). The radiation damage caused by this irradiation also induces structural damage, which becomes effective as color centers. Furthermore, thermally created colors are achieved by heating precious and ornamental gems to temperatures of 400°C to 2,000°C. This color improvement is just as common in the case of agate as it is with aquamarine, amethyst, topaz, and tourmaline but it is also used for ruby and sapphire. An increase in color saturation by applying thermal treatment is possible for all colored gems. Using this technique, the ion valences within the gemstones (electrically charged atoms) are modified: a so-called charge transfer takes place. The charge transfer that takes place in sapphire, caused by heating, transfers bivalent iron + quadrivalent titanium into trivalent iron + trivalent titanium ($Fe^{2+} + Ti^{4+} + Fe^{3+} + Ti^{3+}$).

3. Color Caused by Optical Effects

Optically caused colors are also called colloidal colors. These are caused by light reflected from numerous, often flake- or scale-shaped, needlelike and fine-fibered inclusions that are closely packed in their colorless host mineral and impose their own color imprint on it due to incident light. Some examples of this type of color cause are the red hematite platelets in colorless oligoclase feldspar that, in this form, is called sunstone, and the so-called "bloodshot" cordierite or the green scaly fuchsite in colorless rock crystal that turns it into green aventurine. Many of the fine crystalline (cryptocrystalline) quartzes owe their distinctive appearance to such inclusions.

The breathtaking beauty of colored gemstones loses none of its power of attraction even when explained by physical and chemical processes. On the contrary, it is these secret pathways by which the primeval forces of the elements have paved the way in the formation of the gemstones and that continue to fill us with reverential awe to this very day.

Top: In spite of low refraction and the resultant glassy appearance, citrine can be transformed into a lively brilliant jewel by a well-designed cut. Collection: Gottlieb & Hahn, Idar-Oberstein.

Page 18, from top to bottom:
Smoky quartz: Radiation coloration
The smoke brown smoky quartz owes its color to the admixture of aluminum and lithium as well as to additional radioactive irradiation (color center). Heating transforms it into colorless rock crystal.
Opal: Diffraction coloration
The light penetrating the spaces between the minute globular components of opal is diffracted and fanned into its color components.
Labradorite: Interference coloration
The wavelengths of incident light are mutually displaced on the mineral's thin, twin lamellae. The resultant conflict is seen as combined colors by the human eye.
Moonstone: Scattered coloration (adularescence)
The delicate blue shimmer of the moonstone is based on the scattering of light on submicroscopically fine, regularly-arranged structural faults inside the mineral, the magnitude of which roughly corresponds to the wavelengths of the blue-green section of visible light (400–500 nm).

TOUGHNESS	
Natural glasses	10
Jade/ruby/hematite	8
Sapphire/diamond	7
Chrysoberyl/chalcedony/moldavite	7
Moldavite/obsidian	6.5–7
Quartz, crystalline/spinel	5.5–6.5
Beryl/pyrite	6
Zircon/emerald	5.5–6
Garnet/topaz/turquoise/peridot	5.5
Tourmaline/zircon (heated)/lazulite/benitoite/opal	5
Microcline (amazonite)/feldspar/spodumene	4
Malachite/rhodonite	3

GRINDING HARDNESS	
Scale of hardness (Rosival)	
Talc	0.03
Gypsum	1.25
Calcite	4.5
Fluorspar	5
Apatite	6.5
Feldspar	37
Quartz	120
Topaz	175
Corundum	1,000
Diamond	140,000

SCRATCH HARDNESS	
Scale of hardness (Mohs)	
Talc	1
Gypsum	2
Calcite	3
Fluorspar (fluorite)	4
Apatite	5
Feldspar (moonstone)	6
Quartz	7
Topaz	8
Corundum	9
Diamond	10

A Commitment to Eternity

Humans have left practically no stone unturned in their quest to leave a mark for posterity. They find the ideal symbol of permanence in gemstones, which hand down their sacrosanct beauty and godlike immortality. These characteristics are bestowed on gemstones as a result of their crystalline consistency, their hardness, and their indestructible resistance to chemical attack as well as the color-changing effects of light. They are immune to all harmful environmental influences that could damage their brilliance, their color, and their shape.

Gemstones owe their firmness to the small components that form the crystal as a whole. They are held together by electromagnetic cohesion (attraction) between oppositely charged atoms (positively and negatively charged ions). Their consistency describes the type of resistance with which gemstones resist any separation of their atoms or any change in their external form. Some minerals can be split up (cut or cleaved), others change their shape by hammering. Minerals that do not have sufficient strength break up into small pieces or even crumble to powder if enough force is exerted on them. This brittleness has a negative effect on the strength of minerals. For this reason, gemologists differentiate between tough gemstones and fragile or brittle gemstones. Toughness as a strength component plays a major role both in the processing and in the wearing of gemstones. In actual fact, some gemstones are less valuable than others simply because they are easier to split or break. A stone can be particularly tough without being necessarily particularly hard or vice versa, very hard but not particularly tough. Diamonds, for example, are notable for their hardness but are not very tough. In contrast, nephrite is extraordinarily tough, a feature attributable to the fact that it is not a monocrystal but is a compact, closely packed association of minerals – these are an interlocked mass of fibers and, in the case of jadeite, dovetailed, interlinked grains. A rule of thumb, therefore, for gemstone owners is that very tough gemstones are less of a problem to wear than those that are less tough yet hard, and that toughness and hardness should in no way be confused with each other. Rubies and sapphires have a high degree of toughness and, although they are hard, they cannot be cleaved. For this reason, they are of exceptional durability. In contrast, unpleasant experiences may be encountered with emeralds since they are classified as the most fragile representative of the beryls. Care is also required with topaz, peridot, tourmaline, opal, and spodumene. The cause of this fragility is solely the low level of cohesion along the crystal planes or along any irregular direction. Cleavage is in relation to the inner cohesion of the atoms and molecules. Cohesion might be weak in one particular direction and, when subjected to mechanical forces, a gemstone will more easily cleave parallel to a plane that corresponds to this weak direction. In contrast, however, if the stone has good cleavage and the gem cutter is aware of the direction of the cleavage plane, a slight tap frequently is sufficient to split the gemstone.

In some gemstones, the tendency to cleavage is very strong, in others it

Hardness 6 is considered to be the lower limit on the gemstone hardness scale. It is approximately 200 times harder than talc, the softest mineral, and approximately 5 times softer than corundum (ruby and sapphire). Very difficult to scratch with a knife.

Orthoclase   Moonstone   Labradorite   Spectrolite

Hardness 7, which corresponds to the hardness of quartz, is four times softer than corundum and will scratch window glass.

Rock crystal   Rose quartz   Ametrine   Citrine

Between hardness grades 7 and 8 are beryl (aquamarine, emerald), the garnets, tourmaline, and zircon.

Aquamarine (beryl)   Spessartite   Tourmaline   Zircon

Hardness 8 corresponds to the hardness of topaz and spinel, has half the hardness of corundum, and will slightly scratch rock crystal.

Spinel   Spinel   Topaz   Taaffeite

Hardness 9 corresponds to the hardness of corundum and is twice as hard as topaz but will not scratch it. However, it can be scratched slightly by a diamond.

Ruby   Sapphire   Padparadscha   Corundum

Hardness 10 is the maximum grade of hardness. This is where diamonds are positioned. No other natural substance achieves this hardness. A diamond is 140 times harder than corundum and will scratch all other natural materials.

Diamonds

The Crystal Systems

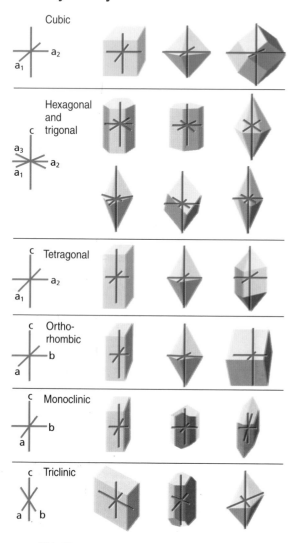

Cubic

Hexagonal and trigonal

Tetragonal

Ortho-rhombic

Monoclinic

Triclinic

This illustration depicts the six crystal systems with their axis arrangements (main axis and lateral axes) as well as the three main growth forms.

is even so marked that they must be treated with extreme care. These include apatite, euclase, fluorite, kunzite, moonstone, emerald, and topaz. A strong tap, for example, if dropped to the ground, knocked while wearing, or bumped together in a jewelry box as well as a sudden change in temperature can all cause cracking and thus substantially reduce the beauty and the value of a gem. For the classification of both raw and polished gemstones, the character of a break can provide decisive indications. The shell-like or conchoidal fracture is widespread among gemstones. Fractures in diamonds are typically stepped, whereas those of amethyst, citrine, and quartz have the finest of ramification lines almost like those on the palm of the hand.

For specialists and keen laypeople alike, the streak method is a safe way to identify stones. The stone is drawn across the rough surface of a harder substance, such as the unglazed edge on the back of a porcelain saucer, where it leaves a trace of the finest powder. This method of investigation is primarily suited to opaque gemstones. Unset gemstones are carefully rubbed with the lower edge of the girdle over the unglazed porcelain. In the case of set gems, a little powder can be scraped off the underside of the stone with the sharp point of a knife without any loss of value and tipped onto a piece of white paper. In the case of ball and olive shapes, this testing method is easily carried out at the edge of the drilled channel.

Hardness is indirectly related to chemical composition and is directly dependent on the strict arrangement of atoms and their inner cohesion. It can be understood as the resistance with which a mineral resists mechanical stresses on its surface. For goldsmiths and jewelers, hardness is synonymous with resistance to abrasion when wearing, that is to say a combination of hardness against scratching and corrosion. An engraver, for his part, relies on the scratch, abrasion, and drilling hardness. Gemstones' typical characteristic of hardness protects them from external damage such as scratching, abrasion, and corrosion. However, there is a scale of hardness specifically applicable to gemstones that was devised in 1812 by the Viennese mineralogist Friedrich Mohs and named after him. The ten degrees of hardness are represented by talc (1), gypsum (2), calcite (3), fluorite (4), apatite (5), orthoclase (6), quartz (7), topaz (8), corundum (9), and diamond (10). However, this method of testing hardness is, at best, a rough comparison of the relative scratch resistance of ten selected minerals. The numbers 1 through 10 on Mohs' scale in no way represent an evenly progressive scale of hardness. They merely mean that the mineral with the higher number is harder than that with a lower number and, in turn, the lower numbered mineral can be scratched by the higher numbered ones. The actual differences in hardness between two adjacent minerals are decisively greater than expressed in this graduated system. Although Mohs' scale shows diamonds with a hardness of 10 and corundum (rubies and sapphires) with a hardness of 9, gemstone research has discovered that the same gemstones from different locations or the varieties of a species of mineral or even one and the same mineral when scratched in different crystal directions can have widely differing degrees of hardness. Thus diamonds from different deposits vary in their hardness, sapphires from Sri Lanka have greater resistance to scratching than do those from Kashmir, and all sapphires are more resistant to scratching than rubies. In the practical processing of gemstones, hardness is of major importance, particularly in the determination of copies and when cutting since all the material used in cutting and polishing must be matched to the individual cutting hardness of the stone being treated. The interplay of the hardness properties also determines from the very start whether a stone can be selected as a gemstone since it has to resist the abrasive effect of minute airborne particles of quartz in order to retain its polish and brilliance forever. A gemstone must therefore be at level 6 or above on Mohs' hardness scale. Together with the rarity and unparalleled beauty of their colors, durability is one of the three main assets of gemstones.

The hardness grade of a mineral is a functional part of its crystal structure, that is, the electromagnetic cohesion of the structural components (= ions). This is clearly demonstrated in the two schematic representations below which show the differing structures of graphite and diamond.

The crystal lattice of graphite (top), which is composed solely of carbon (C) forms parallel layers charged with carbon ions. Within each plane, each carbon ion is surrounded by three others at a distance of 1.45Å (1Å = a ten millionth of a millimeter). The distance from layer to layer, however, amounts to 3.14Å. Cohesion strength between the ions is constantly high, but low between the layers, which is why graphite can be used as a lubricant.

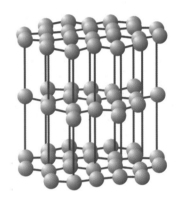

Characteristic Streak Colors in Ornamental Gems

Ornamental Gem	Color	Luster	Hardness	Streak Color
Steel: imitation for hematite	Steel gray	Metallic	6.5	Gray
Pyrite	Brassy yellow	Metallic	6–6.5	Brownish black to black
Marcasite	Pale bronze-yellow			Dark gray-green
Hematite	Black	Metallic	6	Cherry red or blood red
Lapis lazuli (lazurite)	Dark blue azure blue	Vitreous	5–6	Pale blue
Sodalite	Dark blue	Vitreous	5–6	White
Turquoise	Green, greenish-blue, light blue	Waxy	5.25–6	White to pale greenish or pale bluish
Lazulite	Azure blue	Vitreous	5–5.5	White
Variscite	Apple to blue-green	Vitreous	4–5	White, no streak
Malachite	Emerald green, grass green	Silky, dull	3.5–4	Light emerald green to bright green

(Listed in descending order of hardness.)

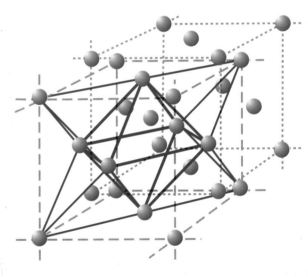

Diamonds have completely different principles of arrangement: The crystal lattice can be imagined as two face-centered cubes, one within the other and displaced by one quarter of the body diagonals. All corners and face centers are occupied by carbon ions. Thus each carbon ion has four immediate neighbors at a distance of 1.542Å. The crystal lattice parameters, that is, the length of the cube edges, measure 3.567Å. This isometric distribution and close stacking of the carbon ions result in the unparalleled hardness of diamonds.

GEMSTONES

THEIR
EXTRACTION
AND
PROCESSING

THE EXTRACTION OF GEMSTONES

Diamond mining takes place in three different types of deposits that correspond to the geographic conditions: in the primary deposits of magmatic rock located in the volcanic pipes (blue ground) as well as in the secondary placer deposits in river beds and maritime terrace deposits in coastal sand close to the shore. The garimpeiros and diggers who single-handedly wrung the precious booty from nature in their own surroundings have largely been replaced by specialists and engineers with all the benefits of advanced technology at their disposal. Africa was the trailblazer in the application of the most advanced diamond-mining processes. Deposits vary widely depending on region. In open-cast mining, the earth is mined to a depth of 350 meters, whereas the stones mined underground are from even greater depths. In contrast, diamonds in the sea are hidden under massive layers of sand between gravel and conglomerate. Nevertheless, the automated processing of the rock masses is very similar in all cases. The excavate is transported on broad conveyor belts to the rock mills and crushers in which the valuable diamonds are separated from the gigantic mass of worthless rock by means of suitable separation methods. The coarse gravel prospect material is first put into a revolving screen and separated according to size on gratings where it is then subjected, depending on dimension, to a whole battery of various roller mills and crushing machines. Only when the gravel mass has been ground down to a particle size of approximately 3 centimeters is it taken by conveyor belts to the processing plant. The first phase of washing makes use of the principle that specific heavy minerals – to which diamond belongs – will sink in a slightly viscous pulp, while specifically lighter material will float to the surface and drain off. The ground gravel and muddy pulp are mixed and stirred several times in washing pans and held in suspension by comblike rakes. This process also serves to separate heavier minerals from lighter ones. After several repetitions of this process, the heavy material undergoing separation is sorted into different sizes by means of various fine strainers and then conveyed to the grease tables. This is the final separation of the wheat from the chaff since the diamonds adhere to the grease while the barren gravel is washed away by the water flow. The gravel finally arrives at a sorting table where hawk-eyed, trained personnel attempt to discover any small remaining diamond crystals – a task that is increasingly being taken over by x-ray fluorescence. In contrast to the primary deposits where approximately 3.6 tons of rock yield 1 carat of diamond (1: 18 million), the ratio in maritime prospecting areas is 1: 80 million (in other words, 16 tons of rock yield 1 carat of diamond).

Color gemstones are found both in primary and in secondary deposits, but never at a depth comparable to diamonds. Only the emerald is mined from its parent rock due to its high sensitivity to external influences. However, the majority of beryls, some feldspars, garnets, opals, many quartzes, tanzanite, topazes, and tourmaline also come directly from primary origins. Mining is done by establishing quarries, whereas in many locations mining takes place underground. In some countries, such as Africa, Brazil, and Thailand, the most advanced, computer-controlled technology is used. In other countries, such as Myanmar and Sri Lanka, traditional excavation methods are used. The widely varying types of secondary deposits of color gemstones result in different methods of excavation, that is, the rocks are extracted from rivers or by mining. On Sri Lanka, for example, in the ancient riverbeds of the

A bird's-eye view of the extensive Argyle Diamond Mine in northwest Australia. Open-cast mining areas are visible on the left. The conveyor belts of the handling system stretch across to the right, and the recovery plant with the administration building on the right is in front of the large water tanks.

Kelani and Kalu-Ganga, particularly at confluences with mountain streams, in inlets, and in shallows formed by strong meanders, a weir of woven branches is constructed straight across the river, so that the water builds up behind it and, beyond the woven barrier, flows faster. In the fast-flowing water, workers with long-handled, rakelike scrapers loosen the alluvial rubble, draw it toward themselves, and pile it up in a furrow in front of the weir to form a small dam. Sand and other worthless gravel are washed out over the dam by the current. After the separation of the lighter material from the heavier precious minerals,

The Argyle Diamond Mine is the most productive source of rose-red diamonds. If the Argyle Diamond Mine is to survive commercially, it must start mining underground by the year 2003.

Top: The large emerald mine near Mingora, Pakistan, which is operated as an open-cast mine as are most of this type. The layer containing emeralds is composed of talc schist, which is intercalated between mica schist and green schist (amphibolite).

Above: In the underground tunnel of an opal mine near Lightning Ridge, New South Wales, Australia, a miner carefully taps away the brittle marl rock along an opal vein.

Right: Special bulldozers remove the immense alluvial sand dunes of the diamond deposits belonging to Consolidated Diamond Mines (CDM) near Oranjemund, Namibia, down to the basic rock containing diamonds.

Photos: Eduard Gübelin, Lucerne.

From top to bottom:
A glimpse into a washing pit on Sri Lanka. A gemstone washer is reaching for a basket filled with illam (gem-containing dredgings), while the others wash the illam by swirling their conical baskets until the heavier gemstones collect at the bottom of the basket.
A colorful concentration of multicolored corundums (rubies and sapphires) from the Swan Brook Mine near Inverell, New South Wales, Australia.
At the end of the washing process on Sri Lanka, the overseer first offers a prayer to Kataragama, the god of minerals, before sorting the gemstones out of the "dullam".
Photos: Eduard Gübelin, Lucerne.

Left: The exquisite emerald crystals from the famous Muzo Mine in Colombia have grown in the quartz-lined cavities of calcite veins running through carbonaceous slate.
Photo: Erica and Harold Van Pelt, Los Angeles.

the washers continue with further separation. The raked-in gravel containing gemstones is scooped out of the dam into a conical basket that is then taken to a deeper spot where it is swirled around so that the heavy minerals sink to the bottom of the basket and the light ones float out over the edge and back into the river. The remaining material is then sorted by the sorters. In the quarry method, the earth is hacked out by workers who frequently stand on dangerously unstable ground. The earth is hoisted up in woven baskets that are occasionally attached to simple rod hoists, then taken apart, painstakingly scanned visually particle by particle and hand sorted in the unremitting search for the precious gems.

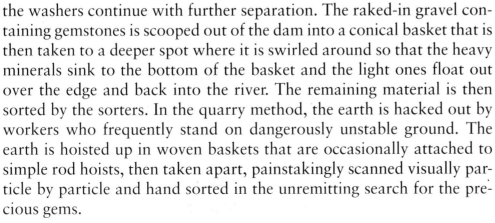

DIAMOND MINING AND PROCESSING

1: Geologic cross-section through the diamond-containing volcanic pipe at the Williamson Diamond Mine near Mwadui, Tanzania. 1 = pithead frame gear, 2 = opencast mining, 3 = gravel and humus, 4 = uppermost adit, 5 = schist, mud and slurry, 6 = uppermost, secondary kimberlite, 7 = lower-lying slate (former lake), 8 = lower-lying, secondary kimberlite, 9 = breccia, 10 = granite, 11 = primary kimberlite (original volcanic pipe).

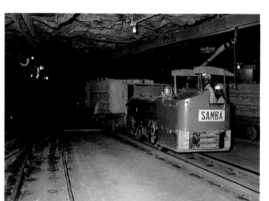

1

2

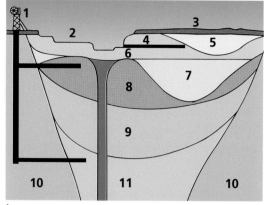

5

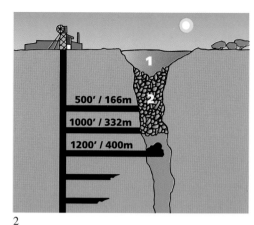

6

7

2: The sides of the volcanic pipes containing diamonds are mined nowadays all around by means of an underground branching shaft and tunnel system. 1 = open crater, 2 = residual broken rock.

3: One of the ways of mining the primary deposits of the volcanic pipes is the block-caving method. The kimberlite filling the pipe is mined from underneath; it breaks off under its own weight and the broken pieces fall through rock funnels into the collection tunnels. 1 = debris that has slid down from the crater rim, 2 = kimberlite, 3 = pieces of broken kimberlite, 4 = pulley, 5 = collection tunnels with hauling excavators, 6 = trucks (dumpers).

4: In the collection tunnels, the blasted material is hauled away with excavators and falls into the waiting trucks that are standing ready in a lower transport tunnel.

5, 6, 7: The trucks, which are controlled from a central switch control, travel to a ramp; there, the trucks are tipped and the blasted material is dumped into the crushing plant in the lower tunnel.

8: (Model of the processing set-up) From the crushing plant, the reduced pieces are conveyed to the recovery plant where they go through a complex system of wash pans and separating funnels until the material has been segregated into its individual components.

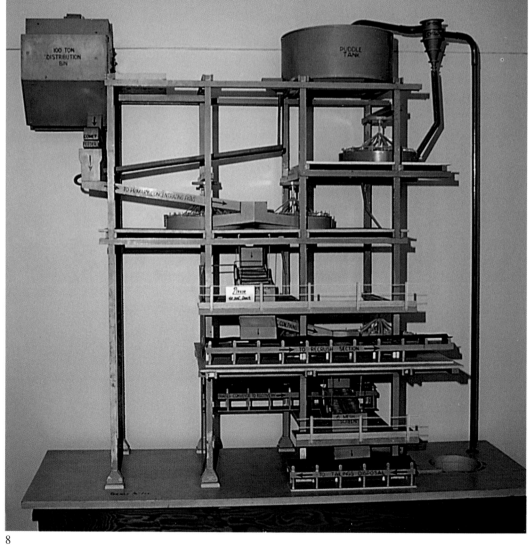

8

28

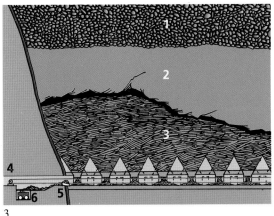

3

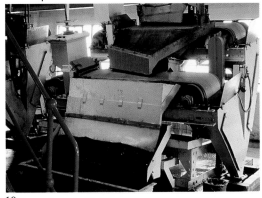

9: In the washing pans, rotating spokes keep the material in motion; it is washed until it disintegrates into its individual minerals.

10 and 11: Toward the end of processing, the now-dried gravel is rinsed over a greased conveyor belt. The diamonds adhere to the grease while the waste material is washed away.

9   10   11

12

12: A modern separation process exploits the diamond's property of fluorescing under x rays. As soon as a diamond on a trough-like conveyor belt comes into range of a narrow x-ray beam and lights up, a photo cell then triggers a blast of wind, which blows the diamond off the conveyor belt and into a collection bag.

13: In spite of all the technical achievements and scientific progress, it is lastly people with their sensitive touch who do the final sorting of diamonds from their worthless accessory minerals.

Photos: Eduard Gübelin, Lucerne

13

1 CANADA
Amethyst, ammolite, diamond, feldspars, garnet, labradorite, lapis lazuli, nephrite, opal, sodalite, collectors' gems

2 USA
Aquamarine, benitoite, beryl, chalcedony, diamond, emerald, feldspars, garnet, nephrite, opal, peridot, quartz, rhodochrosite, ruby, sapphire, spodumene, topaz, tourmaline, turquoise, collectors' gems

3 MEXICO
Agate, chrysocolla, feldspars, garnet, opal, quartz, spinel, topaz, turquoise, collectors' gems

4 GUATEMALA
Jadeite

5 COLOMBIA
Emerald, euclase, sapphire

6 VENEZUELA
Diamond, euclase, jasper, sapphire

7 GUYANA
Diamond

8 BOLIVIA
Ametrine

9 BRAZIL
Agate, amazonite, beryl, chalcedony, chrysoberyl, diamond, emerald, feldspars, garnet, opal, quartz, ruby, sodalite, spodumene, topaz, tourmaline, collectors' gems

10 CHILE
Lapis lazuli

11 ARGENTINA
Rhodochrosite

12 GREENLAND
Nuummite, tugtupite

13 GREAT BRITAIN
Fluorite, jet, morion, smoky quartz

14 NORWAY
Emerald, feldspar, quartz, thulite

15 FINLAND
Chromediopside, spectrolite

16 POLAND
Amber, chrysoprase

17 SPAIN
Aventurine, jet, quartz, sphalerite

18 EGYPT
Emerald, peridot, turquoise

19 GHANA
Diamond

20 NIGERIA
Aquamarine, beryl, emerald, sapphire, spinel, topaz, tourmaline

21 ZAIRE
Diamond, malachite

22 ANGOLA
Diamond

23 KENYA
Amethyst, aquamarine, feldspar, garnet, ruby, sapphire, tsavolite, tourmaline, zircon, collectors' gems

24 TANZANIA
Aquamarine, chrysoberyl, diamond, emerald, garnet, opal, quartz, ruby, sapphire, tanzanite, tourmaline, zircon

25 ZAMBIA
Amethyst, chrysoberyl, emerald, malachite

26 MOZAMBIQUE
Beryl, emerald, garnet, quartz, ruby, sapphire, smoky quartz, spodumene, tourmaline, zircon, collectors' gems

27 NAMIBIA
Aquamarine, diamond, quartz, topaz, tourmaline, collectors' gems

28 BOTSWANA
Diamond

29 ZIMBABWE
Aquamarine, chrysoberyl, emerald, garnet, quartz, topaz, tourmaline, verdelite, collectors' gems

30 SOUTH AFRICA
Beryl, diamond, emerald, feldspar, garnet, quartz, rhodochrosite, sugilite, tourmaline, verdelite

31 MADAGASCAR
Agate, apatite, aquamarine, beryl, chrysoberyl, emerald, feldspars, garnet, ruby, sapphire, spodumene, topaz, tourmaline, zircon, collectors' gems

32 RUSSIA (CIS)
Alexandrite, amber, beryl, charoite, diamond, emerald, feldspars, garnet, lapis lazuli, malachite, nephrite, quartz, rhodonite, topaz, tourmaline, collectors' gems

33 IRAN
Turquoise

34 AFGHANISTAN
Aquamarine, lapis lazuli, quartz, ruby, spinel, spodumene, tourmaline

35 ETHIOPIA
Opal, peridot, quartz

36 PAKISTAN
Aquamarine, emerald, garnet, peridot, ruby, spinel, topaz

37 INDIA
Aquamarine, chalcedony, chrysoberyl, diamond, diopside, emerald, garnet, jasper, moonstone, quartz, rhodonite, ruby, sapphire, sodalite, collectors' gems

38 CHINA
Amber, amethyst, aquamarine, beryl, diamond, nephrite, peridot, ruby, sapphire, tourmaline, turquoise

39 JAPAN
Danburite, jadeite, quartz, rhodonite, topaz

40 MYANMAR
Amber, chrysoberyl, diamond, jadeite, moonstone, peridot, rock crystal, ruby, sapphire, spinel, spodumene, topaz, tourmaline, zircon, collectors' gems

41 THAILAND
Garnet, ruby, sapphire, spinel, zircon

42 SRI LANKA
Amethyst, chrysoberyl, feldspars, garnet, moonstone, quartz, ruby, sapphire, sinhalite, spinel, topaz, tourmaline, zircon, collectors' gems

43 INDONESIA
Diamond

44 AUSTRALIA
Chrysoprase, diamond, emerald, jasper, nephrite, opal, quartz, sapphire, turquoise, zircon, collectors' gems

45 TASMANIA
Sapphire

46 NEW ZEALAND
Nephrite

31

THE CUTTING OF DIAMONDS

From a plain diamond crystal to a sparkling brilliant.

Top right is an octahedral diamond crystal. Its form is made up of two four-sided pyramids with their square bases touching.

To the left of it is a sawed off part that still represents two-thirds of the original crystal. Below that is a round ground diamond. After finishing the "bruting," the diamond is given four so-called "corner facets" top and bottom. Then the remaining forty-one facets are applied all around to the complete brilliant cut, which has a total of fifty-eight facets.

Until the late fourteenth century, only naturally formed diamonds, that is, raw diamonds, were known. The prototype of manually enhanced diamonds is said to have been created in Burgundy around 1400. Initially, wood and copper files coated with diamond powder were used to process existing crystal surfaces until they were evenly convex. Pliny mentions leather cloths that were suitable for smoothing and polishing with the addition of diamond powder. In Gothic times, grindstones provided the necessary symmetry without affecting the characteristic shape of diamonds. The era of diamond cutting started when grindstones appeared in Europe. In 1465, the trade of "Diamantslijper" is documented for the first time in Bruges, Belgium. As an immediate consequence, Antwerp developed to become the center of the diamond trade. In 1610, 164 diamond cutters were recorded within its city walls. At the start of the twenthieth century, Marcel Tolkovsky was the first to devise the criteria for a perfect cut and the ideal proportions based on the laws of the four types of brilliant that are still valid today. The starting point is always the crystal shape created by nature. By cleaving or sawing with a very fine metal circular saw or by laser, the future diamond shape is formed. Four possible cleavage directions and nine different sawing directions can be used. Depending on size and individual resistance, this separating process can take hours or even days. Before the two usually different sized parts of the diamond can be cut, the bruter gives the future gem its shape by rondisting the corners. For cutting the facets and polishing, the diamond is mounted on a dopstick and pressed onto the rapidly rotating grinding wheel that is coated with diamond powder and oil. During this particularly delicate phase of cutting, the diamond is repeatedly applied to the lap and removed in order to precisely monitor the cut. Even with the most careful processing, diamonds lose up to half their weight during this process. With its fifty-eight facets, the brilliant cut is the pinnacle of all cuts. Presently, it is the most popular and, in many colored stones, creates increased radiance and sparkling fire. The natural shape of the crystal dictates, to some extent, the principle of the cut. Of the three primary growth forms – octahedron, rhombic dodecahedron, and cube – the classic cuts have long been feasible using automatic faceting machines. On the other hand, the combined and irregular crystal shapes can offer themselves for the no less beautiful fancy cuts, such as the emerald and step cut, the pendelogue, the drop, the pear pointed at one side, the marquise or navette pointed at both ends, the rectangular baguette mainly used for decorative necklaces, the oval, and the heart. When a sparkling brilliant is finally modeled out of the diamond after days and, occasionally, weeks of struggle between mortal and crystal, the magic transformation of a dull, unpretentious stone into a gemstone with an incomparably gleaming play of light has taken place thanks to the multifacet positions and perfect geometry. Human creative ingenuity is worthy of our deepest respect.

Left: The cut form is mostly determined by the raw shape of the diamond crystal, since as much volume of the precious material as possible should be kept. Since beauty is the prime necessity for a diamond, the cut and the arrangement of the facets must be chosen so that the diamond's high optical properties are fully effective. Collection: Hans Krieger. Photo: Erica and Harold Van Pelt, Los Angeles.

Bottom: Nowadays, the cutting process is carried out in three stages. Formerly, the raw diamonds were cleaved. Today, they are mainly sawed in two parts using a disk-shaped saw blade. Then the two parts are rubbed against each other by turning until they both have the basic round shape desired. The facets are precisely applied at calculated angles using a grinding wheel coated with diamond powder. The same wheel is used to finally polish the facets to brilliance.

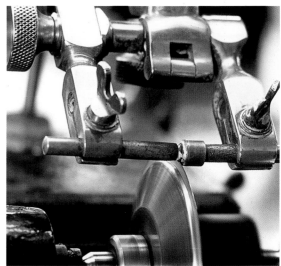

THE CUTTING OF COLOR GEMSTONES

It may possibly be called a form of presumption when humans employ technology to overcome the hardness of gemstones by giving the rough, unassuming pebbles a richly faceted appearance with a polished cut, awakening them from their "sleeping beauty" slumber to radiant beauty and brilliance. The traditional cutting of color gemstones, unlike diamonds, is not based on mathematical calculations but far more on experience handed down and with a good portion of sensitivity. The right

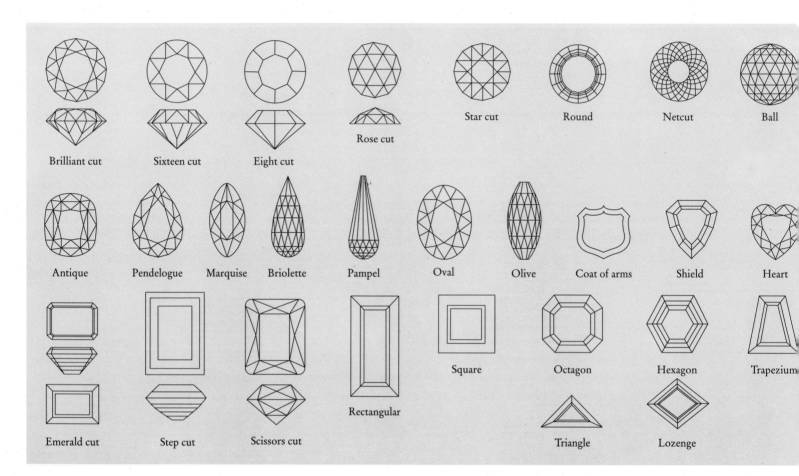

The size and crystal form of the raw gem as well as its intended use generally determine the type of cut. The styles of cut depicted in the top row are mainly used for diamonds but may also be used for color gems.

The fancy styles in the center row are used for unusual pieces of jewelry or for supplementary decoration.

The angular cuts in the bottom row are mainly used for prismatic crystals, but they are also suitable for diamonds.

cut for the stone demands experienced skill and a tried and tested awareness of responsibility since precious material is being processed. Most of the raw stones must first be sawed to a suitable size if they are large or irregular in shape. A metal circular saw, the edge of which is coated with diamond bort, is used for this purpose. A subsequent process, the bruting, gives the rough stone its shape, which is selected after assessing and planning the cut. This is done on a carborundum grindstone. The bruted stone is then cemented to the end of a stick, the lower end of which is pointed so that it can be introduced into a perforated jamb peg for cutting and polishing. The final and most demanding work takes place on a horizontal lap. The dopstick carrying the stone is supported by a perforated jamb peg and put in the correct position by the gem cutter. The angled position for each individual facet is selected by repositioning the dopstick in the different holes of the perforated jamb peg.

The stone receives its final polishing on the polishing lap, which is of identical construction to the grindstone but is used with considerably finer abrasives. Each gemstone is treated individually during cutting and polishing. The material of the disk as well as the cutting and polishing abrasives must be adapted to its original cohesion characteristics. Unfortunately, some leading gemstone countries adhere to the principle of retaining as much weight as possible of the original raw stone. In Sri Lanka, this used to lead to most of the stones having to be recut on arrival in the West in order to correct the coarse shape and to set off the beauty of the precious stone to full advantage by a suitable cut. In

Far left: In the gemstone-cutting workshops, the lapidaries sit side by side at a bench. Those shown here are working on the cut, that is, giving the color gems numerous facets. They press the corresponding part of the gemstone, which is attached to a dopstick, onto the lap coated with diamond powder.

1. In the color gem lapidary workshop, large gemstones are first sawed into smaller pieces using a copper or tinplate disk coated with fine diamond abrasive.

1   2

3   4

contrast, prismatic crystals such as beryls, topazes, peridots, quartzes, tanzanite, tourmaline, and zircons are given their shape – emerald cut *(coins coupés)*, step cut, and occasionally baguette cut – by automatic cutting machines. Other crystal shapes such as garnets, rubies, sapphires, and spinels are also machine cut, but mostly in round, oval, antique forms as well as cushion-shaped (with rounded corners). Fashionable fancy cuts result in stars, triangles, multiple corners (polygonal cut), trapezoids with slightly rounded surface, or even totally nongeometric shapes ("lost forms"). The positioning of the cut is responsible for the internal brilliance, while polishing increases the luster and thus creates external brilliance. The cutting of gemstones is a technique and an art rolled into one. In particular, it requires a great deal of sensitivity toward the nature of the stone in order to give it its corresponding shape and endow it with its much admired beauty.

2. After sawing, the gems are ground to shape and size on a carborundum grindstone.

3. The preformed gems are attached to the dopstick with adhesive. This work requires utmost precision.

4. Using lead horizontal disks charged with carborundum or copper disks with diamond powder, the facets are applied and polished with the help of the dopstick and the perforated jamb peg.

Polishing Agate

Gemstone polishing has its origins in India. Much later, leadership in stone polishing, in particular color stone polishing, was assumed by Idar-Oberstein, the German city on the upper River Nahe and it maintains the leading position today. The city's ascendency in color stone polishing cannot be separated from its agate polishing. The earliest record of the polishing trade in Idar-Oberstein dates from 1453 when the local industry started to develop. The agate was mined from the surrounding hills, mainly from the pits of the Steinkaulenberg, where the old tunnels can still be seen. In the early days of agate polishing, water

From left to right:

Cutting in stomach position
The agate cutter lies on his stomach in a wooden trough and presses the ornamental gem against the water-powered sandstone wheel.

Grinding
Smaller agate and ornamental gems are first cut to shape on the prepolishing wheel.

Hollowing bowls
The bowl-cutter hollows out the agate and other ornamental gems on a carborundum-coated grindstone.

power from the river was used to drive the mighty mill wheels and grindstones in the agate or water polishing shops. The polishers themselves lay on their stomachs on a bench or on a tilting chair to press the heavy agate firmly against the rotating stone. Although some of the polishing processes are still carried out in the old tradition and with the romantic touch of the Middle Ages, modern technology is firmly in control today with new processing methods. The raw stones are first split to the approximate size required and then cut to size on a circular saw coated with diamond bort. The carborundum wheel is used for rough prepolishing, and fine polishing is still done with sandstone. The final polish is carried out with trippel on pewter, lead, or felt rollers or in drums made of beech. Cabochons, the profile stones with dome-shaped surfaces, which are cemented to a stick for safer handling, are polished on narrow grooves on the edges of the grindstones.

GLYPTOGRAPHY

The art of stone cutting is both ancient and ultramodern. Ambitious designers use it to make a name for themselves on the international scene. Glyptography is the skill of engraving gemstones or ornamental stones, including amber, or cutting them in relief. The main focus of glyptic art is on carving and engraving hardstones, the ultimate level of stone cutting, which requires a precise knowledge of the materials and the highest level of precision from skilled artisans. The designation of gem is given to all precious and ornamental stones with engraved pictorial depictions. Pictures for cameos are worked in embossed relief,

Top: View of a gem-carving workshop. Engraving, often called glyptography, is one of the oldest branches of gemstone processing. Using a set of different-sized diamond-tipped tools, the engraver creates artistic intaglios, cameos, or figurative items on a lathe. Herbert Klein workshop, Idar-Oberstein. Photo: Erica and Harold Van Pelt, Los Angeles.

Left: Glyptography is a working technique ideally suited to women with their sense of shape and sensitivity. They understand how to assess and incorporate the natural properties of the ornamental gems, for example, the mysterious courses of color.

whereas intaglio work is the reverse, that is, working down into the stone. However, the technique used is identical in both cases.

The origin of the word *cameo* comes from the Italian *cammeo,* which probably is derived from the Latin word *gemma,* which gave gemology its name and means precious stone. The oldest known use of the designation *gemstone* is in connection with the Mesopotamian seal cylinders, which are small hollow rollers made from jasper, onyx, sard, or agate with engraved symbolic or mythological figures and engravings. One form of seal cherished by the Egyptians was the scarab, a beetle that was revered as a holy insect and worn as an amulet cut in stone. The multicolored layers of the massive quartzes best permit a polychrome depiction. Normally, the gem figures rise in light-colored relief as a sort of silhouette from the darker brown, blue-black, or differently colored background, whereby in view of the small dimensions, the optical effect of strongly contrasting colors is deliberately looked for. The effect of translucent light and dark surfaces increases the living plasticity of the miniature works of art. Nowadays, stone cutters mainly use the wheel or drilling technique with rotating tools. The instruments are generally of soft metal and are coated with a mixture of oil and diamond powder and the cemented stone is directed toward the tool, that is, the stone is fixed to a backing and is cut with mills and drills. The cutting tools are designed in a wide variety of shapes such as points, disks, cylinders, tubes, or balls. Before cutting, the picture is applied to the stone. During the cutting process, an oil-powder coating spreads over the entire surface, distorting and hiding the transferred drawing. Handling the fast rotating, diamond-coated steel tool therefore requires complete harmony between the imagination of the cutter and the valuable material. Glyptography also covers the manufacture of artistic ornaments and small sculptures. In this case, flowers and animals are eminently suitable models – in particular, graceful tropical birds whose plumage is authentically rendered by the stone. Superb rare examples of magnificent gemstones or unusually structured or colored crystals frequently inspire talented stonecutters to create works of exquisite beauty.

Top: Imaginative likeness of a frog made out of ruby sitting on a base of green anyolite (zoisite and hornblende). Collection: Michael Scott. Photo: Erica and Harold Van Pelt, Los Angeles.

Bottom: Elegant figurine of a young heron made of light blue chalcedony (legs and feet of metal). Collection and photo: Eduard Gübelin, Lucerne.

Opposite: Charming still life composed of a variety of gemstones.
Rock crystal vase with flower and berry bouquet of amethyst, ametrine, and tourmaline as well as two kittens made of citrine. Created by Herbert Klien, Idar-Oberstein. Photo: Erica and Harold Van Pelt, Los Angeles.

Striving for beauty is a profoundly human desire. We experience beauty to a particularly intense degree in moments of extreme emotional receptiveness. Wherever beauty makes itself known – either in Creation around us or in a masterpiece created by human hand – it triggers a feeling of oneness, of recognition and admiration. Beauty is the symbol of almighty power, to which human beings spontaneously and immediately respond, without being fully able to comprehend and put it into words. Beauty is a joy to behold and to experience, it elevates the spirits. Nevertheless, no matter how deeply it penetrates into the soul, it barely becomes clear to rational thought.

The beauty of gemstones is revealed in the widest variety of ways: pure transparency, colorlessness, and the fire-radiating sparkle of diamonds; the luxurious wealth of color in rubies, sapphires, and emer-

Portraits of the Gemstones

alds; the impressive clarity of pastel-colored beryls; the bucolic dreaminess of the multihued tourmaline; the magical interplay of light with cat's eyes and starstones; the mischievous color play of opals, and the colorful glow of spectrolites or the fantastic markings found in many ornamental gems. In all these manifestations of beauty that cast their spell over us, light plays the leading role. In spite of all physical findings, it remains an unsolved puzzle that fills us with awe.

The most distinguished of all these gems that unites the properties of light within itself is the diamond – the ice tear. Even in its colorless state, it is considered to be the king of gemstones; the extent to which it corresponds to the ideal gemstone with the addition of color. The beauty of the diamond is not merely attributable to its proverbial transparency and purity but primarily to its radiant brilliance. This is created by the interplay of its adamantine luster, the high level of refraction, its color-radiating fire, and its unique lively sparkle. Naturally, this show is easier to see with colorless stones than with colored ones. The deep gleam is caused by the reflection of light on the polished surface. The fire is the result of the interplay of prismatic colors that are reflected out of the gemstone when the white light is refracted into the colors of the rainbow. In short, the fire of this brilliancy is ignited when light is reflected from the gem.

Opposite: Light awakens the glittering luster in gemstones, brings their superb colors to life and discloses their clear transparency. Tourmalines from the collection of Kalil Elawar. Photo: Erica and Harold Van Pelt, Los Angeles.

THE BEAUTY OF COLOR GEMS

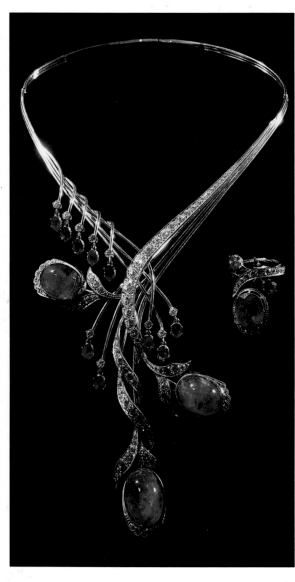

The set of jewelry designed by V. G. Sitnikov and carried out by jeweler B. V. Ivanov represents "Spring." It is composed of a necklace and ring decorated with diamonds, sapphires, and emeralds. Collection: State Treasury of Russia, Moscow.

Opposite: The kaleidoscopic wealth of colors of gemstones finds its unequaled expression in these color gems with their virtually endless tints, shades, and hues. Photo: Erica and Harold Van Pelt, Los Angeles.

Nature is the most talented of painters. It never permits the creation of kitsch by mixing contrasting elements or by the use of daring hues. Any artist would be hard put to mix the colors on his or her palette in a more colorful and cheerful way. There is no question that color is the most beautiful incarnation of light and is one of life's most exquisite experiences. Color adds spice to nature just as salt adds flavor to food. After the gray monotony of winter, our eyes rejoice on seeing the fresh, glowing wealth of colors in the spring. Color is considered to be an expression of dynamism and energy; it conveys vivacious cheerfulness and a pulsating mood. A love of gemstones is also mainly attributable to their colorful beauty.

Again, this comes as no surprise. The world of human fantasy is determined mainly by what the eye perceives and is thus a world of light and colors. Its liveliness and the generous, constantly changing interplay of light not only appeal to widespread sensitivity to beauty but also represent a basic need by humans. For this reason, the highly expressive colors of the three most precious color gems – ruby, sapphire and emerald – are considered to be the most pleasant and beneficial of all.

This intense influence of colors on the eye is undoubtedly a truly modest interpretation of our striving for beauty. Should there be less factual reasons for our desire for color? Might the power of attraction of the color be attributable to the fact that we give up a part of our conscious selves at the sight of a superb, full-colored gem? That we lose ourselves, unaware, in far-envisaged depths? That it will unlock doors otherwise closed to us? Conjure up pictures of peace and paradisiacal bliss in our mind's eye? Indeterminate landscapes of undulating blue in a sapphire, light explosions, consuming fire in the red stream of a ruby; tumbling mountain streams, foam-flecked seas or sunlit gardens growing wild in the green of an emerald. However, not only are the majesty of these incomparable stones capable of arousing our enthusiasm but so also are the less expensive ornamental gems. Ultramarine lapis lazuli reveals a view of the starry sky, whereas opal gives us a glimpse of a merry harlequin, and spectrolite captures a shimmering rainbow. Would not human imagination be impoverished without colors? These secretive interactions create both a releasing and yet oppressive astonishment in us. Mysticism and material have never been as close together as they are here. An irresistible mixture specially for enlightened people, particularly when they discover how the breathtaking color relationships come about in the creation of color that is described in the following chapter.

Nature also reveals astonishing beauty in the realm of flowers, tropical butterflies, in the multihued plumage of parrots, in landscapes, and lively cloud formations as well as in atmospheric moods; such beauty is manifest in gemstones in their unique and unsurpassable, crystalline expressiveness.

THE BEAUTY OF THE PHENOMENON GEMS

Top: The phenomenon of the apparently unreal cat's-eye effect is a special curiosity, seen here at its most attractive as a chrysoberyl cat's-eye. The undulating band of light is caused by the interaction of light refraction on fine parallel fibers or hollow channels and the concentration of light through the curved surface of the gemstone. Photo: Max Weibel, Pfaffhausen.

Above: The two to six times repetition of the phenomenon described above leads to the formation of a star (asterism). This is caused when two to six groups of parallel fibers or hollow channels cross each other inside the gem. The best-known gems of this type are the star rubies and the star sapphires. However, there are also star garnets, star spinels, and star quartzes, and so forth.

Opposite: To its admirers, the opal is the most perfect of gemstones because it unites the colors of the most precious gemstones: the blue of the sapphire, the green of the emerald, the yellow of the topaz, the orange of the padparadscha, the red of the ruby, and the violet of the amethyst. Photo: Eduard Gübelin, Lucerne.

Crystal-clear colored gemstones are revealed to the eye in an almost immeasurable wealth of tones and shades. In view of their unlimited richness, the layperson might easily fall prey to a feeling of confusion. However, this by no means concludes the variety of shapes since this palette is further extended and enriched with the phenomenon stones: cat's-eye and starstones, moonstone, opal, and spectrolite. These impressive effects do not meet with general enthusiasm but appeal much more to individual tastes. The mystique of gemstones and the belief in miracles always find a rich supply in these will-o'-the-wisps flickering with reflected light from within the gem and over the gem's surface. In actual fact, this is a purely optical characteristic of light, which is triggered in phenomenon gems by their special structural composition.

Great acclaim is bestowed on the inclusions in all these phenomenon gems, which achieve the most eye-catching and most amazing phenomenal influence on the light by means of their ordered arrangement – chatoyancy, also called the cat's-eye effect. This is caused by the scattering and reflection of the light on microscopically fine, parallel fibers or hollow channels, which permeate the entire gem. If curved on top to form a dome, the light is concentrated to form a narrow line. To onlookers, the light phenomena of chatoyancy and asterism appear to be floating above the gem. Famous examples of this are the gold-brown tiger's-eye, the blue hawk's-eye, and, in particular, the most precious of them all, the bamboo green to honey-colored chrysoberyl cat's-eye. If chromium oxide is intermingled with the latter, one of the greatest rarities is formed, the alternating red/green alexandrite cat's-eye, which turns up at very rare intervals in the placers of Sri Lanka.

Asterism or star formation is nothing more than a reproduction of a simple chatoyancy by two or three, sometimes even six rays of light crossing each other to form four-, six- or even twelve-pointed stars. This phenomenon is seen to best advantage in the star ruby and star sapphire. The star spinel and star garnet are less well known but just as sought after.

The delicate blue, flitting shimmer of the moonstone is termed adularescence. The cause of this effect is the scattering of light through the fine lamellar structure. This was caused during the cooling of the moonstone in the bosom of the earth when two minerals that were originally intermingled – orthoclase and albite – became exsolved and thus formed lamellalike platelets over which the penetrating light scatters to create the blue shimmer.

Light interferences cause the blue-green glow of the common labradorite as well as its brightly colored variety, spectrolite.

The colorfully flecked carpet of flames that is opal is caused by light diffraction in the spaces between tiny spheres arranged in a network. This is comparable to the light diffraction of a streetlight when seen through an open umbrella during a rain shower.

DIAMOND

KING
OF
GEMSTONES

Chemistry: C (crystallized carbon)

Crystal system: Cubic

Habit (form): Octahedral, cube, rhombic dodecahedron, and combinations of these forms.

Colors: All colors in many shades and tints as well as black and white.

Refractive index (R.I.): 2.4175 (isotropic/highly constant)

Specific gravity: 3.52 (3.51–3.53)

Hardness (Mohs' scale): 10 (hardest natural substance on earth)

Consistency: Brittle, eminent cleavage; conchoidal, stepped fracture

Occurrence: In metamorphic, ultramafic rocks (lherzolite, harzburgite, websterite, etc.) and eklogite.

Extraction: From kimberlite and lamproite in volcanic pipes and craters, from alluvial beds and littoral deposits, from conglomerate beds and other sedimentary rocks; occasionally from meteorites.

The mystery and magic of diamonds are attributable to two equally alluring characteristics of this gem: its beauty and its lasting value. With its radiant beauty and its lasting value, the diamond is one of the best known, most popular, and much sought after precious stones. In many respects, it is the most unusual and most interesting mineral in the material world we know and bears witness to the geologic conditions at the time of its formation in the earth's mantle, which has never been directly accessible to us.

Diamonds are a symbol of brilliancy and dignity; they decorate crowns and religious objects and serve as adornment for queens – for centuries, diamonds have been synonymous with unparalleled value and sublime beauty. Diamonds have been linked to the fates of rulers and adventurers, as well as with the fortune of peoples, families, and distinguished personalities. Diamonds are gemstones that mark the momentous occasions in our lives with their brilliancy and remind us of them anew – birth, engagement, marriage, first child, and anniversaries, to name but a few important events. A diamond's unclouded transparency and spectacular clarity, combined with its fascinating sparkle, the flash of rainbow-hued fire and its strong, lively brilliancy rightfully elevate it to the "king of gemstones."

From ancient times until the eighteenth century, India was the only known source of diamonds. The first mythical images linked with diamonds also originated there: "It protects those who are threatened by snakes, fire, poison, illness, thieves, water and black magic." The ancient Greeks extolled the diamond as *adamas,* steely and invincible, insuperable. This word developed into the Medieval Latin *diamas* and *diamant* in Middle English and Old French. All the major Indian deposits are spread over the eastern part of the Deccan plateau. They can be subdivided into the following main sources: Golconda with the most significant deposits along the Pennar and Kistna rivers; the Brahamani and Mahanadi group with placer beds on the rivers of the same name; the Panna group with two smaller, primary sources as outcropping "pipes." Occasionally, diamonds are found in loose alluvial gravel in India. Of far more importance, however, are the concentrations in alluvial terraces and deposits at higher elevations, in which the diamonds are embedded in secondary deposits between conglomerate layers and varieties of sandstone.

The weight of all gemstones, including diamonds, is given in carats. The carat is based on a unit of weight found in nature: the seed of the carob tree (1 seed corresponds to 1 carat). From time immemorial, the Indians determined the weight of the "fruits of the earth," which is what they considered diamonds, on simple scales using the "cattie," as they call the seed of the carob tree. The current designation of carat, which is now standardized to the equivalent of 0.2 grams, is based on the Arabic word *qirat* and the Greek *keration.*

The start of the eighteenth century saw the dawning of a new era for diamonds. The sources in India had been almost completely exhausted when the Portuguese royal family officially announced the discovery of Brazilian diamonds in 1729. Only a few years prior to this, men pan-

1. The *Sancy*, a colorless (white) diamond has a weight of 55.23 carats. It is currently in the Louvre in Paris.
2. The *Portuguese* weighs 127.02 carats. It once belonged to the Portuguese royal family. It has been on display at the Smithsonian Institution, Washington, D.C. (USA) since 1963. Photo: Erica and Harold Van Pelt, Los Angeles.
3. The *Eugénie Blue* was once owned by Empress Eugénie of France. It weighs 31 carats. Mrs. Merriweather Post donated

ning for gold in Brazil had been using the crystal-clear pebbles as gaming tokens, unaware that these were worth far more than the minute amounts of gold they toiled for day after day in the river. Initially, the European market was highly skeptical about the new Brazilian diamonds. The Brazilians resorted to trickery and transported their diamonds to the Indian port of Goa, which, like Brazil, was another Portuguese colony. From there, they were smuggled into India, and, by means of this detour, they found their way unhindered into Europe.

The discovery of the South African diamond deposits resulted in a powerful upswing in diamond trading. The discovery by a farmer's

1 2 3 4

the gem to the Smithsonian Institution as a gift. Photo: Erica and Harold Van Pelt, Los Angeles.
4. The *Régent* was stolen by a slave in India. It originally weighed 400 carats. but, after cutting, only 140.50 carats. When it subsequently reappeared in 1793, it was doomed to an eventful fate, only coming to rest in the Louvre in Paris after the Second World War.
5. The *Koh-i-noor* weighs 108.93 carats and, of all the famous diamonds, bears the most appropriate and finest name since it means "Mountain of Light." The first mention of it was in 1304, when it was in the possession of Rajah Malwa. Today, it radiates from the crown of the British queen and can be admired in the Tower of London.
6. With its 128.51 carats, the *Tiffany* is one of the largest yellow diamonds (the Red Cross diamond weighs 204 carats). It was discovered in the Kimberley Mine in South Africa in 1878 and has been on display at Tiffany's, New York, since 1879. Since then, it has been admired by more than 30,000,000 people.
7. The *Wittelsbacher* comes from India and weighs 35.32 carats. After being in the possession of the Spanish royal family for a long time, it became the property of the Austrian Hapsburgs in 1667 and, in 1722, of the Bavarian Wittelsbacher. It disappeared in 1931, only to be rediscovered in

son, Erasmus Stephanus Jacobs, was confirmed by mineralogist Dr. W. Guybon Atherstone as the first genuine African diamond in 1866. In order to control the chaos of the ensuing diamond fever and to counteract mine disasters and fights between companies and diggers, the Englishman Cecil John Rhodes gradually acquired the farmlands of the De Beers and Kimberley mines. As did their neighboring farmers, the De Beers moved to a quieter region. Today, their name stands for the world's largest diamond company. Rhodes registered the De Beers Consolidated Mines, Ltd. in Kimberley as early as 1888. Since then, the production and sale of diamonds have been subject to a monopoly cartel. Via its Central Selling Organization, located in Lucerne, Switzerland, the diamond syndicate controls 80 percent of the total raw diamond trade, regulates what is available, and thus ensures extensive price stability for the exporting countries and trusting customers. The most productive diamond mines in South Africa were the De Beers, Kimberley, Wesselton, Dutoitspan, and Bulfontein mines.

In the twentieth century, too, the African continent has opened up to treasure seekers. Until that time, fate had had a hand in all the discoveries of diamonds. Now, a planned approach was taken. The first diamond occurrence systematically probed and discovered in 1940 with the help of precise geologic research was the highly productive deposit at Mwadui in Tanzania, which contains the largest primary deposits of

9

12

13

Antwerp in 1962. In 1964, it was sold to a private owner by Christie's.

8. The *Condé* diamond has a weight of 50 carats. Louis of Bourbon received this pink diamond in 1643 from the French King Louis XIV as a gift for his services in the Thirty Years' War. In 1892, the Condé family donated it to the French nation, which keeps the diamond in the Musée Condé in Chantilly.

9. The *Green Dresden* is an apple-green, pendelogue-shaped diamond and, at 41 carats, the largest green diamond in the world. It originated in India and was acquired by Elector Frederick August II of Saxony at the Leipzig fair in 1743. It is among the treasure in the *"Grünes Ge-*

wölbe" (Green Vault) in Dresden. Photo: George Bosshart, Horgen.

10/11. The *Cullinan* was the largest diamond crystal that history has ever known. It was discovered on January 26, 1905 in the Premier Mine. The Ascher company in Amsterdam cut nine smaller jewels from this diamond, which weighed 3,106 carats. The largest of these, the *Star of Africa* or *Cullinan I* (in the lower half of the photo) decorates the British Royal Sceptre. It is the largest cut diamond in the world and weighs 530.20 carats. The next smaller in size is called *Cullinan II*, weighs 317.40 carats, and adorns the front of the British state crown.

12. The dark blue *Hope* diamond is one of the most famous historical diamonds. Its story is linked with many tragic events. After having changed owners several times, Harry Winston donated the 44.50 carat Hope to the Smithsonian Institution in Washington, D.C. (USA) in 1958. Photo: Erica and Harold Van Pelt, Los Angeles.

13. The *Centenary* shares most of the superlatives with the *Cullinan*. Like the latter, it originates from the Premier Mine and, with its 273 carats, it comes immediately after *Cullinan II* and before *Cullinan III* (94.40 carats). In addition, the *Centenary* is the largest diamond with a modern cut and of flawless quality. It is owned by the diamond company of De Beers in London.

49

if

vvs 1

vvs 2

CLARITY GRADING OF DIAMONDS

In accordance with international practice, the clarity of a diamond is established by a skilled specialist using ten times magnification under normal light conditions with an achromatic and an aplanatic lens. Classification is made on the following basis:

Internally Flawless (if)
A diamond that is absolutely transparent and, under 10x magnification, has neither inclusions nor internal features.

Very, Very Small Inclusions (vvs 1/vvs 2)
Very, very small inclusions that are still very difficult to see under 10x magnification.

Very Small Inclusions (vs 1/vs 2)
Very small inclusions that are visible under 10x magnification but still difficult to see.

Small Inclusions (si1/si2)
Small inclusions that are easily visible under 10x magnification. Not visible to the naked eye, at least through the crown.

Piqué I (P I)
Larger inclusions. Visible to the naked eye through the crown of the diamond. Brilliance, however, ms not affected.

Piqué II (P II)
Larger and/or numerous inclusions. Easily visible to the naked eye through the crown of the diamond. Brilliance is slightly affected.

Piqué III (P III)
Large and/or numerous inclusions. Very easily visible to the naked eye. Brilliance is clearly affected.

After the grade of P III, only diamonds rich in inclusions follow and these are already considered industrial diamonds.

Photos: Eduard Gübelin, Lucerne.

vs 1

v

si 1

si

P I

P

P III

P

50

exceptionally fine jewelry diamonds. However, new deposits are continually being developed in the classical diamond area in South Africa, for example, the Finsch mine, which is currently considered to be the queen of the South African diamond mines.

Recently, Zaire has supplanted South Africa as the leading supplier of diamonds. With an annual production of 17 million carats, the former Belgian Congo is the largest producer of diamonds and is responsible for 80 percent of world production of industrial diamonds. Conducted over a long period of time, systematic investigations of the earth in Zaire led to the conclusion that there is an almost incredible wealth of diamonds still to be exploited. The dark continent might yet yield further surprises as diamonds have also been found in Angola and Sierra Leone.

In the middle of the twentieth century, however, Russian diamonds, in particular, were very much in the news. The country's need for industrial diamonds increased sharply after the meteoric rise of the steel industry. In 1954, a young mineralogist, L. Popugaeva, following garnet rock scree, discovered a kimberlite pipe containing diamonds, which she named "Sarzina." Other mines opened since then include the Mir, Udacznaya, and Aichal mines. The Siberian pipes largely contain industrial diamonds of ideal size. In recent years, Russia has become the world's second-largest producer of industrial diamonds after Zaire and, after South Africa, similarly the second-largest producer of jewelry-quality diamonds.

Discoveries of diamond deposits seem to succeed each other at an ever-increasing pace. Currently, the most recent discovery was made in the Kimberley area in northwest Australia. After prospecting was carried out systematically in 1972 with a great deal of investment, the annual production at the beginning of the 1990s had already reached between 35 and 40 million carats. The Premier mine in South Africa thus relinquished its position as the world's largest diamond mine to the Argyle mine. Argyle owes its fame to its rare and high-priced pink diamonds.

The diamond is undoubtedly the best known precious stone and the mineral most investigated. It is the only gemstone that is comprised of only one element, quadrivalent carbon (C). It differs from simple graphite and coal merely by the extraordinarily close, cube-shaped stacking of the carbon atoms that, together with the strong cohesion bonds responsible for the diamond's particular hardness – with 10, at the very top of Mohs' scale – and for its superb light refraction, from which the lively brilliancy and the powerful sparkle emanate. Due to the relative lightness of carbon, its density is only 3.52. The shape of the unit cell of the cubically crystallizing diamond forms a tetrahedron (shape limited by four triangular surfaces). The most common growth forms are the octahedron (a geometric shape comprised of a double pyramid with a square contact plane), the cube, and the rhombdodecahedron (limited by rhomb twelve faces).

The discovery of the South African deposits finally solved the mystery of diamond formation. First of all, the diamonds were found in kimberlite, that is, in the volcanic eruption vents, the "pipes." The explanation at the time was based on the conviction that diamonds were formed in a

This precious diamond weighs 36.65 carats and has an oval fancy cut. Collection: Sotheby's, Geneva.

Rising from the deepest night
The diamond rests in the light.
God Himself still needs it,
In order to break it.

very early epoch under extreme PT-conditions that reached 40,000 to 60,000 atmospheres and 1,250–1,300°C, respectively. These conditions only occur in nature at depths of around 150 to 200 kilometers or for brief moments when meteorites impact. In the course of tectonic displacements and metamorphic transformations, a differentiation occurred in the basic magma at great depth. A change occurred in the original uniform igneous rock suites resulting in new, metamorphic rocks. The sequel to this was new rock-forming minerals as well as accessory minerals, which include diamonds.

In a third phase, the diamonds were explosively driven to the surface from the depths of the earth by sporadically triggered eruptions, to be-

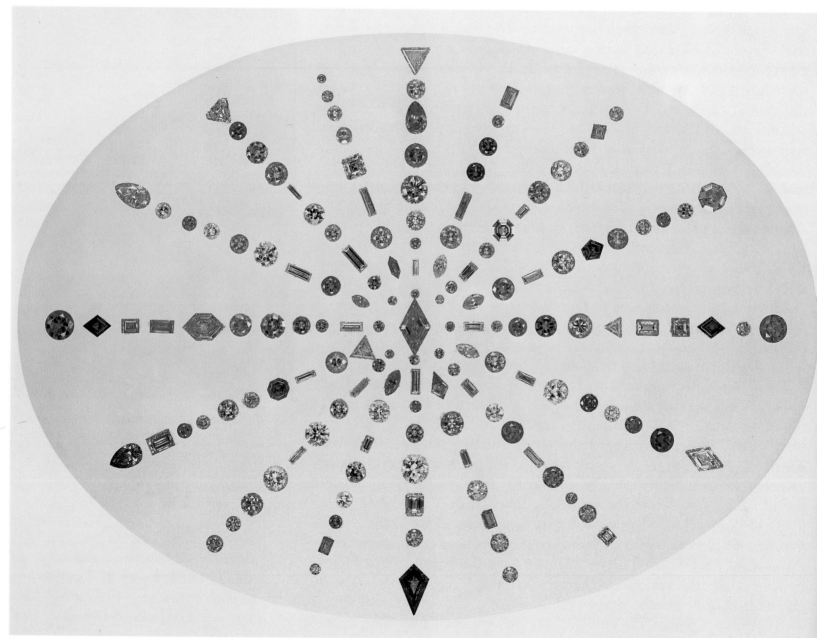

Top: Two yellowish, transparent gem diamonds, crystallized in perfect octahedral form. The larger one weighs 162 carats, the smaller one 65 carats. Photographed at De Beers in Kimberley by Eduard Gübelin, Lucerne.

Above: De Beers' diamond color palette contains all the colors in which diamonds are available. Collection: De Beers, London.

come embedded in the kimberlite rock formed during the cooling of the magma mass. Thus, kimberlite is only a means of conveyance. During the last 200 million years, the soft kimberlite crumbled away due to weathering. The diamonds thus released were deposited in alluvial gravel or carried as far as the seacoast where they were deposited either in coastal banks or in offshore shelves. Diamonds are therefore recovered from quite different deposits: from the primary infill rocks of the volcanic pipes (the "blue ground"), from the secondary placers of river gravel, and from the littoral deposits of coastal formations.

Diamonds make fools of human eyes: glassy and unappealing, unshaped and rough, diamonds can barely be distinguished from normal

Top: Typical example of a "sight": a batch of raw diamonds of different sizes, color, and quality, as they are presented to buyers at the Central Selling Organization (CSO) in London, Lucerne, and Johannesburg.

Center left: At the Finsch Mine, a grab excavator loads excavated, diamond-containing earth into a truck for transportation to the processing plant.

Center right: Concessionaire diamond diggers still work in the valley of the Vaal river using methods and equipment similar to those used after the discovery of the diamond deposits in the second half of the nineteenth century.

Left: View of the gigantic Premier Diamond Mine, which was split in two sections by an enormous, sterile quartzite reef. The reef was later blasted away. The 3,106 carat *Cullinan* diamond was found in the Premier Mine in 1905.

Photos: Eduard Gübelin, Lucerne

The four Cs:

Clarity

Color

Cut

Carat

Below: The photographic reproduction of the color grades corresponds to the color shades of E, J, Q, W, Z, and Fancy yellow in the table on the right. Photo: Gemological Institute of America (GIA), San Diego, California (USA).

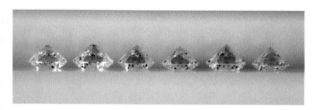

Opposite, top left: Decorative diamond brooch, with a large, cushion-shaped, yellow diamond, that weighs 34.54 carats. This piece of jewelry was created in the mid-nineteenth century. The two cushion-shaped yellow diamonds underneath weigh 23.76 carats and 49.14 carats, respectively. Photo: Christie's, Geneva.

Opposite, right: At the time of the Renaissance, the crystal's form determined the type of cut and, for this reason, the square table cut was preferred. This brooch set with diamonds was created in the first half of the seventeenth century. Collection: Victoria and Albert Museum, London.

Opposite, below left: The lavish and artistic use of different styles of diamond cut makes this jewelry set of necklace and earrings radiate in magnificent beauty. Collection: Van Cleef and Arpels. Photo: Erica and Harold Van Pelt, Los Angeles.

pebbles. Only human rationality and technology can transform a diamond into a work of sparkling light and bring the unique interplay of optical properties described as brilliancy to life. Brilliancy is the result of the joint effect of the adamantine luster (reflection of light from the cut surface), the high level of refraction (diamonds have a refractive index of 2.42, which means that light in diamonds is transmitted 2.42 times slower than in the air), and the total reflection of the rays reflected from the interior of the cut stone, the flashing fire of the light refracted by scattering into its constituent colors as it leaves the gem, and its lively sparkle.

Diamond cutting is both a science and an art. The brilliant cut with its fifty-eight facets, created on the basis of the laws of refraction, is unrivalled among cuts. As important as the cut may be for the incomparable beauty of the brilliant, it is only one of the four Cs that together are the quality factors that determine the value of a diamond.

The diamond's color is a decisive factor for the evaluation of a jewel diamond. Only the "white (colorless) color group" as it is known is subject to a precise color scale. The richly colored varieties are called

Color Grading System of Colorless (White) Diamonds

Exceptional white + D	Exceptional white E	Rare white + F	Rare white G	White H	Slightly tinted white I/J
Tinted white K/L	Tinted color 1 M/N	Tinted color 2 O/P	Tinted color 3 Q/R	Tinted color 4 S-W	Tinted color 5 X-Z

"fancy diamonds" in the trade, attaining exceptionally high prices because of their great rarity. The fine shades within the white color group can be very precisely measured scientifically from exceptional white down to the merest tint. In the trade, however, a comparative method based on measured sample diamonds is sufficient.

Diamonds frequently bear within themselves the distinctive features of their troublesome birth in the form of inclusions that may in future demand high respect as valuable characteristics of authenticity. Inclusions are vagaries of nature: minerals, twin brothers of diamonds, that were created with the latter, accessory minerals or fractures, opaqueness, cloudiness, and structural irregularities. These inclusions adversely affect a diamond's market value and, for this reason, its degree of clarity is of decisive importance. A diamond is considered to be "internally flawless" (i. f.), as it is called, if absolutely no inclusions, that is, no internal flaws, can be seen under ten times magnification with an achromatic lens. Inclusions that are only visible with greater magnification have no influence on the degree of clarity. Internal features that are visible under ten times magnification reduce the commercial value of the diamond in a variety of ways.

Those intending to buy diamonds as a means of capital investment should only buy i. f. brilliant cuts.

From time immemorial, this "fragment of eternity," as diamonds are called in India, has always been the embodiment of power and boldness thanks to its exceptional hardness. As the birthstone for April, it is supposed to free the spirit of fears, render poisons ineffective, and make its owner insuperable if his way of thinking is pure, his mind is lofty, and his thoughts are noble. With its radiant clarity, it continues to personify the highest of virtues and is considered to be a symbol of good luck down to the present day. Throughout every age, humans have unwaveringly revered the diamond as a most precious jewel as well as one of the most reliable and smallest investment assets. The diamond has not fully disclosed itself to the scientific world. It

remains surrounded by secrets and will continue to baffle in the future. In this respect, it is also ADAMAS, the invincible.

55

CORUNDUM

THE COLORFUL PALETTE

Chemistry: Al₂O₃ (alumina)

Crystal system: Trigonal

Habit (form): Hexagonal, narrow to stumpy prisms or rhombohedral tablets, often with steep dipyramids, frequently barrel-shaped.

Colors: All colors (except for red = ruby and blue = sapphire) in all tints and shades as well as colorless and black (pink-orange = Padparadscha).

Refractive index (R.I.): 1.76–1.78 (very constant)

Birefringence: -0.008 (very constant)

Dichroism: Distinct, dependent on body color

Density: 3.99 (3.96–4.01) very constant

Hardness (Mohs' scale): 9 (very constant)

Consistency: No cleavage, weak parting, tough, conchoidal fracture.

Occurrence: In crystalline rocks such as granite, nepheline syenite, gneiss, mica schist, chlorite schist. Widespread worldwide.

Extraction: Gem corundums are usually obtained worldwide from placers, rarely from primary deposits since most of the parent rock is susceptible to weathering.

The extensive corundum family is presented in a bright array of rainbow colors. It repeatedly invites you to make an amazed comparison with a majestically unfolding nature. Like an Alpine meadow in full springtime glory, this mineral group showers crystallized droplets of color in all conceivable shades of blue, yellow, orange, pink, green, violet, and brown. Like delicate buds, some slumber in restrained light shades; others, kissed by the sun and called to a sprightly and glowing existence, dazzle the beholder. These colorful flowers of a charming May bouquet are of clear transparency, as if washed clean by a strong mountain rain. Their colors are genuine and of unequivocal clarity. The yellow corundums radiate a perfect yellow, the reds blaze with purest red, the blues shine in finest blue, and the purples imitate precisely the color of the cardinals. The name of this colorful gemstone family originated from the Sanskrit word *kuruwinda* and the Hindu word *kurund*. The gems are of exquisite beauty and rarity: the red ruby, the blue sapphire, and the orange padparadscha. These are commonly referred to as yellow, green, or orange sapphires although the name sapphire is reserved exclusively for the blue variety of corundum. Correctly speaking, the other color corundums require the adjectival prefacing of the color, that is to say yellow, green or violet corundum, as well as pink or purple corundum, and so forth.

The colorful corundums have one thing in common: They are crystallized alumina, which means they are composed of a combination of aluminum and oxygen (Al₂O₃). Aluminum is well known as a light metal, and oxygen is a very lightweight gas. Nevertheless, this combination results in a specifically heavy, hard, and durable mineral. The strict arrangement of one aluminum atom above and below three oxygen atoms lying in one plane in the corundum's crystal lattice leads to the formation of a trigonal crystal architecture that finds its external expression in a sixfold surface. The shape of the sapphire is frequently several hexagonal double pyramids with or without intervening prisms. This shape combination results in barrel-shaped crystals that are typical of sapphires from Sri Lanka. In contrast, the ruby frequently favors a compact shape that originates from the combination of a short, hexagonal prism with large end faces, whose edges are truncated by small rhombohedral faces. The corundum group's level of hardness on the Mohs' scale is 9. However, its scratch hardness is around 140 times lower than that of the diamond but around 7 times higher than that of the topaz, which is the next softer gem on the scale of hardness. Its high density makes extraction from extensive placer deposits easier. As it sinks, the corundum is separated from the lighter, less precious accompanying minerals. The corundum owes its powerful, full-bodied shine and its sparkling brilliancy to its high level of refraction, which has an average index of 1.765. Corundums are distinguished from the members of other colorful gemstone families by the purity of their color and their lively interaction with light.

Corundum's basic substance, chemically pure, crystallized alumina (alumina/corundum) is completely colorless and corresponds to some extent to the leucosapphire, a variety of corundum that always has a slight tinge of color thus differentiating it from the synthetic colorless corundum. The leucosapphire is extremely rare, even rarer than rubies and sapphires. However, it is less valuable since the beauty, and thus the value, of a corundum lies in its array of colors. The colors are caused by allochromatic, alien coloration. These are color-providing additions that occur as finest metallic mist distributed in the atomic lattice of the crystals. The color is determined by the proportional quantity of these alien pigments. Blue, brown, yellow, and green corundums are colored by iron, which gives them their different colors depending on the degree of oxidation: trivalent iron predominates in the yellow and brown corundums, bivalent iron and titanium are present in blue sapphires. Green sapphires have bi- and trivalent iron, probably in identical quantities. Depending on color intensity, these corundums have an iron content of between 0.005 and 1 percent. The padparadschaah (from padma-rad-schaah – the color of the lotus blossom) is a remarkable exception, distinguished by its unusual color and extreme rarity. When the setting sun touches the snowfields with its last rays, nature shows an image of its warming shades constituted by soft orange and a delicate pink tinge.

Along with the wealth and variety of colors in corundum, it also possesses one of the most puzzling light effects – asterism. Asterism refers to a six-rayed white star effect that appears to hover over a dome-shaped surface and, when the gem is moved, travels over the convex surface as if released. The cause of asterism is based on light scattering over hair-fine mineral inclusions. Microscopically minute rutile fibers have crystalized due to exsolution within the corundum and arranged themselves parallel to the crystallographic main axis in three directions that dissect each other at angles of 120 degrees. Due to the convex shape of the surface, which acts as a converging lens, the light is concentrated into three narrow lines that likewise dissect each other at an angle of 120 degrees. The more concentrated the embedded rutile needles are, the more striking the appearance of the star. This effect is particularly eye-catching in the parallel beams of sunlight or of a spotlight. In the diffuse light of lamps and neon tubes, the star fades into insignificance. On the other hand, the sharpness of the star has a considerable influence on the gem's value. Although the transparency of the star corundum is affected by the fine "silk" of the rutile needles, the pale-colored corundums generally have the most distinct stars. The color of a gemstone plays a central role in determining its value. Full-colored red or blue star gems are exquisitely rare, much sought after objects and they fetch very high prices. Blue star sapphires originate mainly from Sri Lanka, the finest dove's blood red star rubies have consistently been supplied for decades from Mogok in Myanmar. While the six-pointed star tends to be standard, the fine silver threads can also manifest themselves as four-, eight- or twelve-pointed stars. It is not just the classic cabochons of star sapphires that enjoy great popularity among collectors – in the second half of the twentieth century, star gems in other gemstone families have also found favor with collectors. These include the star beryl, the star garnet, and the select rarity of mostly modest size, the ruby-red star spinel.

Corundums can in no way be considered rare, since alumina, their

The corundum family offers lovers of colorful gemstones a sumptuous horn of plenty in the widest variety of colors, which are due to the color effects caused by different trace elements. Photo: Hugo and Andreas Frutig, Berne.

Center left: In the province of Sabaragamu-va on Sri Lanka, numerous thatched gemstone pits are located close together.

Center right: Gemstone diggers fill so-called *illam* (gem-containing dredgings) from the excavated piles into conical washing baskets in order to wash it in the washing pit.

Bottom left: After washing, the overseer offers a prayer to Kataragama, the god of minerals, and then sorts the gemstones collected in the basket.

basic crystallized substance, is very widespread in the earth's crust. Deposits of gem corundum are thus found on all continents and the most important among these always also contain the colorful fancy corundums. The sites famed for the wealth of colors of their corundums are Mogok in Myanmar, Chantaburi and Bo Phloi in Thailand, Ratnapura on Sri Lanka, Anakie in Queensland, Australia, in the Umba valley, along the Tunduru River and around Morogoro in Tanzania, at Lodwar on Lake Turkana in Kenya, and at Yogo Gulch, Dry Cottonwood Creek, and Rock Creek in the state of Montana (USA), and last but not least around Ilakaka, Madagascar.

Right: A gemstone cutter on Sri Lanka makes an interesting subject. With his left hand, he is pressing the raw gem against the grinding disk that is attached on the left to a notched wooden shaft. Using a fiddle-bow, whose cord runs around the wooden roll, he sets it in alternating turning motions.

Photos: Eduard Gübelin, Lucerne.

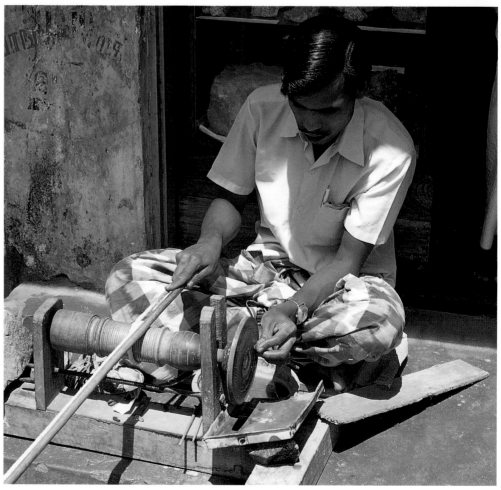

58

The most important occurrences of colorful corundums are the extensive placers on Sri Lanka from which gemstones have been extracted for thousands of years. Sri Lanka's corundums were definitely not formed in a single process but are more likely to be products of a correlation of pegmatitic, metamorphic, and metasomatic processes that, as a result of weathering, finally came to rest in sedimentary deposits.

Over millions of years, this process also ensured a certain amount of qualitative selection. The soft and thus worthless rock did not resist the long hard strain and crumbled. In contrast, the hard minerals collected into gemiferous (meaning "carrying gems" deposits, the placers, as they

are called (the local people call them *illam*), in rubble heaps, in alluvial beds, and wherever terraces formed on mountain slopes and talus hills. The formation of these alluvial gemstone deposits was largely completed around one million years ago. They lie over a much older, partly decomposed basic rock – the former, original surface of the island.

The most precious concentration of gemstones is located in the old river beds of the Kelani and Kalu-Ganga, particularly where they are joined by mountain streams, in bays, and in the shallows of large meanders. The digging methods – river and pit mining – are extremely backward by modern standards. However, any attempts at modernization have met with resistance from the native population as they cling to the profession handed down to them through the generations. The simplicity, even primitiveness of mining in Sri Lanka is in stark contrast to gemstone excavation in Thailand. There, mining operations use the most advanced technical equipment. The jungle is becoming a major construction site. The mining methods that are almost akin to overexploitation have led experts to anticipate the depletion of the Thai deposits at the start of the third millennium.

Left: Typical corundum crystal (sapphire) intergrown in horizontal direction with a flat twin (Sri Lanka).
Below it, three faceted corundums in different colors. Photo: Erica and Harold Van Pelt, Los Angeles.

Center: The most charming and precious member of the corundum family is the orange padparadscha with its delicate pink tinge. Collection: Gebr. Bank, Idar-Oberstein. Photo: Erica and Harold Van Pelt, Los Angeles.

Right: Close-packed, multicolored concentration of corundum crystals, which is how they mostly occur in large quantities in corundum deposits. Photo: Eduard Gübelin, Lucerne.

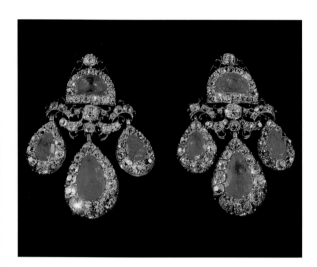

Chemistry: Al₂O₃ (alumina with traces of chromium oxide)

Crystal system: Trigonal

Habit (form): Hexagonal, narrow to stumpy prisms or tabular rhombohedral prisms, often with steep dipyramids.

Colors: All tints and shades of red. The most precious color is considered to be carmine red, called "pigeon's blood red."

Refractive index (R.I.): 1.76–1.78

Birefringence: -0.008

Dichroism: Yellow to orange-red and purple-red

Density: 3.99 (3.96–4.01)

Hardness (Mohs' scale): 9

Consistency: Tough, no cleavage, conchoidal fracture.

Occurrence: In crystalline limestones, dolomites, and dolomitic calcite marbles as well as in basic metamorphic rocks (amphibolite); also in contact zones and volcanites.

Extraction: From the above-mentioned rocks in primary and valley floor deposits as well as alluvial deposits (placers).

RUBY: DIVINE CRYSTAL SPARK

Red magic and color extract from a "drop of the heart's blood of Mother Earth" is how the ruby is described in the effusive language of the Orient. These characteristics have enabled the gemstone to rise as a paramount favorite among those in power and those in love. The glorification of this proud representative of the color gemstones often borders on the charmingly irrational. Hardly any other gem can inspire such emotional vibrations as does the ruby. Among most peoples, it has symbolized since time immemorial the highest of earthly possessions – love. To children born in the month of July, it promises the much sought after benefits of freedom, goodness, respect, and dignity. This "flaming beacon" owes its popularity to the majestically glowing color of a fiery red ember under a surface with a lacquered sheen. Its name, derived from the Latin word *ruber* (red), represents the embodiment of the most beautiful red conceivable. Light and velvety shades change from pink to darkest purple. The highlight of all beauty, however, the finest and most precious shade is the dove's blood red, a full-toned shading of carmine red. The brighter, the livelier the red sparkles, the more exquisite and precious is the ruby.

Even a serious look at rubies falls prey to superlatives. Together with the sapphire, the ruby belongs to the noble corundum family. It is also composed of crystallized alumina (Al_2O_3) and thus has the same superb properties. The high degree of hardness (H = 9), its high density (D = 3.99), and its high refractive index (n = 1.765) safeguard its position just below the diamond. Nevertheless, it has no need to acknowledge any superior authority. The Indians put this sentiment into words and named it in Sanskrit *ratnanäyaka*, the lord of gemstones.

Its outstanding color is attributable to the introduction of chromium oxide (Cr_2O_3, dependent on saturation of 0.10–1.6 percent), which found its way into the crystal lattice of the crystallized alumina an infinite number of years ago and replaced several percent of alumina. The color intensity is substantially influenced by the chromium percentage. The preferred dove's blood red coloration appears with 0.30 percent pure chromium oxide. If the oxidation condition of the chromium changes, orange-colored shades occur. Other shades of red, brown-red, or purple-red can be ascribed to traces of iron and vanadium, respectively. Increased proportions of iron cause a brownish touch, whereas the vanadium content determines the blue coloration. It is precisely this chromium pigment that is in such short supply in the upper regions of the earth's crust that makes the ruby one of the rarest gemstones. During the creation of the ruby, therefore, a very unusual chance occurrence must have taken place for the chromium oxide, which originates in the very depths of the earth, to be present at the exact moment of crystallization of the alumina.

The ruby's time of birth is surrounded by secrecy. Basalt, marble, metamorphic rock (amphibolite, gneiss, and others), as well as pegmatite were all involved in its crystallization. In the hilly surroundings of Mo-

A magnificent specimen of marble with a large ruby crystal. Beside it, a heart-shaped ruby. Both from Jagdalek, Afghanistan. Collection: William Larson. Photo: Erica and Harold Van Pelt, Los Angeles.

Opposite, top left: View of the Inkyauk Mine, the largest ruby mine near Mogok, Myanmar, showing excavation operations. Bottom center in the picture, the miners are clearing away the valley floor, which contains rubies. The pump on the left-hand slope sucks the excavated material upward and transports it to the processing plant, to which the excavations from top right and from the background are also taken. In the early morning, the landscape is still misty. Photo: Eduard Gübelin, Lucerne.

gok in Myanmar, where the most important occurrences of rubies are located and the finest rubies are discovered, an almost classic example of this type of formation can be found. The mother rock is a white, coarse-grained, partly dolomite limestone marble of extreme age (over 500 million years old), which is embedded in a formation of crystalline schist. It is a contact rock that is the result of contact with granitic magmas and limestone conversions. It is a well-known fact that highly active, pneumatolytic mineral solutions have a preference for penetrating limestones and related carbonatic adjacent rock where they cause the formation of new and amazingly varied combinations of minerals. In the generation sequence of gemstones that crystallized in succession, the ruby is the youngest. It was created when only alumina and a little chromium were left of the solution substances. Chromium is not normally a component of the rocks involved in these precipitation processes but has to be transported up from the depths by the rising melt or solutions and added to the rubies' crystallization process at the right time and place. In the mother rock, rubies occur mostly as beautifully developed crystals. The blood red examples in contrasting white marble make an overpowering impression. All the more so, since rubies are rarely found in their host rocks, while they are to some extent very heavily concentrated in the weathered residues of marbles and the resulting alluvial valley floors where they are preferably extracted nowadays.

In Mogok, admirers of rubies will find examples of unsurpassable beauty. The discovery of this richest of ruby treasure vaults is lost in the mystery of a legend. In the fifteenth century, a Burmese king is said to have seized the Mogok valley through trickery. A band of thieves who were serving their sentence in the inaccessible valley reported the red stones for the first time. The king imposed the strictest secrecy. Through the already tortuous paths of diplomacy, he exchanged the rich Mogok valley of the unsuspecting Shan prince for a worthless piece of land. From then on, the Burmese rulers accumulated a fabulous treasure. A royal edict from 1597 contains the first known indication of the ruby deposit in Mogok, which was the exclusive property of the Burmese crown. The heirs had the remote district militarily blockaded. Access is prohibited to outsiders. Trading is conducted nowadays at the annual auction of the Gem Emporium in the capital of Yangon and via smugglers' routes to Bangkok.

With Mogok as the most important deposit, it is occasionally equalled by Hunza (Pakistan), which likewise provides gems of the finest color although on much rarer occasions. In Hunza, too, the mother rock is dolomite marble. The rubies frequently have a large number of inclusions and are therefore primarily used as cabochons. Further occurrences are in Thailand, Sri Lanka, Cambodia, Tanzania, Afghanistan, and North Carolina (USA). Even Switzerland has a small deposit of rubies and sapphires on Mount Campolungo in the canton of Ticino. Thailand is the second most important supplier of rubies. The occurrences are in the southeast on both sides of the border with Cambodia. They are to be found only a few meters deep in basalt rubble that covers extensive areas due to the erosion of ancient, long-extinct volcanoes.

Below: Two top-quality rubies with weights of 10.55 and 8.75 carats. They are different shades of red and originate from the valley floor of Mogok, Myanmar, which is rich in gemstones.

Above: A satisfied ruby washer shows a handful of rubies that she has sorted from the gravel in her washing basket. Near Bang Tun, Thailand.

Left: Against the background of a graceful pagoda, ruby traders (kanesema) haggle over the prices of their gems. Picturesque scenes of this type are encountered on the streets and mining fields of Mogok.

Photos: Eduard Gübelin, Lucerne.

*We see rubies born of the Earth
in a far country;
Processed with the gemcutter's hand,
selected by Mankind as a jewel.*

Eduard Gübelin, Lucerne.

Only the intervention of a lapidary can turn the unattractive red stones into radiant, glowing rubies, precious jewels to delight humans.

Thai (Siam) rubies, which only rarely achieve the lively color tones of Myanmar rubies, are darker and often have a purple or brown tinge. The rubies of Pailin (Cambodia) are more beautiful. The mainly light to raspberry red rubies of Sri Lanka, which are noted for their uncommonly lively luster, are extracted from placers in the southwest of the island near Ratnapura. The examples found are mostly so light-colored that differentiating between light-red rubies or rich-colored pink sapphires becomes difficult. The ruby deposits in Tanzania have increasingly attracted attention. In the valley of the Umba River, which empties into the Indian Ocean between Tanga and Mombasa, beautiful transparent rubies, comparable in color to the Siam rubies await their release together with a large number of colorful corundums from primary and secondary deposits. Farther to the northwest, at the foot of the extinct volcano of Longido, miners excavate opaque yet deep red rubies embedded in green zoisite rock from small pits. The small, magnificently red rubies are eminently suited for use in gold items of jewelry if used in larger numbers.

In the second half of the twentieth century, the earth yielded further as yet unknown ruby occurrences at short intervals. These include Kenya with deposits at the southern foot of Kilimanjaro, Luc Yen and Quy Chao in North Vietnam, and Mong Hsu in the state of the Karen in Myanmar. The rubies from Luc Yen and Mong Hsu, together with those from Mogok and Hunza, have a characteristic similarity: all are embedded in the same mother rock, dolomite marble. Externally, therefore, the rubies are confusingly similar. However, internally, they differ by their inclusions and trace elements. The term of Burma ruby used for a single geographical location now includes, in addition to Mogok, the second deposit of Mong Hsu.

Sticking doggedly to provenance should strongly be warned against since, although the different colorations are apparently typical for the various sources, they can never serve as features of origin. The source names, such as Burma ruby and Siam ruby, frequently used in the trade as designations of quality are misleading and incorrect, since every deposit has rubies of high quality as well as less valuable ones. An important criterion for the appreciation of rubies and their origins, however, is provided by their inclusions. Rubies are hard to imagine without them, since pure rubies are discovered only on extremely rare occasions. They almost always contain minute foreign crystals. These originated either from the surrounding mother rock or they developed at the same time as the ruby or were formed inside the ruby subsequently such as the delicate rutile needles. The rutile fibers create an ultrafine network called *silk*, which creates a delicate, silvery shimmer of light that can be bundled together on rubies with a domed cut to form a star. Other inclusions are "feathers" of liquid drops, which are reminiscent of dragonfly wings in their delicate netlike arrangement. Beyond the determination of origin, inclusions serve as unmistakable recognition features to distinguish between natural rubies, which are born of the Earth, and synthetic (artificially manufactured) products. Advanced technology enables the production of gems of such harmonious chemical, physical, and optical properties that only the type of inclusion can provide convincing information about their origin. In contrast to diamonds, where maximum clarity can be demanded as a sign of excellent quality, the inclusions in rubies as in all other color gemstones provide a valuable certificate of authenticity.

With rubies, nature is not nearly as generous as it is with diamonds: rubies very rarely form large crystals. Examples weighing more than 5 carats are sparse; rubies of over 10 carats are considered to be exceptions to the rule. Some of these exceptional gemstones are in the posses-

Rubies are your lips,
no finer can be seen.
Thrice happy is the man,
to whom you confess your love.

Heinrich Heine *(Heimkehr 59)*

sion of oriental princes, since the Eastern belief in miracles ascribes magical powers to rubies, too; it is suggested that rubies have the ability to foresee terrible events or that their countenance darkens at the approach of evil and lightens once again as it retreats.

Given the generally small size of rubies, news of the discovery of gigantic examples spreads like wildfire. These are correspondingly honored by the specialists' world and courted by museums. The *Rosser Reeves* ruby weighs in at the seemingly legendary 138 carats. This is a star ruby of perfect shape about the size of a walnut and is currently at the Smithsonian Institution in Washington, D.C. (USA). The 100-carat *Delong* ruby once fell victim to a robbery and was only recovered in return for the payment of a high ransom. It is on display at the Museum of Natural History in New York (USA). In the armistice year of 1918, a 41-carat gemstone discovered in Myanmar and dubbed the *Peace* ruby caused excitement. Incomparable in every way, however, is a ruby crystal of 1,743 carats from the Dat Taw mine, which the author was fortunate enough to admire in 1993 in Mogok, Myanmar.

Right: An attractive, classic necklace and a pair of earrings set with rubies and marquise diamonds. In addition, a ladies' ring with a drop-shaped diamond weighing 9.03 carats. Private collection.

Left: Diadem from the ruby jewelry of Queen Theresa, created by Caspar Rieländer and commissioned by King Ludwig I of Bavaria (1786–1868) for his wife. Gold, silver, rubies, spinels, and diamonds are arranged in the form of blossoms and leaves. Munich 1830. Treasure Chamber of the Munich Residency. Photo: Claus Hansmann, Munich.

65

SAPPHIRE: SYMBOL OF THE FIRMAMENT

Sapphires are your eyes,
so lovely, so sweet,
Thrice happy is the man
you greet with love.

Heinrich Heine *(Heimkehr 59)*

Precious, cornflower blue sapphire weighing 20 carats from deposits at an altitude of 5,500 meters in the Zanskar Mountains of Kashmir, India. The cornflower blue color is considered to be the finest of the sapphire colors. Photo: Eduard Gübelin, Lucerne.

The blue sapphire, which displays its charms with dignified restraint, is surrounded by a sacred aura. It superbly enacts the symbiosis of elegant distance and spiritual depth. For this reason, the sapphire is involved, like no other among its noble brothers, in heathen and Christian magic, which attempted to harness psychic powers with the help of this celestial gem. In actual fact, the sapphire was the jewel of choice in past centuries for the high dignitaries of the church and worldly regents as is eloquently witnessed by their treasure chambers even today.

The name sapphire came into being through the languages of many peoples. In Sanskrit, it is called *sauriratna*, which means dedicated to Saturn. In Chaldean, it was called *sampir*, in Greek *sappheiros* (blue), in Latin, *saphirus,* and in Arabic safir; all designations that are testimony to its widespread occurrence. There is no doubt that the blue sapphire is far more widespread than its more spectacular brother, the red ruby; in some locations, it is so abundant that, as is the case with diamonds, lesser qualities are used for polishing purposes.

Rubies and sapphires are very closely related to each other and the admiration for the one is as old as the esteem for the other. However, while the temperamental, fiery brother woos the favors of dusky women in such princely fashion, the more discreet, more restrained sapphire enjoys the favors of the entire world of females, particularly blondes. As an exalted member of the same family of corundums, the ruby and the sapphire both share the same characteristics. The sapphire is also chemically a crystallized alumina (Al_2O_3) and shares with the other corundums the same data for light refraction, density, and hardness. As they are created from the same substances, the occurrence of the blue sapphire is frequently identical to that of the ruby. The mountains of Myanmar sometimes yield a specialty, a willful combination of both, namely a red ruby with a core of plum blue sapphire (e. g., from Mong Hsu).

If the ruby is allowed to have the most beautiful color in its most sensual impression as its watchword, the sapphire is satisfied with the more restrained blue, but compensates for this supposed modesty with a much more lavish wealth of shades. The majestic cornflower blue is the most sought after color, both gentle and demanding at the same time, both gleaming and flattering, ennobled by a delicate admixture of regal purple. No less in demand is the royal blue sapphire. A silky shimmer of velvet radiates over it, diverts the eye to hidden depths where a tiny touch of cobalt gives it the bottomlessness of mountain lakes. Almost akin to elfin beauty, the marine blue sapphires blaze dramatically yet are still filled with a warm glow. They are reminiscent of crystallized drops from the deep blue oceans of the Orient. But there are still more: The shades range from the opulent, dark blue of gentians to a cool ice blue, from dancing, frivolous azure blue and a light, cheerful sky blue through to crackling, exciting electric blue. Words cannot precisely describe the many possible varieties of blue. Nature has been so inventive with them that it is presumptuous to talk of sapphire blue as

Chemistry: Al_2O_3 (alumina with traces of iron-titanium oxide)

Crystal system: Trigonal

Habit (form): Hexagonal, narrow to barrel-shaped prisms, usually with small basic surface, often with pointed ends and combined with steep dipyramids that, in combination with the prism surfaces, form steps and ledges, resulting in so-called "barrel-shapes."

Colors: All tints and shades of blue, from light blue to dark blue and from green-blue to violet-blue. The color most appreciated is the corn-flower blue.

Refractive index (R.I.): 1.76–1.78

Birefringence: -0.008

Dichroism: Blue and greenish blue

Density: 3.99 (3.96–4.01)

Hardness (Mohs' scale): 9

Consistency: Tough, no cleavage, conchoidal fracture.

Occurrence: Widespread in pegmatite veins, in metamorphic and metasomatic rocks as well as in volcanites.

Extraction: From the above-mentioned rocks in primary and valley floor deposits as well as alluvial deposits (placers).

Above: Elegant sapphire set called *Astroline*, made of white and yellow gold with blue baguette sapphires and large, oval pink sapphires weighing between 2.98 carats and 11.00 carats, surrounded by white and yellow diamonds. Création Gübelin AG, Lucerne.

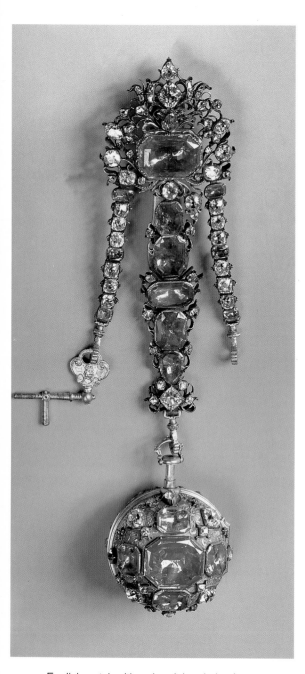

English watch with a chatelaine dating from the eighteenth century, made by master craftsman Charles Cabrier, London. The watch and chatelaine are set with eighteen sapphires and ninety-nine diamonds cut in the old style. Watches of this kind were worn on the belt as jewelry. Gallery of Treasures, St. Petersburg.

the quintessence of a quite specific color. It is equally misguided to express this nature-given difference in the colors in the descriptions of origin, since, without exception, Providence strewed light and dark, pure and mixed-color sapphires in all corundum deposits. It is undoubtedly questionable to limit interest to the cornflower blue shade, as the rarest, due to its price category. Is it not more the case that sapphires conceal the reflection of heavenly blues inside themselves at all hours of the day and over all continents?

The secretive blue of vanishing daylight and the onset of night's shadows – unmatched in these graduated color modulations by any other gemstone in nature – are granted to the sapphire by ultramicroscopic additions of the trace elements iron and titanium oxide. As the main pigment, bivalent iron is responsible for the blue color. Very slight deviations of approximately only one hundredth of a percent in weight in the iron and titanium content and their resultant interaction determine the brilliance of the colors and are thus answerable for the enhanced values of cornflower, royal, and marine blue . The more frequent occurrence of the blue sapphire in comparison with rubies is explained simply by the colorant. Combinations of titanium and iron are more prevalent in the upper rock-forming segments of the earth's crust, precisely where sapphires have their birthplace. Just as rubies, most sapphires can be called metasomatic minerals. Blue sapphires are the result of highly disparate rock-forming processes: sapphires in Kashmir were formed in pegmatites rich in aluminum and boron. The requisite iron and titanium for the blue coloration originate from the adjacent rock. Sapphires from Australia, Cambodia, and Thailand were subjected to completely different conditions: Created as a reaction by aluminum-rich, molten carbonatite in the deep layers of the earth's crust under high pressures and temperatures, they were transported as the accompanying minerals of volcanic basalt eruptions to the earth's surface to be deposited as a result of weathering in the sedimentary rubble of the valley floors. The sapphires discovered just a few years ago in the sapphire deposits at Andranondambo on Malagasy were created in yet another way: In the contact zone of very ancient, metamorphic formations, impure marbles were transformed under metasomatic conditions into coarsely crystalline, aluminum-rich skarns (calcsilicates), accompanied by the crystallization of blue corundum thanks to the admixture of traces of titanium and iron. As is the case with rubies, the inclusions in sapphires are the result of their style of formation and structure. Their internal life is a true wonderland in the most compact of spaces, enjoying their reputation as welcoming hosts who will house their invited guests eternally. In exceptional cases, the sapphire embraces other, individual gemstones of microscopic minuteness, that were created before or at the same time. One of nature's caprices is to allow the integrated colorant titanium oxide (TiO_2) to appear as the finest of rutile needles. This creates the so-called "silk" on which twinkling, iridescent reflections sparkle. This quirk of nature reaches its zenith in an enchanting spell, when the silvery gleam of a star shines out over the silky blue background.

The most important sapphire occurrences are on Sri Lanka, in Myan-

Left: A magnificent classic set of jewelry, set with brilliant-cut and marquise-cut diamonds as well as royal blue sapphires from Myanmar. Alongside, three sapphires from Kashmir and one from Myanmar. Création Gübelin AG, Lucerne.

Bottom left: This hair ornament, called an "aigrette," is designed in the shape of a fountain. From its swirling base of large sapphires and brilliant-cut diamonds, a fountain sprays a cascade of brilliant-cut diamonds, which fall down again as heavy sapphire drops. Style: Rococo, 1755. Treasure Chamber of the Confederation of Independent States (Russia).

Above: Classic modern necklace with Myanmar sapphires, brilliant-cut and marquise-cut diamonds. Création Gübelin AG, Lucerne.

Right: A sorter divides up the raw sapphires according to size and quality in a sapphire-cutting workshop in Inverell, Australia,.

Far right: Small-scale gemstone trading in a street in Elahera, Sri Lanka.

Center: As shown by the two rows, the sapphires (corundums) from deposits near Tunduru (top row) and Umba valley, Tanzania (bottom row), come in a wide variety of colors.

Photos: Eduard Gübelin, Lucerne.

Above: Near Andranondambo, Madagascar, the snow-white skarn that contains sapphires is mined in narrow, closely packed shafts.

Right: The sapphire mine of Yadana Kadè near Kyaukpyatthat, Myanmar, is considerably more spacious. Photo shows miners transporting diggings containing sapphires from a pit to the processing plant by means of hooks.

mar, Thailand, Tanzania, Cambodia, Australia, Madagascar, and in the state of Montana (USA). Extraction is mainly from alluvial weathered rubble or, in some cases, directly from the mother rock, for example, on Madagascar. At Kyaukpyatthat in Myanmar, in the Umba valley in Tanzania, and at Yogo Gulch in Montana as well as in the poorly accessible deposits of the famous cornflower blue Kashmir sapphires in India, both primary and secondary deposits are mined simultaneously and alongside each other. In each case, however, the placer deposits prove to be much more productive. The sapphire deposits in Australia, Thailand, and Cambodia are coarse-grained, alluvial rubble banks that are the result of weathered volcanoes. They are strikingly rich in black star sapphires and dark, blue-black sapphires with very similar inclusions. In addition, blue, yellow, green, and pink corundums, garnets, zircons, and black spinels are extracted. The most beautiful of all these volcanic sapphires from Australia, Cambodia, Thailand, and Vietnam are those from Pailin (Cambodia). However, they are generally small and are rarely seen on the market. The other volcanic sapphires take second place to some extent due to their timid darker blue.

The cultural centers of the ancient world, Rome and Egypt, revered the sapphire as the holy stone of truth and justice; to Buddhists, it means peace, friendship, and permanence and is therefore honored as a talisman for marital bliss. The sapphire found its way into the Christian church at a very early stage. Innocence III decreed by papal bull that every cardinal and bishop should wear a sapphire ring on the right hand that was used for blessing. Oddly enough, at the same time the sapphire was also the medium of the necromancers. They believed it would make them capable of hearing voices and uttering prophecies. From time immemorial, it has also been honored as the stone of chastity and fidelity.

The treasure houses of all the world's rulers vied for the privilege of showing the finest and most brilliant "tears from the eyes of the goddess Saitya." This must have been a very sad goddess that the Hindus honored since she shed many large tears! Godly tears were not always used to adorn majestic jewelry or to decorate eighteenfold the famous crown of Wenzel, the Bohemian king, for example. In the United States of America, a different and unusual possibility of working the gem was thought up. The heads of presidents George Washington, Abraham Lincoln, and Dwight Eisenhower were carved out of three superb sapphires of around 2,000 carats each.

The largest sapphire in the world was, until recently, a find of 6,000 carats. It was discovered, as the annals are pleased to record, in Mogok in 1972. This record has only recently been broken by a find of truly remarkable size. The exciting event occurred on Madagascar. The gemological certificate of April 1996 that attested the authenticity of the find amazed the trade: this latest and, at the same time, the heaviest sapphire ever brought to light by human hands was 89,500 carats or a weight of no less than 17.5 kilograms.

As a birthstone, the sapphire is assigned to September. Its inherent powers of peace of mind, cleverness, and fidelity multiply the benefits of ownership.

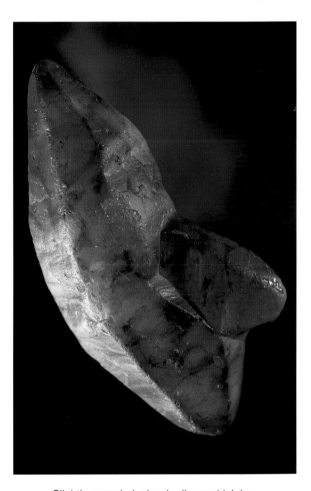

Slightly corroded, classic dipyramidal, barrel-shaped, trigonal crystal form of a sapphire from Sri Lanka, grown together with a smaller, similarly formed sapphire. Collection: A. Ruppenthal, Idar-Oberstein.

BERYL
THE PALETTE
OF
PASTEL COLORS

Aquamarine, golden beryl, yellow and green beryl, morganite and red beryl, heliodor and emerald.

Chemistry: $Be_3Al_2Si_6O_{18}$ (beryllium-aluminum silicate)

Crystal system: Hexagonal

Habit (form): Stumpy to narrow, hexagonal prisms usually with flat end pinacoids or inclined pyramid faces.

Colors: All colors in all tints and shades, even colorless and black.

Aquamarine: blue; morganite: pink; emerald: green.

Refractive index (R.I.): 1.56–1.57 (morganite: 1.59–1.599)

Birefringence: -0.005 (morganite: -0.009)

Dichroism: Weak to clear, differs according to body color.

Density: 2.65–2.75 (morganite: 2.8–2.9)

Hardness (Mohs' scale): 7.5–8

Consistency: Brittle (emerald more so than the other beryls), conchoidal fracture.

Occurrence: Mainly in granitic pegmatites, emerald also in metamorphic rocks as well as pneumatolytic and hydrothermal rocks.

Extraction: From the parent rock in primary deposits, rarely from placers.

Widespread worldwide.

With beryls, we meet yet another large gemstone family among the endless color palette of gemstones, which please the eye with springlike, fresh, and lively pastel colors. The designation *beryl* comprises gemstones that have a striking, almost inconceivable wealth of colors. It is a little known fact that, in olden days, beryls were used as eye glasses as Pliny reported in his *Historia naturalis*. The name might be Indian in origin and a development of the Prakrit word *veruliyam* before passing via the Latin *berullus* into English as *beryl*. It is said that the Emperor Nero viewed the gladiator fights through an emerald. The emerald is the rarest and finest member of the beryl group. In the Middle Ages, beryl was also used as a magic mirror in which, it was claimed, the future could be glimpsed. Monstrances and reliquary vessels were decorated with cut disks of beryl at that time, too.

The actual environment for these cheerful beryls are pegmatites, the liquid molten rocks that, in their rise through the passageways and cracks of older rocks, carried substances that were necessary for the formation of beryls. The beryls belong to the large group of silicates. Silica (SiO_2) forms six-membered rings, as they are called, that are firmly bonded together by the layers of beryllium and alumina molecules ($3 BeO$ and $1Al_2O_3$) between them. This leads to a combination of beryllium earth and clay with silica [$Be_3Al_2(SiO_3)_6$]. The close cohesion between the crystalline modules makes beryl highly resistant to mechanical stress (Hardness = 7.5–8). The remaining properties – density (D = 2.72) and refraction (n = 1.58) – are fairly low. In spite of their lively glassy luster, beryls compensate for their weak brilliance with their pastel colors of refreshing luminosity and untiring variety.

Similar to most gemstones of this type, the cheerfulness and dainty idyll of these gemstones are typical examples of allochromatic coloring since a beryl of the pure chemical composition as described above is colorless. It is a characteristic of a pegmatite mineral that, out of the numerous, highly volatile components in the molten parent rock, it has incorporated all those that might contribute toward enhancing its beauty. The beryl is certainly no exception here. The pink beryl is a treasure trove of rare elements that serve to heighten its exceptional characteristics. If it develops not only the delicate color of peach blossom but a fine cyclamen red, it is unrivalled by any other gem for its graceful beauty. The astounding intensive pink is sometimes caused by manganese. In honor of the American gemstone patron, J. P. Morgan, this symphony in pink was named *Morganite* by the Swiss gemologist G. F. Kunz at Tiffany's in New York (USA). Like an ice floe, the dewy blue of the aquamarine is attributable to the addition of bivalent iron. Legend has it that seahorses carried these pale and watery riches from the treasure chests of the nymphs to inhabited shores. With the transparent clarity of all beryls, the aquamarine or sea-blue remains permanently associated with water in myths: It accompanies seafarers and ensures them a safe return home; and round the ship of marital fortune, it weaves a ribbon of faithfulness. The aquamarine is the gemstone of all young people and all those who have remained young at heart. It takes particular care of those born in March. Trivalent iron pours the

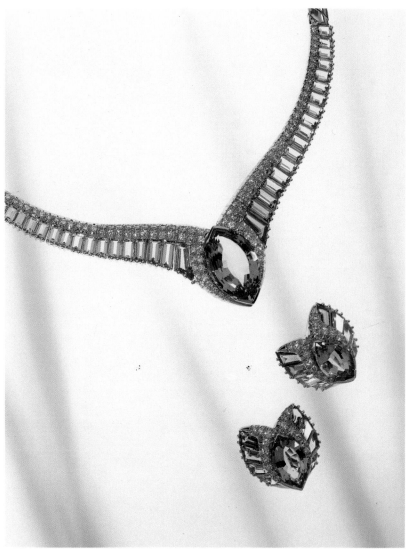

color of liquid gold into the warm luster of golden beryl, whereas the mixture of bivalent and trivalent iron produces shades of green. The original inhabitants of South Africa call the sunshine yellow heliodor a "gift of the sun," and it would be difficult to find a better name for it. They are seriously convinced that this rare gemstone fell to earth in a mighty shower of meteorites. Its color is enhanced by a slight admixture of uranium oxide, which makes the heliodor as irresistible to collectors as an apple in Paradise.

As a typical accompaniment to pegmatite, that most industrious of gemstone producers, beryls occur in many of the deposits on all continents, but mainly on Sri Lanka and Madagascar, in Myanmar, India, and California (USA) as well as in the Urals and Siberia. The most important occurrences of these widely varying gems are in Brazil in the gem-rich states of Bahia, Espirito Santo, and Minas Gerais. There, they are found in coarse-grained pegmatites and their weathered remains, also in crystalline schist, mostly together with other characteristic minerals of pegmatitic paragenesis such as topaz and tourmaline, in druses not to mention veins of quartz that permeate granite, gneiss, and mica schist.

From these primary deposits, beryls are extracted from quarries as

Right: Idiomorphous, many-faced aquamarine crystal intergrown with muscovite on pegmatite from the Palmital Mine, Minas Gerais, Brazil. Collection: Hein Gärtner, Idar-Oberstein. Photo: Karl Hartmann.

Far right: Four small specimens with bluish and greenish beryl crystals from the Naipa Mine, Alto Ligonha, Mozambique. Photos: Eduard Gübelin, Lucerne.

Below: In a pit shored up with wooden planking, gemstone diggers wash their diggings containing aquamarine crystals. Minas Gerais, Brazil.

Bottom: In a gallery of the St. Anne's Mine in the large pegmatite shield near Karoi, Zimbabwe, a miner breaks off protruding lumps of rock containing aquamarine and tourmaline crystals.

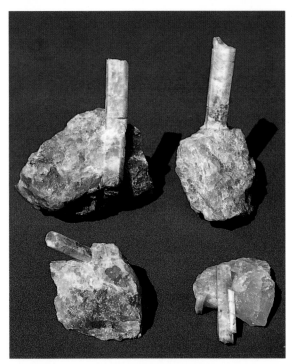

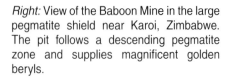

Right: View of the Baboon Mine in the large pegmatite shield near Karoi, Zimbabwe. The pit follows a descending pegmatite zone and supplies magnificent golden beryls.

Photos: Eduard Gübelin, Lucerne.

74

well as from mines in many places. Since the beryls were formed from liquid molten rock, enormous crystals frequently developed, achieving lengths of up to 2 meters and weights of 30 hundredweight. The placers – slope rubble and debris – often located in the vicinity of rock faces are always broken up by powerful jets of water and made to collapse wherever these heaps of pebbles have accumulated and solidified. Together with the loose deposits, the gravel released in this way is carried away using shovels and rakes and processed in nearby flowing rivers. From the interior of the country, the beryls and all Brazilian gemstones are taken for processing to their two most important trading locations. These are traditionally Rio de Janeiro and Idar-Oberstein in Germany.

Beryl prices vary just as much as their colors. Prices fluctuate widely depending on color and quality. Youthfully pale examples are cheaper than those with vivid colors; pure and transparent gems are more expensive than cloudy ones.

Top right: Idiomorphously crystallized prism of a red beryl on its parent rock of rhyolite from the Wah-Wah Mountains, Utah (USA). Collection: Senckenberg Museum, Frankfurt/Main.

Left: These beryls owe their different colors to the admixture of small quantities of iron of different valences. Collection: William Larson, Fallbrook, California (USA). Photo: Erica and Harold Van Pelt, Los Angeles.

Right: Necklace studded with diamonds and a pendant made of a drop-shaped aquamarine. Photo: Erica and Harold Van Pelt, Los Angeles.

EMERALD: GLITTERING LIKE LEAVES IN MAY

There are few words in human speech to describe the green of an emerald, no matter how rich in imagination or expression. Its green is filled with almost unrestrained dynamism. It is a green of unique perfection that effortlessly conquers spatial distances due to its short waves. The untamed wildness of this color splits people into ardent fans and decided opponents. "We delight in feasting our eyes on the pleasant green of the grasses and leaves, but the enjoyment of beholding an emerald is incomparably greater, for its green is the most soothing," was how Pliny's cheerful hymn of praise described the fine head of the beryl family. Chromium oxide is decisive for the creation of this extravagant green. Only those beryls that have chromium and/or vanadium as colorants can be considered to be emeralds. Similarly, green gemstones, for example beryls containing iron oxide as the dominant coloring admixture, are assigned to the normal beryls. Even minute traces of chromium are sufficient to create the unmistakable emerald color that can be easily distinguished from the green color of beryls caused by iron oxide. The intensity of the color depends on the quantity of chromium, which can amount to several percent. The trace elements of iron and vanadium that frequently accompany chromium create yellow and bluish tones. The almost imperceptible graduations of the strongly shaded green palette range from pale leaf green to bright green or heavy pine green. The most beautiful and richest colorful shade is the green of tingling, dewy Maytime grass. The emerald is one of the few gemstones that allows the luster of its natural green to sparkle even in the dark when festively illuminated with lamps or candles.

The explanation for the rare occurrence of beautifully colored emeralds lies in the fundamentally different geochemical behavior of the two elements beryllium and chromium that are almost never encountered together in nature. In the atomic structure of the beryllium-aluminum silicate, which corresponds to the chemical composition of the beryl, trivalent chromium oxide replaces an alumina molecule. Its volume is greater than that of alumina. For this reason, the adhesion between the silica rings is loosened and the inherent brittleness of every mineral is increased in the emerald. Despite its hardness of 7.5–8 against mechanical stress, the emerald is more sensitive than other gemstones of equal hardness. It therefore requires special care when being handled, processed and worn. Inner tensions that easily occur during its growth phase favor the formation of fissures and, during its life as jewelry, the formation of fractures. Flawless emeralds of more than 3 to 4 carats are therefore extremely rare. And we are fortunate that inclusions do occur, say connoisseurs, since they are the type of inclusion that permits the unequivocal identification of an emerald's origin. The high price of emeralds, teamed with their exclusive rarity, result in an unusual volume of impure qualities being cut and more artificial stones being offered by dealers of little repute.

The inclusions again bestow the gemstone with an infallible certificate

*Springtime has lit up the roses
on sconces of emerald in the
cathedral
and every soul swells and flows
into the river of victims.*

Lenau, *Liebesfeier (Celebration of
Love)*

An emerald vessel of inestimable value.
Commissioned by Emperor Ferdinand III
(1637–1656), the fist-sized, high-quality
emerald originating from Muzo in Colombia
was hollowed out and decorated in 1641 by
Dionysio Miseroni in Prague over a period
of two years. In order to keep material
losses as low as possible, the outline of
the vessel follows the shape of the natural
gem. The lid is cut from the "heart" of the
emerald. Emerald weight: 2,680 carats.
History of Art Museum, Vienna.

of authenticity. Moreover, inclusions are a work of sheer poetry in emeralds. The exciting inclusions and secrets express themselves in multifarious ways. Minute, pale glittering that shines out from inside the stone, a wealth of fine channels containing minute quantities of liquid or serrated liquid-filled cavities in which a gas bubble or a tiny salt crystal floats. Often there are microscopic crystals that have been taken from the parent rock or that thrive in intimate contact with the host crystal and are visible as a mossy formation. Reminiscent of an idyllic, sun-dappled arbor, the poetic designation *jardin* came into use to describe these inclusions. Particularly where natural emeralds are concerned, it cannot be sufficiently emphasized that inclusions are a part of their existence. In view of their exquisite color and their select rarity, speaking of "flaws" is therefore a deprecation of the reality and the negation of the purposeful meaning of inanimate nature. On the contrary, inclusions that are visible to the eye are actually expected in natural emeralds. Their absence is immediately suggestive of a fake or a synthetic stone.

The most illustrious member of the beryl family has the same physical traits as the other members of the family. However, refraction and density vary considerably according to birthplace. A low refractive index emphasizes the balanced effect of its green. Since this lightweight and fragile mineral does not accumulate in placers, emeralds are only recovered at their primary location straight from the parent rock.

According to tradition and in the course of historical events, the emerald – how could it be otherwise with a gemstone of this challenging color? – set scintillating accents. In ancient times, this name was not merely assigned to a single gemstone but apparently included minerals of a green color in general. It is known that Caesar hoarded emeralds because of their supposed healing powers, and, even today, this gemstone is mentioned in pseudomedical literature as a so-called healing stone. The crown of Charlemagne as well as the famous iron crown of Lombardy was studded with emeralds. Henry II, the king of the Irish, was presented with an exceptional emerald ring as a symbol of power on his accession to the throne in 1171. Through to the late Middle Ages, emeralds were of great rarity and of high value. They all originated from the only two deposits known at the time – the Cleopatra mine on the Red Sea in the Wadi Sikait (Egypt) and Habachtal (Austria). This only changed when the Spanish conquistadors Cortez and Pizzaro conquered South America in the sixteenth century and the riches plundered from the palaces and temples of the Aztecs and the Incas flowed to Europe. A chronicler of the time reported an emerald the size of a hen's egg that enjoyed divine veneration. The pride of the Viennese treasury is a 12 centimeter high emerald jug, weighing 2,205 carats, that was cut from a single enormous crystal and came into the possession of the Hapsburgs in the seventeenth century. Indian, Turkish, and Persian rulers also possessed wonderful collections of emeralds. The Topkapi Museum in the former seraglio in Istanbul contains a wealth of emerald jewelry and items that were among the sultan's possessions and that render observers virtually speechless. The Iranian crown jewels are reputed to unite some of the finest and most precious gemstone artifacts, including a box made of

emerals and diamonds and a globe made of 51,000 emeralds, rubies, sapphires, and diamonds.

The *Crown of the Andes* also achieved worldwide fame. It was presented by the inhabitants of the Colombian town of Popayán to the "Holy Virgin Maria, Queen of the Andes" in 1593 in gratitude for being spared a three-year plague. Twenty-four goldsmiths worked continuously for six years to complete a richly ornamented crown finely chased from a solid lump of gold. This exceptionally sumptuous piece of jewelry was decorated with 453 emeralds weighing a total of 1,521 carats.

Neither torture nor fear of death could coerce the Inca priests to reveal the secret of the emerald deposits. Quite the opposite, in their powerless thirst for revenge, they erased all traces. The Muzo mine was only rediscovered by chance. It lies about 100 kilometers northeast of the capital Bogotá and is the most prolific location for the most superb emeralds

Left: Superb example of a hexagonally crystallized, pure emerald prism from the famous Muzo Mine, Colombia. In front of it, a faceted, splendidly pure emerald from the same location. Photo: Erica and Harold Van Pelt, Los Angeles.

Right: A particularly fine set of emerald necklace, bracelet, ear pendants, and ring with drop-shaped emeralds and diamonds in various cuts. Sotheby's, Geneva.

found at present. Close to the village of Somondoco and almost 100 kilometers east of Bogotá, the Chivor mine was only rediscovered at the start of the twentieth century. Since then, the development of a few other emerald occurrences has been noted in Colombia. While most of the emerald deposits are attributable to volcanic activity but are of metamorphic character, the occurrences in Colombia belong to a completely different type geochemically. These gemstones of a singularly beautiful, green color obviously owe their creation to hydrothermal processes. Among the various deposits, the one at Muzo is exemplary. Here, the emeralds occur in a black shale clay rich in organic substances that dates from the Lower Cretaceous period and is around 120 million years old. They crystallize in veins that are several centimeters in diameter and are mainly of calcite, sodium feldspar albite, and the iron sulfite pyrite. The richly abundant organic substances and sulfur compounds permit the assumption that, during metamorphism, the biogenic mass attributable to decayed sea organisms was transformed into a type of bitumen.

Below: In a sector of the Mingora Mine in the Swat valley, Pakistan, composed of dolomitic limestone and quartz, miners sort emeralds out of the blasted rock.

Bottom: Fist-sized blocks containing emerald crystals are taken to the workshop where the emeralds are carefully removed from their surroundings. All clear pieces of emerald are valuable enough to warrant cutting.

Right: In the immense emerald mine of Maji moto on the west bank of the Manyara lake, Tanzania, large numbers of miners dig precious emeralds out of the crumbly biotite schist, while a bulldozer clears away waste material. This deposit produces enormous quantities of small emeralds that are suitable for cutting.

Photos: Eduard Gübelin, Lucerne.

The genesis of emeralds is the consequence of the hydrothermal oxidation of bitumen containing trace elements and elementary sulfur. In the process, beryllium ions were released that entered the hydrothermal water as complexes. These were then pressed into veins and cracks where emerald was deposited at the same time as calcite, albite, and pyrite during the rising and cooling phase. The color-inducing elements of chromium and vanadium that were present in the bitumen were released during the decay of the organic material. However, beryllium, chromium, and vanadium were only liberated where sulfur was able to oxidize the bitumen, which means in the circulatory area of the hydrothermal waters. It was decisive that a maximum proportion of the available iron did not enter the emerald crystal but was precipitated in the form of pyrite and entered the emerald as large multifaced crystals. Otherwise, the color of the Colombian emeralds would have been severely impaired. In addition to the mines at Chivor and Muzo, Colombian emeralds are found in the mines of Burbar, Cosquez, Gachala, and others. The occurrence in veins, which is absolutely unique to Colombia and is not seen anywhere else, contrasts with the emeralds found worldwide in chromium-containing, metamorphic, crystalline schists. As already mentioned, these occurrences are the result of volcanic activity. They were created during the contact of chromium-bearing rocks, for example, biotite or actinolite schist, with layers containing beryl, for example, pegmatites, whereby the emeralds received their color due to the diffusion of chromium (and vanadium). Good examples of this type of deposit are those in the Urals. They lie on the Siberian side of the mountains on the Tokovaya River, northeast of Yekaterinburg. The mother lode is an actinolite schist, that is intercalated by talc and chlorite schists and has been transformed by contact metamorphism through a neighboring granite massif to the west and penetrating pegmatites. The accessory minerals are typical of the pegmatitic-pneumatolytic phase.

Further important metamorphic emerald deposits are found at Leydsdorp (Transvaal), Sandawana (Zimbabwe), Kafubu Feld (Zambia), Mingora (Pakistan), Itabira and Santa Terezinha (Brazil), Panjsher Valley (Afghanistan), Maji moto on Lake Manyara (Tanzania), Mananjary (Madagascar), and many other less important locations. But emeralds are also occasionally mined in the Habachtal in Austria. In all these other deposits, emeralds are mainly found in mica or actinolite schist, into which pegmatites have penetrated. The pegmatites provided heat and beryllium. But it was initially the reaction with adjacent rocks rich in alumina that provided the chromium/vanadium oxide, that led to the ideal mixture of alumina, beryllium, silicium, and chromium/vanadium oxide and thus to emeralds.

Mining this metamorphic parent rock in which the emeralds are embedded is carried out almost everywhere in terraces arranged in steps, and the entire mountain or hill is quarried until the mine is exhausted. The compact rock masses must be worked with extreme caution so as not to run the risk of missing an abundant pocket by only a few centimeters or even destroying it.

Above: A specimen of actinolite schist with a pretty cluster of well-developed emerald crystals from Habachtal, Austria. Photo: Eduard Gübelin, Lucerne.

Center: Waste excavated and washed material is disposed of via a ramp. A small valley near Santa Terezinha, Brazil, is gradually being filled with the material.

Bottom: Two sorters separate emerald crystals from the conveyor belt at the emerald mine of Belo Horizonte near Itabira, Brazil.

Photos: Eduard Gübelin, Lucerne.

CHRYSO-BERYLS

AN EXQUISITE TRIO

Alexandrite, chrysoberyl, cat's-eye

Chemistry: $BeAl_2O_4$ (beryllium aluminate)

Crystal system: Orthorhombic

Habit (form): Flat to thick tablets, compact prisms, interpenetrated triplets.

Colors: Alternating green and red (alexandrite), yellow, green, brown, and combinations of these (chrysoberyl). Yellow, honey-colored, or bamboo green (cat's-eye).

Refractive index (R.I.): 1.745 (1.748) – 1.757

Birefringence: +0.009

Pleochroism: Dependent on body color; alexandrite: green, orange, red.

Density: 3.75 (3.68–3.78)

Hardness (Mohs' scale): 8.5

Consistency: Prismatic cleavage, brittle, conchoidal fracture, uneven.

Occurrence: Granitic pegmatites, gneiss, mica schist, and dolomite marbles.

Extraction: Both from primary deposits (parent rock) and placers (alluvial).

In the gemstone firmament, the chrysoberyls shine out as three highly dissimilar stars. They rarely display themselves in a fitting manner to the unknowing, but to those in the know they are an inexhaustible source of continuous wonder. Almost unknown, jealously guarded by the earth and only surrendered in homeopathic doses as it were, they have garnered themselves a place in the gemstone stronghold. Combined with three totally different forms of appearance, the rareness of chrysoberyls predestines them to become collector's items for the keenest connoisseurs. The foundation for the fame of the chrysoberyls was laid by alexandrite and cat's eye, two precious yet unusual varieties, neither of which is sparing when it comes to surprising effects.

Chrysoberyls are on the boundary between the multicolored corundums and the high-minded beryls. The chemistry of the chrysoberyls – beryllium-alumina – forms the link between the alumina of the corundums and the aluminum silicate of beryls. Its distinctive features also single it out as a border crosser. Its refraction (n = 1.75) is close to that of corundum (n = 1.76) and clearly above the beryls (n = 1.58). The density of the chrysoberyl (D = 3.71) lies between that of corundum (D = 4) and beryl (D = 2.72). In terms of hardness, it once again assumes the intermediate position: Corundum, which claims the highest properties of all color gemstones as its own, dazzles with a hardness of 9, chrysoberyl competes with 8.5, and beryl together with the emerald is satisfied with 7.5.

Among the three special features, the clear, transparent chrysoberyl is unusual for its unaccustomed and frequently mixed color broken by green-yellow shading. Cheerful, even slightly impish, its siskin yellow to lime green and leaf green shades range from opulent chartreuse and olive green through to the warm, smoky golden shades of tobacco. Its Greek prefix *chryso* (golden) indicates its noble origins and its predominantly golden color shades. Chrysoberyls contain beryllium, comprised in equal parts of beryllium oxide (BeO) and alumina (Al_2O_3) and are thus a beryllium aluminate ($BeAl_2O_4$). This combination is crystallized in beautifully formed columns with the irresistible tendency to interlace as triplets that lead to the formation of hexagonal, starlike crystal shapes. Its highly individual color is attributable to allochromatic foreign coloration since the combination of the two molecules beryl and alumina is colorless in itself. Iron (up to 6 percent Fe_2O_3) and chromium (only 0.6 percent Cr_2O_3) have been identified as the chromophoric metals. Titanium is only occasionally diagnosed in traces. Thanks to its high level of hardness, chrysoberyl takes a superb polish, which bestows it with a sparkling surface luster. Supported by its high refractive index, it develops a noticeably lively brilliancy that has a bewitching attraction for the eyes, especially in the case of large gems. Its high density carries it to the bottom of the secondary alluvial deposits and thus once again to the vicinity of the corundums.

The second in the trio of chrysoberyls is the cat's-eye with its silky luster. This chatoyant offspring (chatoyancy being a play on words with the French word *chat* [cat] or the slitlike line of cats' pupils) is of exceptional nature. It is distinctive for its exceptionally eye-catching, uncom-

Below: A family portrait of the chrysoberyls.
Left: A cabochon-cut cat's-eye with a distinct straight line.
Right: A faceted, highly transparent yellow chrysoberyl.
Bottom: A color-changing, brilliant-cut alexandrite.

Above: The classic crystal form of the chrysoberyl is the triplet, that is, three individual orthorhombic crystals have interlaced (an interpenetrated triplet, as it is called).

Photos: Eduard Gübelin, Lucerne.

monly attractive light effect that together with the rarity of its occurrence, makes it appealing to connoisseurs.

Weightless and disembodied, a silver glow of light hovers for a brief moment over the surface of a gem cut *en cabochon*, released from earthly fetters, and yet fully connected to the material in enchanting delusion since, on the gentlest tilting of the gemstone, the ray of light is set in undulating motion whereupon it withdraws, stealing away as lithely as a cat, from its static location to skip unrealistically over the curved surface. The cause of this ghostly and delicate phenomenon is the diffusion of parallel bundles of light rays on ultrafine parallel sillimanite fibers. The diffused light forms a cone, which nestles against the elongation of the ray of light. If the light strikes vertically, it is diffused in one plane around the mineral fiber. The corundums star ruby and star sapphire have, corresponding to the trigonal symmetry, three systems of parallel diffusing inclusions. But a cat's eye is only formed with one system as is the case with chrysoberyl. Cat's-eyes are transparent to cloudy and normally have a domed-shaped cut as cabochons. The layout of the convex curve does most justice to its sublime beauty as it confines a rather diffuse band of light to a sharp, precisely defined strip. The more exact and precise the light trace rises from the center of the gem, the greater the increase in value. Occasionally, other types of gemstones develop similar chatoyancy. Nevertheless, chrysoberyl stands out as the finest and by far the most valuable gem among all these similarly named cat's-eye varieties. Its name alone expresses its difference in status: "Cymophane" is derived from the Greek *kyma* (wave) and *phanein* (appear). Bestowed with little favor until the twentieth century, the chrysoberyl cat's-eye is not connected with any mystification, although its individual color and, even more, the unreal magic of its evasive and wavering ray of light warns us of the incalculability of the Felid, who was already holy in ancient times to the Egyptians but still remains slightly sinister.

The third exciting chrysoberyl is slightly more unfamiliar. First among equals, it owes its puzzling fascination to various light properties alone. Like a chameleon, alexandrite changes its color in artificial light or daylight, which makes it highly desirable for connoisseurs and collectors alike. Alexandrite is not just a particularly precious gemstone but also a very individualistic one. Daylight entices from it a mossy green with delicate bluish tinges that is transformed into raspberry red to amethyst purple under artificial illumination. Its color is a characteristic chromium oxide coloration. The cause of its phenomenal day and night enchantment does not lie in a light-dependant change in the chromium oxide, however, but is solely the result of the composition of the light. Daylight mainly contains blue rays, whereas artificial light has more red rays. Whatever the prevailing color is, the alexandrite will reflect it. This behavior in which it changes color from green to red with an increase in the longer-waved proportion of the rays is called change of color. The alexandrite is the classic color-changing gemstone, which is why other color-changing minerals are also described as being alexandritelike.

In the 1830s the stone was apparently discovered on the slopes of the Urals northeast of Yekaterinburg on the same day that the future Czar

Alexander came of age and, in his honor, was named alexandrite. It was considered to be the national gemstone of Russia since it united the czarist colors of red and green. Despite its coloration caused by chromium/vanadium, it is a mineral of pegmatitic-pneumatolytic descent. Solutions based on a pegmatite and rich in beryllium permeated the adjoining metamorphic schist and permitted the formation of three different beryllium minerals on the boundary with this pegmatite. These are the beryllium silicate phenacite, the beryllium aluminum silicate emerald, and finally the beryllium aluminate chrysoberyll. Remarkably, the minerals occurring in the pegmatite are colorless, whereas those lying in the schist are green. It can thus be concluded that the chromium that was already present immigrated to the contact zone from the mica schist and contributed to the formation of alexandrite (and emerald, of course). The phenacite formed in the pegmatite does not contain any coloring substance. For almost one hundred years, the Urals supplied the finest alexandrites with their velvety, bluish-green daylight color and highly intense color change to red. Today, the deposit is being exploited again. Other occurrences are in Zimbabwe where, in the northeast near Novello, the zone of mica schist rich in chromium adjoins the emerald deposits of Novello, Sandawana and Filabusi as well as in Brazil at Malacacheta and more recently high quality alexandrites have been found at Hematita near Itabira, Minas Gerais. New alexandrite occurrences have been opened up at Tunduru and Lipatu in Tanzania. The latest discovery of very fine alexandrite was made at Kakaka on Madagascar in 1998.

Once again, the relatively small Sri Lanka, which has an area of only a little over 65,000 square kilometers, distinguishes itself as a location for top quality alexandrite as well as chrysoberyls and chrysoberyl cat's-eyes with their own coloration. No place is more justified in being termed the *Shining Isle* than Sri Lanka. The parent rock consists of granite pegmatites in the central massif from which they were carried away due to erosion and left to accumulate in the secondary deposits of the ancient river sediments and the alluvial valley floors over the course of millions of years. Even from a distance, the gemstone locations are easy to spot from the bamboo scaffolding or small huts rising from the midst of paddy fields. The excavated shafts go down as far as 15 meters in the sandy-clayey ground and reach the level of the gem-bearing *illam*. These illam seams form irregular layers, one above the other, of thicknesses varying from a few centimeters to 1.5 meters. Horizontally, their widths can range between 10 centimeters and 2 meters and stretch to 100 meters in length. The illam is easy to recognize because it is always accompanied by fine-grained to coarse quartz gravel. At the bottom of the shaft, a digger excavates the earth and gradually widens the pit until all the excavated illam deposits have been exhausted. On the first washing day, again predetermined by the fortune-teller, the employer gives symbolic alms to his treasure seekers before the start of work, which replace sacrifices to the gods in former times. The overseer hunkers next to the pile of baskets, utters a quick and fervent prayer to Kataragama, the god of minerals, and then examines the remaining extract with a practiced, hawk-eyed look.

Below: Rakelike scrapers are used for the collection of gemstones in the rivers of Sri Lanka to heap up the gem-containing gravel along a fascine weir.

Above: Heaped up by rakelike scrapers, the gravel is washed with the help of the river current. The washing basket is swirled so that the light minerals are washed away and the heavier gemstones remain in the center of the basket.

Photos: Eduard Gübelin, Lucerne.

FELDSPARS

A MAJOR
COMPANY

The feldspar group of minerals is the most widespread on earth and is found in highly diverse types of rock: plutonic, magmatic, sedimentary and metamorphic. According to their chemical composition, there are three compounds of alumina and silica with potassium, sodium, and calcium that can mutually replace one another by an exchange of substantial ions and thus produce completely different variaties. The feldspars are subdivided into two main groups: the alkali feldspars and the plagioclase feldspars. In the case of the alkali feldspars, there is a mutual exchange between potassium and sodium. This category includes auspicious names such as the noble orthoclase from Madagascar, the smoky-brown sanidine from the Eifel Mountains in Germany, the shimmering blue moonstones from Brazil, Sri Lanka, and India as well as the speckled, blue-green microcline (amazonite) from South Africa. In contrast, among the plagioclase feldspars, it is the interchange between sodium and calcium that leads to the creation of a multiplicity of different gems. The percentage content of ions present also results in the names bestowed. In this way, we meet the colorless to white albite from Myanmar, the delicate blue and green albite from the Kioo hills of Kenya, the red-brown glittering aventurine feldspar (sunstone) from India, the transparent yellow, green, and red plagioclases from Plush and Ponderosa in the state of Oregon (USA) and, last but not least, the iridescent pearl gray and spectral colored labradorite (spectrolite) from Labrador, Madagascar, and Finland.

This impressive listing is not a matter of large-scale economic potential as one might assume. Most of the feldspars can be seen as pretty collectors items, but the labradorite and moonstone, in particular, are the ones favored by buyers, although individual markets indicate a conformity of their very own. Thus the transparent, facet-cut, green and red plagioclases are a secret tip among experts in the United States, their country of origin, while they suffer from a lack of popularity in Europe. Sri Lanka, the treasure vault of the world, supplies the most charming moonstones; their color a crystallized misty veil changing from cloudy gray via neon blue to a limpid, silver-shimmering white. In the southwest of the island, at Meetiyagoda, they are burrowed out of secondary deposits in clayey earth and broken out of primary mother rock in pegmatitic veins with quartzes as accompanying material. The moonstone finds in India attracted great attention since the locations in the area of Kangyam in the south of the country also provided moonstones with cat's-eye effect and four-rayed stars. Their colors range from brown to red-brown, lead gray to black, and yellow, green, and pink-colored shades also appear occasionally. Engraved as artistic cameos, they appeal to an American clientele. Smaller moonstone deposits are located near Mogok in Myanmar, and also in Brazil, Australia, and in several locations in North America. The moonstone is not a uniform mineral but is built up of microscopically fine lamellar structures alternating between potassium feldspar orthoclase and sodium feldspar albite. It has the lowest density (D = 2.56) of most of the feldspars and a low refractive index (n = 1.52), which cannot rival the delicate sfumato.

The blue shimmer deftly racing over the curved surface is caused by

Opposite: Elegant necklace and matching earrings with blue shimmering moonstones, accompanied by tourmaline baguettes and brilliant-cut diamonds. Création Gübelin AG, Lucerne.

The feldspar group comprises several independent minerals that form a vivid example of a so-called "isomorphous group," that is, they have similar crystal structures and similar crystal forms (morphologies) but different chemistry, by interchanging either potassium and sodium or sodium and calcium in differing proportions (please refer to the triangle diagram). The end members contain either only the cation potassium or sodium or calcium. There is thus a range of mixtures of the relevant end members, each with its own name.

Chemistry:
Orthoclase: $KAlSi_3O_8$ (potassium-aluminum silicate)
Albite: $NaAlSi_3O_8$ (sodium-aluminum silicate)
Plagioclase: Mixed crystal of albite and anorthite: $Na(AlSi_3O_8)/Ca(Al_2Si_2O_8)$, for example, labradorite
Anorthite: $CaAl_2Si_2O_8$ (end member of the plagioclase feldspar)

Crystal system:
Orthoclase: monoclinic; albite: triclinic; plagioclase: triclinic; anorthite: triclinic.

Habit (form): Narrow to compact prismatic, also tabular.

Colors:
Othoclase: colorless, but mostly yellow.
Moonstone: white, yellow, green, orange with whitish to bluish adularescence (sheen).
Amazonite: green to blue-green.
Aventurine (sunstone): brown-red to orange, glittering (due to inclusions of hematite platelets).
Labradorite (spectrolite): anthracite colors with multihued play of colors.

Refractive index (R.I.): 1.52–1.53
(Labradorite: 1.56–1.57)

Birefringence: -0.008 to +0.01
(Labradorite: +0.01)

Pleochroism: Dependent on body color, usually weak in lighter and darker shades.

Density: 2.54–2.65 (Labradorite: 2.70–2.72)

Hardness (Mohs' scale): 6–6.5

Consistency: Good prismatic cleavage, brittle, conchoidal, uneven fracture.

Occurrence: As one of the most important rock-forming minerals, feldspar is widely distributed worldwide. It is present in many basic and acid rock types. In magmatic rocks (granite, pegmatite), crystalline schist (gneiss and other metamorphic rocks), and even in sediments.

Extraction: Mostly from primary deposits, rarely from alluvial placers.

light diffusing through the thinly separated albite layers. This enticing appearance is called *adularescence* and comes from the mineralogical name *adularia* that in turn, the moonstone received from its previously classical site of discovery, the Adula massif (Rheinwaldhorn) in the Swiss Alps. Under the microscope, moonstones may show minute tension cracks (perthitization, as it is called), which are known as "millipedes." From time immemorial, people have considered the gem as a protege of the moon. It is said to arouse gentle passions when loving couples lay it under their tongues during a full moon. Associated with June, this gemstone promises good fortune and prosperity to those born in that month.

In its color and appearance, labradorite is far more down to earth. This fundamentally stolid, dark gray rock of the plagioclase feldspars

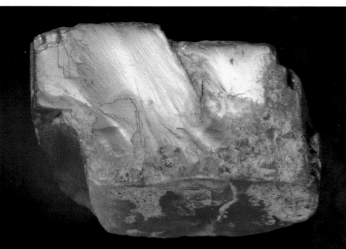

Above: It is astonishing how delicately blue, shimmering moonstones – the favorite of young women – can be created out of a plain-looking raw gem thanks to the skilled artistry of the gem cutter. This raw gem comes from Meetiyagoda, Sri Lanka. Collection: Hein Gärtner, Idar-Oberstein. Photo: Karl Hartmann, Sobernheim.

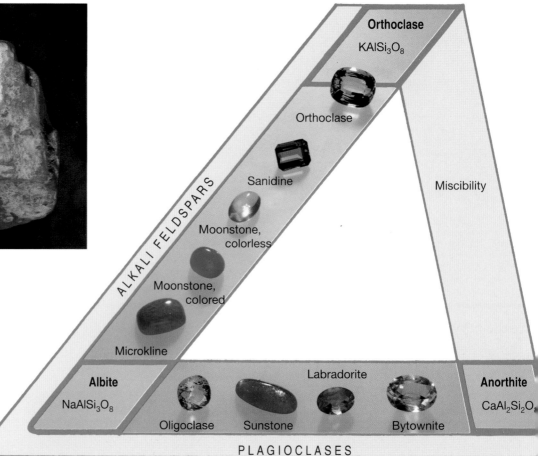

Above: The spectrolite called labradorite from the Lammenpää deposit near Ylijärvi, Finland, form patterns in the combined spectral colors. By moving the spectrolite or the light source, these colors are transposed. Photo: Eduard Gübelin, Lucerne.

Top right: This diagram shows the mixture relationships within the feldspar group: The names of the relevant end members are in the corners, while the bars contain those of the mixed crystals. Those inside the triangle are the names of the actual gem feldspars. Photo: James G. Perret, Lucerne.

Right: A beautiful unique example of a spectrolite-labradorite in rainbow colors in an unusual arrangement of concentric circles. The gem comes from Madagascar and is of magmatic origin. Collection: Fritz Loosli, Adliswil. Photo: James G. Perret, Lucerne.

(sodium-calcium feldspars) only becomes an object of desire in its iridescent, spectrally shimmering version, which is perfected by the skill of the gem cutter. With good fortune as an ally and advance studies that promised good prospects in his luggage, the Finnish mineralogist Laitakari received a pleasant surprise. During the Finnish/Russian winter campaign of 1939–1940 and while erecting defenses not far from the border, he came across granite blocks whose feldspar insets revealed the unmistakable iridescence of labradorite. With this discovery, he opened up the Finnish source of a mineral that, until then, was mainly to be found on the Labrador coast in Canada. And what is more, the new find turned out to be a variety of labradorite belonging to the calcium-rich feldspar of the plagioclase group (with triclinic crystals) outshining, with its much more colorful and lively reflections, the common blue and green iridescent labradorite. In the trade, hardly any difference is made between geographic provenance, since the respective finds are of equal importance. Both were created in the liquid magmatic phase as the main compounds of granites. With a suitable angle of inclination to the incident light, unexpectedly intensive lustrous, colorful fireworks burst forth from the dark ash, anthracite to silver gray rock hues: pure-toned, intensive spectral colors from blue and green to yellow and fiery orange through to flickering red. This fulmination of hidden magnificence and self-dynamism was honored with the name of spectrolite. The color iridescence typical of labradorite – the "labradorescence" that fools the eye as does a glittering tropical butterfly's wing – appears even more perfectly in the rainbow-hued spectrolite and changes according to the incident light. This is the result of the interaction of light interference and submicroscopically fine, polysynthetic twin platelets partly composed of albite and labradorite. Blocks weighing up to almost a ton are sawed out of the rock faces of the parent granite of the spectrolite near the village of Ylijärvi in the Ylämaa district. The relatively small, colorfully iridescent blocks find their way to all parts of the globe. In the color-hungry Scandinavian countries, the glittery granite slabs are in great demand as decorative cladding on facades and walls. This appealing and effective mineral is likewise found on Madagascar.

Highly original necklace with four blue shimmering moonstones set in diamond frames. Collection: David Humphrey. Photo: Erica and Harold Van Pelt, Los Angeles.

Among the feldspars, the oligoclase and its aliases represents a curiosity. In gemologists' jargon, it is called the *sunstone*. The glittering inclusions are small hematite platelets and are a guarantee of its origin. Glass imitations of this gem are manufactured in Murano. It owes its new designation of *goldstone* to small copper crystals with triangular, speckled surfaces. Between Greece and India, travelers will encounter it under the name of *star stone* – ergo, caveat emptor!

Orthoclase also has its own special history. Until the discovery of green and red feldspar near Plush in Oregon (USA), orthoclase gems were particularly popular in France where the renowned mineralogist Alfred Lacroix paid tribute to them in his *Minéralogie de Madagascar.* Madagascar or, more precisely, the town of Itrongay is considered to be the best supplier of the lustrous light to honey-yellow variations of orthoclase. In contrast, however, there is less demand for its pink-colored version.

GARNETS

A COURTLY HOUSEHOLD OF NOBLE VASSALS

Above: The flaming orange of the spessartite garnet is impressively effective on its own, but it is heightened to breathtaking intensity by the addition of numerous diamonds. Collection: Michael M. Scott. Photo: Erica and Harold Van Pelt, Los Angeles.

Opposite: In the garnet family, all colors are represented together with colorless and black. However, blue is only rarely encountered and only in garnets that change color. Photo: Erica and Harold Van Pelt, Los Angeles.

The garnet family comprises a proud variety of the noblest and finest gemstones. Despite its great wealth of colors, the classic garnet is red, as its name promises. The Latin name *malum granatum* is a reference to garnet's resemblance to red pomegranate seeds embedded in glossy red fruit pulp. However, there are also garnets of different coloration. Under the cloak of this unifying umbrella term, there is a mineral group of widely differing appearance and known by its own name. Just as with feldspars, the group forms a clear example of the so-called idiomorphic series or "solid solution": although the internal structure of a mineral determines its outer shape (all garnets crystallize according to the cubic system), its color is subject to change owing to a certain amount of mutual exchange of ions (cations), and thus to the physical characteristics of this group of gemstones. As a result, completely new types develop.

Pyrope $Mg_3Al_2(SiO_4)_3$

Pyrope is a complex aluminum silicate that is colored ember red by chrome as an allochromatic pigment. It is widespread all over the world. Among other places, the "fire-eye" (from the Greek *pyropós* [fiery]) that is suitable for jewelry purposes is mainly found in Bohemia, South and East Africa, and Arizona (USA). Pyrope developed as a typical representative of mafic mineral formation as did the diamond. Among diamond miners, therefore, it is highly regarded as a guide mineral. Queen Victoria also played the role of trendsetter for this gemstone. She enhanced pyrope's popularity substantially, and was in appropriate company in this respect. After all, these gemstones had been taken for rubies for centuries due to the remote similarity of their color and had already decorated the jeweled panoply of the Bohemian king Wenzel. The always tempering effect of magnesium provides the golden mean of its features: the refractive index of pyrope is 1.75 and its density is 3.80.

Almandite $Fe_3Al_2(SiO_4)_3$

Almandite is an aluminum silicate with iron, which as an idiochromatic element is responsible for the brown-red to red-violet color graduations. Wherever iron appears in the chemical composition of a gemstone, it creates a saturation of color and an intensification of its general characteristics. This "nutritious foodstuff" elevates the almandite to a higher refractive index (n = 1.795) and greater density (D = 4.1) than pyrope. Almandites are the result of a variety of rock-forming processes. They are minerals of the deep and contact rocks as well as crystalline schist, which explains their extensive presence in almost all important gemstone deposits. Pliny the Elder derived the name of *carbunculus alabandicus* from the city of Alabanda in Asia Minor, which gave the name to the almandite in the familiar circles of the carbuncle. The knights of the Crusades wore them as talismans against poison and wounding. Emperor Otto received from his son the valuable carbuncle gem that adorned the former German emperor's crown under the name of "the wise one."

Rhodolite $(Mg, Fe)_3 Al_2(SiO_4)_3$

Rhodolite is the link between pyrope and almandite with which it forms the red garnet series of the pyrandine. Magnesium and iron maintain a balance and provide it with its highly appreciated pinkish-red color and its lively luster. Rhodolites are the garnets that are the best quality for gemstones, and, for this reason, they are the ones most encountered in the trade. The most economically viable deposits are found in Kenya, on Madagascar, in Zambia, Tanzania, Brazil, and the United States.

Spessartite $Mn_3Al_2(SiO_4)_3$

Spessartite is an aluminum silicate idiochromatically colored by manganese. Its glowing hot orange color embodies the fire in the earth's core. Large, transparent, and cut with a large number of facets, it is one of the most attractive garnets and one of the most superb gemstone varieties since its high level of refraction (n = 1.8) promotes its sparkling luster. Its high density (D = 4.16) makes its recovery from alluvial deposits decisively easier. Sri Lanka, where it is well represented in combination with hessonite in the alluvial placers, was the mecca for spessartite until the mid-twentieth century. Since then, other providers have emerged: Tanzania, Madagascar and Brazil. Baja California, Mexico, and the state of Virginia (USA), are blessed with particularly fine examples of spessartite. The highest accolade, however, goes to the most recent discoveries in the Marien stream near the village of Kunene in northern Namibia as well as to the region of Josh in Nigeria. Due to its pure, distinctive orange sparkle, it has been awarded the noble title of *mandarine-spessartite*.

Chemistry: The general chemical formula is
$A_3B_2(SiO_4)_3$, *whereby*
$A = Mg, Fe^{2+}, Ca$ *or* Mn^{2+}
$B = Al, Fe^{3+}, Mn^{3+} Cr^{3+}$ *but can also be Si, Ti, V^{3+} and Zr. Si is partly replaced by Al or Fe.*
Colors: Pyrope: $Mg_3Al_2(SiO_4)_3$, dark red
Rhodolite: $(Mg,Fe)_3Al_2(SiO_4)_3$, rose red
Almandite: $Fe_3Al_2(SiO_4)_3$, brown-red to violet-red
Grossularite: $Ca_3Al_2(SiO_4)_3$, colorless, yellow to red-brown (hessonite), emerald green (tsavolite)
Spessartite: $Mn_3Al_2(SiO_4)_3$, orange
Andradite: $Ca_3Fe_2(SiO_4)_3$:
green = demantoid
yellow = topazolite
black = melanite

Crystal system: Cubic, isometric

Habit (form): Several combination forms in the cubic system result in a rounded appearance (with numerous faces; often called garneto-hedra).

Refractive index (R.I.): Pyrope 1.74–1.76 (1.75, isotropic)
Rhodolite: 1.75
Almandite: 1.75–1.82 (1.795, isotropic)
Grossularite: 1.74–1.748 (1.745, isotropic)
Spessartite: 1.79–1.81
Andradite: 1.82–1.89 (demantoid: 1.88–1.89)

Density: Pyrope: 3.80
Rhodolite: 3.84
Almandite: 3.90–4.20
Grossularite: 3.55–3.68
Spessartite: 3.95–4.20
Andradite: 3.80–3.90 (demantoid: 3.84)

Hardness (Mohs' scale): 6.5–7.5

Consistency: Very good. No cleavage. Uneven fracture.

Occurrence: Dependent on variety, in different types of rock. Pyrope in metamorphic deep-seated rocks (serpentinite, frequently in combination with diamonds in peridotite).
Almandite: Widespread throughout the world in crystalline schist, gneiss, and other metamorphic rocks.
Grossularite: Typically in metamorphosed impure limestones, particularly in contact zones, also in crystalline schist and serpentinite.
Spessartite: In granitic pegmatite, gneiss, quartzite, crystalline schists, rhyolite, and so forth.
Andradite: Mainly in chlorite schists and serpentinite (demantoid, topazolite) and in metamorphic limestones or contact zones.

Extraction: Especially from the parent rock in primary deposits, as well as from sedimentary deposits and placers.

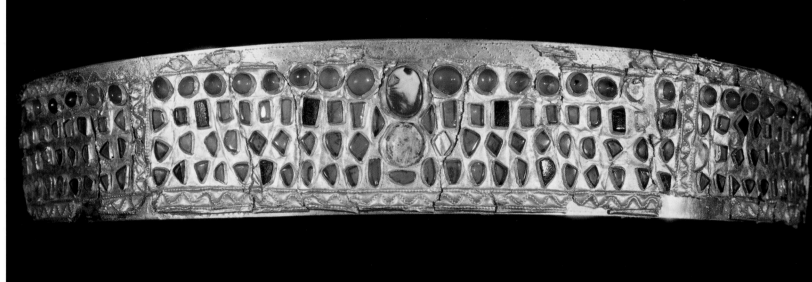

Above: The characteristic "garnetohedron" crystal form is clearly recognizable on this green demantoid garnet. Demantoids largely have clear crystal forms. Found: Bobrovka River in the Urals.

Right: Two gem collectors trying their luck on a search for demantoid garnets in the Bobrovka River south of Yekaterinburg in the Urals. Photo: A. Peretti, Adligenswil.

Grossular Ca₃Al₂ (SiO₄)₃

Grossular garnet is an aluminum silica with calcium. The garnets known by this name are, with one exception, not particularly spectacular but of wide variety. The longest known is the dull brown to dull red-brown hessonite (cinnamon stone) from Sri Lanka, Brazil, and Madagascar. At the end of the twentieth century, a new, this time gold-colored variety of hessonite was discovered in Sri Lanka. Its high refractive index and low cleavage make it a serious rival to the topaz of the same color. Hessonites are distinctive from other grossular garnets due to their mosaic structure as they are a monogranular aggregate composed of numerous, microscopically small hessonite crystals. Around the mid-twentieth century, the grossular group was extended by a transparent, lustrous copper-gold version from Quebec, Canada, and a light green version from Tanzania. The discovery of light to deep green grossulars was a major surprise for the gem world. The exceptional appearance of their powerful colors comes sensitively close to that of the emerald. They were called tsavolites after the Tsavo National Park in Kenya where they were discovered. The freshness of the green and the greater price flexibility in comparison with emeralds give tsavolite first-class market prospects. Chromium (light green) and vanadium (deep green) pigments are responsible for tsavolite's wonderful color. The two paladines from the Transvaal are of opaque constitution – one is gooseberry green and speckled with black dots, and the other is a raspberry red grossular.

Andradite Ca₃Fe₂ (SiO₄)₃

Andradite is a silicate of calcium and iron. The most unusual variety of andradite is the glittery green demantoid. The superior pigment chromium, which creates the luxurious wealth of color in rubies and emeralds, as well as an astonishingly high refractive index (n = 1.89) and a fire that is even more intense than that of diamonds (dispersion = 0.057) provide demantoid with a luster of radiant splendor. Demantoid could even endanger the emerald if it were not so soft and so exclusively rare. It is only excavated from the depths at three locations in the world: south of Yekaterinburg in the Urals, near Kunene in Namibia, and in Val Malenco in Italy. No other type of gemstone has developed anything like the wide variety of garnets over the past few years. Just before the turn of the millennium, two additional, as yet unknown subgroups of andradite came to the fore. One of them was clearly transparent with grayish-green, yellowish-green, to greenish-yellow and yellow-brown to brown color variations. They were discovered in Mali. The andradite garnet from Hermocillo, Mexico, is of a completely different type. Basically, black and opaque, its crystal surfaces mutate due to surface decomposition into the whirling color array of a rainbow. This *rainbow garnet* requires a sensitive and highly qualified cutter so that a dome-shaped cabochon is endowed with the attributes of the lively iridescent weather phenomenon.

The birthstone of those born in January, the garnet symbolizes loyalty, friendship, and steadfastness.

Above: Garnet jewelry from the second half of the eighteenth century. The cherry red pyrope garnets from Bohemia with diamonds are designed to represent a bundle of feathers, with a large brilliant-cut diamond holding them together. Collection: Treasure Chamber of Russia (CIS).

Opposite, center: A diadem from Csorna, Hungary, of beaten gold set with gemstones, in the middle an oval carnelian, green glass ornamentation in between. Originally, the gold plaques were attached to an underlay of bronze. Hunnish, first half of the fifth century. Hungarian National Museum, Budapest. Photo: Claus Hansmann, Munich.

OPAL
HUMMINGBIRD
AND
FIREBIRD

A variety of the quartz group

Chemismtry SiO_2+nH_2O (hydrous silicium dioxide. n = variable water content)

Crystal system: Opal is not crystalline but amorphous. In a gel-like, firm basic mass, unequally sized blocks of submicroscopic silica spheres are closely and irregularly cemented together.

Colors: Body colors: white, gray, yellow, orange, brown, and blue as well as black and colorless. Diffraction colors also create a bright play of color. This is caused by light diffraction in the spaces between the tiny spheres; the general term for this is "play of colors." Preference is for all the spectral colors to light up.

Opalescence: Milky, whitish, yellowish, greenish, bluish, and orange shimmer as the result of reflective effects on the wavy surface of the blocks of tiny spheres in the gel-type basic mass.

Refractive index (R.I.): 1.39–1.47 (1.45), isotropic

Density: 1.95–2.20 (2.10)

Hardness (Mohs' scale): 5–6.5

Consistency: Brittle. Conchoidal, glassy fracture.

The water content can gradually evaporate, which results in cracks. Should be kept in water. Opal is particularly at risk under hot window-display lighting.

Occurrence: Widespread in a variety of rocks. In Australia, in sedimentary deposits (marl). In Mexico, in volcanic rocks (rhyolite).

Extraction: Mostly from primary deposits in open-cast and underground mines.

Early cultural civilizations fell under the colorful spell of the opal. Depending on geographic location, the Mayas and the Aztecs called this gem with its sensual pleasures captured within pictorial spaces the *Quetzal-itzlipyollitli* (bird of paradise stone) or *Vitzitziltecpatl* (hummingbird stone) to reflect the multicolored shimmering plumage of these tropical birds. Although the precious opal with the most vivid color play was introduced decades ago from the sixth continent, Mexico still remains the undisputed top supplier for transparent to translucent fire opals with their famous color range from wine to resin yellow (sherry opal), from orange to hyacinth red (fire opal), and orange red to dark red (cherry opal). In the iridescent shimmer of the precious opal, the earth has presented us with an additional gemstone whose lively colorfulness is not created by the inclusion of colorants but by an energetic apparition of light. The color play of the precious opal is the most spectacular and unique case in the mineral kingdom in which a play of light is created by internal diffraction in the spaces of ultramicroscopically tiny spheres arranged in layers and blocks, resulting in the dispersion of the light into its spectral colors. In addition, the opal is one of the few gemstones that does not have a definite atomic lattice and is therefore not a crystal. It is composed of a gel-like compound that, in contrast to its environment, is not delineated by any geometrically definable shape. Such substances are described as being amorphous, which means shapeless. The opal's basic structure of amorphous silicium dioxide is a dense accumulation of myriads of the minutest aggregated siliceous spherolites. If these minute spheres – their diameter is less than 0.0005 millimeter – are regularly arranged and of the same size throughout all sections, they are able to diffract incident light and fan it into its prismatic colors. Arranged in rows, yet aligned in different directions, these fields create the speckled distribution of color that appears to be randomly positioned as if dabbed with a brush. When an opal is tilted, individual sectors can immediately change their spectral colors from red through yellow, to green, blue, and violet. The actual substance of opal, which is covered by the glowing rainbow hues, is either white or colored by trace elements. The actual color of the gemstone is only shown where no color is applied. A distinction is made between a range of opal varieties based on their body pigmentation: white opals or white precious opals in their narrower definition, black opals as the most precious design by nature, the transparent water opal, the "crystal opal" as a translucent gemstone noted for its intense play of light and, in addition, the flame-throwing fire opal.

Geologically speaking, the opal is relatively young since it would not have lived to survive the pressure of tectonic movements nor the effects of surface erosion. The genesis of these rare beauties – each in itself a unique example in design and color play – takes place, together with slow displacements, close to groundwater level. Most occurrences of opal are volcanic in origin. In the volcanic deposits of Honduras, California, Mexico, and Slovakia, the basic substance was an aggregate of calcite grains, which filled spaces and veins in lava rock. As a consequence of vulcanism, hot, watery brine solutions containing gelatinous, dissolved silica ascended from the volcano epicenter or neighboring ther-

Right: Imaginative jewelry set consisting of a necklace, bracelet, ring, and brooch in yellow gold set with light to dark orange fire opals from Mexico. Création: Gübelin AG, Lucerne. Photo: Claude Mercier, Geneva.

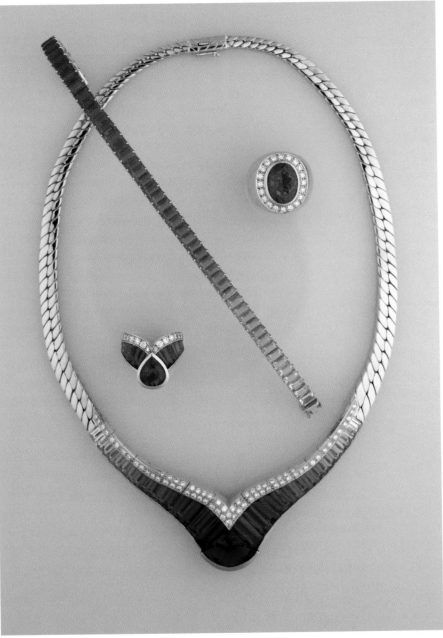

Above: Opalized fossil shells provide unequivocal proof that the Australian opals were created in a watery environment. Fossils and shells coated with opal are prized collectors' items. Photo: Erica and Harold Van Pelt, Los Angeles.

Page 95: Opals from different locations. The two opals with the brownish-yellow body colors are fire opals from Mexico. The two dark, multicolored opals are black opals and the two light opals to the left and right are so-called "crystal" opals – all four come from Australia. The colorful cabochon at the very front is a water opal from Mexico. Collection: American Gemtraders Association (AGTA). Photo: Erica and Harold Van Pelt, Los Angeles.

mal sources, decomposing the calcite filling, leaving behind in its place a mixture of colloidal silica and water ($SiO_2 + nH_2O$), which will later become the opal. Particularly fine examples of this process are the Mexican and former Hungarian opals. In 400 B.C., opals were already being extracted from what are now the east Slovakian volcanic deposits. Many examples on display in museums are proof of their exemplary quality.

In Australia, however, a paradise for opals with 95 percent of world production, occurrences are linked with finely grained marl layers that are rich in clay through to roughly grained banks of conglomerate that solidified during the Cretaceous period (135–70 million years ago). The deposition process of the silica, which occurred in the Tertiary period, that is, during the last 70 million years, took place over eons of years. Subterranean runnels and groundwater channels leached the silica out of the weathered sedimentary rocks and carried it with them until they found a new resting place in cracks or depressions of impervious layers of clay. The silica collected there on the bottom where, due to the interaction of continued accumulation and water evaporation, it gradually solidified to form opals. This is the classic theory of the genesis of opals. In recent times, some doubts have been cast about this theory however. The scientific dispute has arisen due to several aspects: the period of formation (by no means as long ago as previously assumed), the pressure conditions (close to the surface), the accumulation process, and the formation temperature. So, even today, one of nature's mysteries requires solving. Opal is the typical gemstone of Australia and was elevated to the position of national gemstone by that country's government in 1993. Along with recognition for its economic importance, the fact was also emphasized that the Australian earth produces the most magnificent opals in the world. In a competition of the best, the sparkling fire of the black opal gets first place. Truly excellent gems are, admittedly, reaching the market with diminishing frequency. They receive the highest offers, which put them practically on a par with the finest diamonds. The main production of the light opals extends across the state of South Australia (Andamooka, Coober Pedy – which claims the title of "World Capital of Opals" for itself – which is almost elitist in comparison with "white man in hole" in the language of the aborigines), while New South Wales (Lightning Ridge) created a name for itself with its elegant and now extremely rare black opals. Boulder opals are typical of Queensland (Quilpie, Yowah, and, in particular, Jundah). The interesting specialty of this stone, the "church window" is mainly to be found in collections. Many of the boulder opals are in dark shades and with a temperamental interplay of colors on a brown marbled matrix of ironstone. These rare and classy pieces possess finely nuanced structures in compact material in which phantomlike elements throng in an ever-changing set of motifs.

A few years ago, Tanzania astounded gemstone connoisseurs with an unusual variety. The prase-opal as it is called (Greek prasis [leek]) obtains its green coloration from its slight nickel content deposited in weathered serpentine. Even more recent discoveries, however, awaken the curiosity of the specialist world. Lovers of fine gemstones enrich their collections with gemstones from the United States, Honduras, Saxony in Germany, Denmark, Turkey, Ethiopia, Mali, and Indonesia. South America has two deposits in Peru and Brazil. The new Brazilian finds in the state of Piaui, however, can in no way match the quality standards of Australia. Mexico holds second place in world rankings. Whereas the black opal is the pride of Australia, Mexico, in turn, has the unsurpassably beautiful fire opals. The fire opals excavated in Querétaro in open-cast mines are of esthetically pure, clear transparency. Iron gives them their own red shading. The best examples are in a fire-red, orange color. Recently, Kazakhstan and the Ukraine are attempting to gain a share of the world market with new occurrences of fire opals. Opals with a color play are cut flat or into cabochons and fire opals are generally faceted, whereby the wearer of a ring gem must be aware of the sensitivity of the mineral.

Too forceful handling of the opal is inadvisable in any case. The noble gem with its delightful colors needs diligent care in all its shadings. Its strengths are not to be found in its hardness (6) or in its durability.

Austerely designed pendant with a color-showering black opal weighing 17 carats from Lightning Ridge, New South Wales, Australia. Setting of brilliant-cut diamonds. Collection: J. Zanger. Photo: Erica and Harold Van Pelt, Los Angeles.

Page 98:
6. The dizzying height of this mine face near Querétaro, Mexico, gives an indication of the work required to mine opals in Mexico. Photo: Eduard Gübelin, Lucerne.
7. On the floor of the mine near Querétaro, Mexico, the blasted rocks are carefully broken apart to remove the valuable fire opals. Photo: Eduard Gübelin, Lucerne.

1. Two handfuls of opals of cutting quality, only a few of which are of top quality, are the result of a strenuous day's work in intense heat. Querétaro, Mexico. Photo: Eduard Gübelin, Lucerne.

1

2

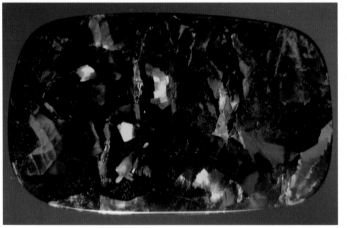

3

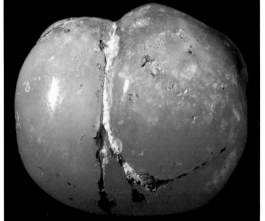

4

5

2. The screen drums loosen the marl and separate clay and earth from the hard stones such as sandstone and opal nodules at Lightning Ridge, New South Wales, Australia. Photo: Eduard Gübelin, Lucerne.

3. The black opal named *Aurora Australis* from Lightning Ridge lights up in all the spectral colors even when at rest. Photo: Eduard Gübelin, Lucerne.

4. This apple created from a large fire opal originates from rhyolite rock near Querétaro, Mexico. The white vein indicates a natural cementing by rhyolite. Collection: Zoltán Buzas, Munich. Photo: Karl Hartmann, Sobernheim.

5. This black opal flashing in intense spectral colors is from Lightning Ridge, New South Wales, Australia, and has the impressive name of *Red Heart of Australia*. Photo: Eduard Gübelin, Lucerne.

6

7

During its lifetime as a piece of jewelry, it may dry out and craze (hairline splits). Chemical influences (acids, lye, grease), full sunlight and high heat are anathemas to this gemstone. Unfortunately, it is beset by insignificant prejudices. The victim of superstition, it came into disrepute as a presumed bringer of bad luck. This stigmatization, however, cannot prevent the precious opal with its unique and delightful glittering colors from becoming the Mount Olympus of gemstones.

The opal – in Sanskrit *upala* (precious stone) – is found everywhere as a secondary mineral. It was deposited in rocks long after the rocks had been formed. Once again, therefore, the opal is in contrast to the majority of gemstones, which frequently crystallize out simultaneously as the rocks solidify. This explains both its proximity to the surface as well as the low age of the opal occurrences. Opals are only very rarely exploited in alluvial placers but are generally excavated from their primary parent rock. For this reason, the opal does not depend on high density (D around 2.0). As a precious opal, it can high-mindedly dispense with the favorable optical features of the other gemstones, as a fire opal even just a trifling amount more would be sufficient for higher esteem. Its refractive index of 1.45 is only slightly above that of water ($n = 1.30$); if it were any higher, it would adversely affect its flickering sheaves of light. With nature's clever providence, each gemstone was thus endowed with those properties that would later turn it into a jewel for people to enjoy. The individual basic colors of the opal's substance – white, gray, blue, green, orange, and black – are determined by the chemical differences in the sedimentary rock and thus by the trace elements of iron, cobalt, copper, nickel, silver, and so forth, with which the opal is provided by the adjacent rock. The characteristic play of colors is completely independent of this. The different color accords are given a variety of labels: mosaic, surface, and scattered fire. Among these, the designation of the valuable harlequin opal takes a special place. The evenly distributed chessboard pattern over the entire surface of the gemstone provides new, spectral color symphonies that spring from each of the colorful squares when struck by incident light. "The Opal Village," on its own authority the most significant location worldwide for opal production, is not situated as one would imagine in the Australian outback. Kirschweiler, a neighboring district of Idar-Oberstein, the respected trading center for South American beryls, currently plays an important role in the processing and world trade in high-class opals due to its highly qualified cutting industry and a group of prudent dealers.

The ancient Greeks used the *ophthalmos* (eye stone), as a universal means of curing eye troubles and considered it to be a lucky charm, comparing it to *cupid paideros*, "a child as beautiful as love." Pliny said that it was the vessel of unity, from which the carbuncle had drunk its glowing embers, the amethysts their deep purple, the emeralds their cheerful sea-green, the topazes their golden yellow, and the sapphires their deep blue. No other gemstone like the opal has been equipped with the ability to unfold the shades of the universal spectral wealth of colors of the other gemstones in such glittering and colorful arrays.

Below: Exemplary opal formations in botryoidal cavities of the parent rhyolite. Shortly after excavation, the damp halos around the opals are still recognizable. Photo: Eduard Gübelin, Lucerne.

Below: 15,000x magnification with a scanning electron microscope captures the densely packed sphere structures in the precious opal. These tiny spheres, with a diameter of less than 0.0005 millimeter, are minute amorphous silica spherolites that are joined together more or less regularly into individual lattice surfaces or blocks. The color play of the opal is caused by the multiple diffraction, refraction, interference, and scattering of light in the gaps of the sphere structures. Photo: H. U. Nissen, Department of Solid-State Physics, Federal Institute of Technology, Zurich.

PERIDOT

GREEN-GOLDEN RAY OF SUNSHINE

The gemstone peridot is the middle member in the olivine isomorphic group. The end members are the magnesium silicate forsterite (Mg_2SiO_4) and the iron silicate fayalite (Fe_2SiO_4), respectively.

Chemistry: $(MgFe)_2SiO_4$ (magnesium-iron silicate)

Crystal system: Orthorhombic

Habit (form): Thick-tabular, often with vertical striations. Edges frequently wedge-shaped.

Colors: Yellowish green, green, olive green.

Refractive index (R.I.): 1.654–1.690 (1.672)

Birefringence: +0.036 (very constant)

Pleochroism: Olive green, green, yellowish green

Density: 3.30–3.40 (very constant at 3.34)

Hardness (Mohs' scale): 6.5–7

Consistency: Brittle. Imperfect cleavage. Conchoidal fracture.

Occurrence: In basic and ultrabasic magmatic and metamorphic rocks (peridotite, dunite, serpentinite, etc.) as well as in thermally metamorphosed, impure dolomitic limestone marbles. In lava on Hawaii.

Extraction: Usually from the parent rock, rarely from placers.

Transposed into the language of music, the green of peridot is equivalent to the sounds of reed pipes. Like the sun's golden rays filtering through sparse foliage at an oblique angle, peridot's green catches the gold of the day star. Its family name of *green gold* reflects its green gold color tone, which is special among all gemstones. In early times, peridot was associated with the sun. It was said to store the bright rays of the sun and thus guard against imminent eclipses and blindness. The peridot is the most important member of the olivine family. After the feldspars and the garnets, this is the third clan from the kingdom of the isomorphic solid-solution series. This term refers to the ability of exchanging inherent (relevant) materials without any change to the crystal structure. The peridot is approximately in the middle of this series, flanked by two end members of insignificant minerals. The determining factor is its iron content, which, as an idiochromatic colorant, is part of the chemical composition. It is a magnesium-iron silicate, $(Mg,Fe)_2SiO_4$, in which magnesium and iron are linked with silica in changing quantities. At the end of the mixed series that is low in iron, there is the colorless forsterite and, at the iron-rich end, the black fayalite. Although olivines are a very important rock-forming mineral from the basic magmas of the earth's mantle, they are rarely fortunate to have gemstone format.

The rich potpourri of greens ranges from yellow-green to brownish – but bottle and olive green are the ones most frequently encountered. In its most perfect form, peridot has a velvety green-gold color, shimmering like damp moss in the fall sunshine, an effect attributable to its nickel content of several tenths of one percent. Peridot is an early crystallization that took place during the hardening of igneous rocks in the liquid magmatic phase. In the form of microscopically small minerals, it even played a considerable role in the formation of diamonds. It is a constituent component of kimberlite, its subsequent means of transportation, which is responsible for the blue-green color of the famous "blue ground" in the primary diamond deposits in South Africa.

Since time immemorial, peridot has played an important role in history. Fifteen hundred years before Christ it was released by Egyptian slaves from its dark dungeon on the dry and barren island of Zabargad in the Red Sea. On this classic primary location it is surrounded by basic igneous rock called gabbro, which was extremely slow to harden in the gigantic masses of molten magma. During this process, large crystals that had no real competitors for millennia were able to grow and mature undisturbed. The island, which was highly inaccessible due to frequent fog, was called *Topazos* by seafarers after the Greek word for seek. The designation *topaz* was commonly used for many centuries before being gradually superseded by the French name *peridot*, a derivation of the Arabian word *faridat*, which means gemstone. Peridot gained entry to Europe during the Middle Ages as a result of the Crusaders. The church rapidly recognized its particular suitability for sacred purposes. Peridot finds a suitable purpose as altar ornamentation or, as among Egyptian women, as showy earrings, but also as precious neck jewelry. Since its hardness is only 6.5, it is susceptible to wear and tear.

Like green fragments on a sandy beach, small peridots are scattered

Right: View from the peridot mountain on the island of Zabargad across the former mining area in which the waste dumps are still recognizable toward the northeastern foothills.

Below: Multifaced crystallized peridot crystal from Pyaunggaung near Mogok, Myanmar.

Bottom: Light green, similarly multifaced peridot protrudes from the parent rock into a cavity in which it could freely develop. This specimen was found by the author on the island of Zabargad in the Red Sea.

Right: Lisu children in the village of Pyaunggaung in the vicinity of the peridot deposit in Mount Kyaukpon, Myanmar, stare inquisitively at the white visitor who returned after thirty-four years to this remote region. Photos: Eduard Gübelin, Lucerne.

carelessly in a secondary deposit of fine black basalt sand near Hilo on Hawaii. In the primary deposits, peridot forms insets in a fine-grained compact basalt against whose dark basic mass the olive green crystals clearly stand out. Excavation from the basalt itself is impossible due to the extreme hardness of the rock. Although the peridots on Hawaii have little weight in terms of carats, careful collection still results in a worthwhile proportion of stones for cutting.

Also lavishly provided for by nature, Myanmar is a productive source of peridots. They are found near the legendary valley of the rubies, located a few kilometers to the north of Mogok, near Pyaunggaung, on the northern slopes of Mount Kyaukpon, which is 2,250 meters high. There, peridot appears as a lustrous green inset of small to quite substantial proportions in a loose, weathered, greenish serpentine, which was formed by metamorphism of a ferruginous gabbro. Like sparkling owls' eyes, bright, well-formed peridot crystals blink here and there out of the aqueous serpentine. Transformation of the former basic rock probably by hydrothermal action changed the parent rock without influencing the huge, magnesium-rich gemstone crystals. In this way, the clear, green crystals lie well preserved in the lap of their rock for millions of years. Among other things, the green crystals were also protected from seismic earthquakes until humans allowed them to be brought from their pitch-black accommodation into the golden sunlight. Excavation from the loose serpentine is relatively easy and is mainly implemented by exploding quarries in the mountain slopes or by sinking pits. The fragments are manually broken using rock hammers and the peridot crystals released, some weighing up to 100 carats, are collected in baskets.

The fact that peridots can actually fall out of the sky was proved in 1749 by a large meteorite that landed in the eastern Siberian district of Jenissejsk. Named the *Meteor Stone of Krasnojarsk* after the capital of the province, it contained very respectable crystals suitable for jewelry production. The event was all the more remarkable since, although other gemstones are thrown to earth, they are always minute and peridot is not very frequently represented. After the Second World War, its rarity was aggravated by the fact that a gemstone that was long considered to be a "precious olivine" and to which it is only related, was declared to be a mineral in its own right. Because of its sole occurrence on Sri Lanka and with reference to the old Sinhalese name of its homeland, it was given the name of sinhalite. Important localities for peridot also recently include San Carlos, Arizona (USA), Arendal in Norway and Suppatt in Pakistan. The peridots produced there in no way resemble those of the island of Zabargad, which has been exhausted in the meantime, and replace them completely. In addition, peridot is found in Ethiopia and in the Antarctic.

The fiery grace of peridot made it the favorite gemstone of the Baroque period. The golden olive green corresponded perfectly to the mentality and the color preference of the style of the period. An olive green peridot of crystal clarity and weighing 192 carats is said to have been part of the czar's insignia at some time. The largest peridot the author ever feasted his eyes on weighed over 250 carats.

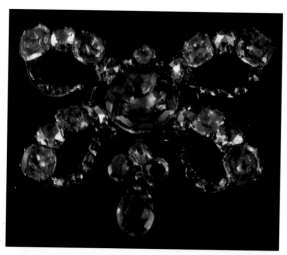

Below: A brooch set with diamonds and peridots from the eighteenth century. State Treasury of Russia (CIS).

Above: With a weight of 192.60 carats, this peridot is among the largest gems of this type ever found. It is set as a pendant in a wreath of thirty-two brilliant diamonds of old mine cut. State Treasury of Russia (CIS).

QUARTZ
BUSTLING GLOBETROTTER

Amethyst, rock crystal, smoky quartz, morion, citrine.

Chemistry: SiO_2 (silicon dioxide)

Crystal system: Trigonal (hexagonal)

Habit (form): Six-sided prism with ends of three large and three small rhombohedral faces each. Often interpenetration twins (Dauphiné, Brazil and Japanese).

Colors:
Amethyst: violet
Citrine: yellow
Morion: dark brown
Rock crystal: colorless
Smoky quartz: smoky brown, smoky gray

With heat treatment, amethyst can be transformed into yellow citrine or green prasiolite.

Refractive index (R.I.): 1.544–1.553

Birefringence: +0.009

Dichroism: Clear to weak, lighter and darker body colors.

Density: 2.65 (very constant)

Hardness (Mohs' scale): 7

Consistency: Brittle. No cleavage. Conchoidal, striated fracture.
Occurrence: Quartz is the most common of all minerals. It is found in very many rocks of all ages. It is one of the rock-forming minerals and is an important constituent in many magmatic, metamorphic, and sedimentary formations. The finest quartzes originate in pegmatitic and hydrothermal deposits.

Extraction: Mostly from primary deposits, veins and fissures, but also from placers.

As a quick-change artist of renown, quartz is found everywhere on earth, on every continent, in the lofty heights of mountains or in the depths of valleys. Its claims on space are thus by no means inferior to those of the feldspars. Its worldwide presence was facilitated by the widespread abundance of silica (SiO_2). This permeated the entire magmatic area and was present as quartz at every rock-forming stage. Gemstone quality, however, was only guaranteed by the pegmatitic and, particularly, the hydrothermal phase. The best quartzes are excavated from primary birthplaces, since its low density of 2.65 is no match for water and mud masses. The low refractive index of only 1.545 makes rich faceting desirable in order to put gleaming miniature floodlights on its luster. Perfectly formed quartz crystals are by no means rare. Their weight varies from microscopic size to real giants weighing a hundredweight or more. The wide variety of inclusions are a striking feature. Along with the inclusions in diamonds, these have been the subject of intensive investigation. In the quartzes retrieved from Alpine fissures alone, over forty types of distinct inclusions have been identified. Study of the liquid inclusions in the Swiss Alps resulted in detailed findings about the pressure and temperature conditions at the time of their formation and the crystallization phases. The umbrella term for phanero (or coarse) crystalline quartz is derived from *Querz* or *Quaderz*, old German mining expressions for crosswise vein quartz. Some subvarieties of quartz have achieved considerable levels of popularity. They include rose quartz (frequently cloudy, with traces of titanium), prasiolite (amethysts of Brazilian origin heated to become green), smoky quartz (brown), and aventurine (rock crystal with close-packed inclusions of green, glittering chromium mica [fuchsite]).

Rock Crystal

As clear as water, firmly bonded, apparently fragile and ethereal in its hovering lightness, rock crystal is the bearer of a long tradition. It goes back to the days when ancient Greece was at its zenith as is expressed in its name *krystallos*. This refers to the petrified, earthly ice palace of the Olympian gods, which could not even be destroyed by the heat of the sun.

Amethyst

The amethyst (from the Greek *améthystos*) is the most valuable and highly prized variety of quartz. Its lilac to rich violet color is attributable both to the allochromatic pigment of iron as well as to its interaction with color centers, which are electromagnetically disturbed sites. The color is often unstable and can be altered by heating. The crystals frequently are colored in zones, rather stumpy and compact and grown on a base. The coloration is mostly strongest at the tip – an authentic sign that amethysts were created at low temperatures. The process is very easy to explain: During their growth, they fended off the impurity of iron until the solution was saturated and then, in the final stage, had to be accepted by the quartz tips at temperatures that had already fallen.

In sources in the northern Brazilian state of Bahia, amethysts are found in fissures that are very similar to those of the Alpine mineral fissures. In Minas Gerais, they are found in pegmatites in conjunction with smoky quartz. In the two main occurrences in Rio Grande do Sul (southern Brazil) and near Catalan in neighboring Uruguay, they form the lining of cavities inside almond-shaped tagates grown in magmatic rocks. Additional abundant and lucrative deposits have been found on Madagascar and in Zambia as well as at various localities in Russia and Siberia.

Citrin

In nature, citrine only develops as a pale yellow to lemon-colored gemstone. When heated, it can undergo a color change from dark yellow to light brown. Many amethysts are sacrificed for transformation into yellow-brown citrines by heat treatment. The color induced by the effects of heat cannot be determined in advance. Powerfully colored citrines are also traded under the false designation of *topaz* – an interesting career development from amethyst to citrine to disguised topaz. In all cases, heating serves to upgrade the color and has no negative influence on the assessment of a stone, as long as the stone does not fade when exposed to light. The gemstones should therefore only be exposed to sunlight for a limited period of time. Natural-colored citrine comes from Brazil, Madagascar, and Myanmar.

The most elegant member of the worldwide quartz group is the violet amethyst, which owes its violet coloring to the interaction of iron and the color centers. The illustration shows a harmonious specimen from Guanajuato, Mexico. Photo: Karl Hartmann, Sobernheim.

Left: The design of this set of jewelry with its blossoms, leaves, and fruit combines fairy tale and reality and a picturesque arrangement with decorative ornamentation. The artist, N. V. Rostovzeva, was inspired by old Russian embroideries and named this set *Strawberries.* The amethysts are offspring of the Urals. Collection: V. V. Niko-layev, G. F. Alexachin.

Ametrine

Nature always provides a few capricious surprises. The most recent quartz foundling from the central Cordilleras of Bolivia, near the village of Anay in the province of Santa Cruz, is comprised of a coexistence of violet amethyst and yellow citrine. Words alone cannot convey the graceful attraction of this color symbiosis, which has been produced by Creation with unerring delicacy for a successful, harmoniously colorful composition: Two completely disparate color fields sharply delineated from each other are wedded together in one and the same gemstone. Ametrine is the composite name for this unusual hybrid being, which is excavated from cavities in a quartzite field.

Page 106, top right: Yellow citrines are extremely rare in nature. Their color is mostly created by heating amethyst to over 350°C. The original color determines the richness of the citrine's yellow. Collection: Hein Gärtner, Idar-Oberstein. Photo: Traudel Sachs, Sobernheim.

Page 106, bottom right: Smoky quartz (also called morion) is a typical example of gems colored by radiation. The smoky brown shade is the result of the interaction of structural inclusions of the foreign ions aluminum and lithium together with radioactive radiation from uranium and thorium in the accessory rocks. Senckenberg Museum, Frankfurt am Main. Photo: Karl Hartmann, Sobernheim.

Left: Magnificent rock crystal group from the Maderanertal, Uri, Switzerland. Pliny the Elder (24–79 A.D.) reported on the mining of rock crystals in the Alps. Photo: Max Weibel, Pfaffhausen.

Above: The cross-section of a multicrystalline amethyst group reveals the growth phases from its core to the perimeter. Photo: Karl Hartmann, Sobernheim.

Left: Since rose quartz is usually found in massive shape, well-formed crystals are highly prized. Large crystals recognizable to the naked eye are called "phaneroquartzes" as opposed to the massive grainy to fibrous "cryptocrystalline quartzes" such as chalcedony, agate, jasper, and so forth. Photo: Traudel Sachs, Sobernheim.

107

SPINEL
THE CORUNDUM'S DISGUISED TWIN

Chemistry: $MgAl_2O_4$ *(magnesium aluminate)*

Crystal system: Cubic

Habit (form): Mostly octahedral (rarely cubic or dodecahedral)

Colors: All colors with varying tints and shades. Mixed colors are frequent. The most popular colors are pure red and cobalt blue.

Refractive index (R.I.): 1.712–1.736 (isotropic) (1.72)

Density: 3.58–3.75 (the highest values apply to gahno spinel with zinc content)

Hardness (Mohs' scale): 8

Consistency: Tough. No cleavage. Conchoidal, uneven fracture.

Occurrence: Mainly in metamorphic and metasomatic rocks such as crystalline limestones, in dolomite marble as well as in gneiss and serpentine.

Extraction: Both from primary and secondary deposits, that is, from the parent rock and placers.

Modesty is not one of the spinel's strengths. In past centuries, before gemology had its current, detailed knowledge at its disposal, many a spinel made a self-assured appearance in public as a ruby. With the help of modern detection methods, practically all red gemstones that were recorded in history as rubies, were later discovered to be red spinels, which was detrimental to their reputation. Since then, spinels have languished, barely noticed, in the shadow of the corundums. Quite undeservedly, as proved by their impressive personal data. Above all other gemstones, our benevolent earth fairy provided the spinel with a considerable share of enviable features. Its high refractive index (n = 1.72) provides it with liveliness and temperament; its good dispersion (0.021) gives it vibrant fire; its remarkable hardness (8) makes it resistant and durable; it has no cleavage, which makes it tough; it has no birefringence, which leaves it wonderfully clear and transparent internally. The sum of these generous features elevates it to the status of a downright ideal gemstone, the equal of corundum and chrysoberyls and a close neighbor of the diamond. Its name might be derived from the Greek root *spinter* (spark), whereby one of its above-average properties would be confirmed. On the other hand, the Latin word *spina* refers to a thorn, probably a reference to the pointed crystal shape of the spinel. Particularly good, clear gemstones of more than 10 carats tend to be rare. As is the case with the corundum, beryl, and tourmaline families, spinel encompasses a variegated mixture of superb varieties that are represented in practically all colors. In the magic garden of crystalline flowers from the earth's depths, the spinel blooms in a picturesque bouquet of glowing colors full of southern intensity. It is notable for its wealth of delicate color nuances from pink to ruby red and from lilac to sapphire blue. Although the red spinel succeeds with stupendous facility to pass itself off as a double for the red corundum – fine red spinels are identical in color to first-class rubies – it is difficult for the blue spinel to compete in the color contest with the blue corundum. Instead of the delicate sapphire blue, the spinel tends toward gray-blue, violet blue, or mellow colors. One recent item of news is the discovery of cobalt spinel on the tropical island of Sri Lanka. It did not receive its name from the chemical element – cobalt is not present in natural gemstones – but from a silvery midnight blue, distantly related to the Virgin Mary's robes of the Middle Ages. Similar to alexandrite and chrysoberyl cat's eye, the cobalt spinel can be expected to develop into a cult gemstone for collectors. The voluptuous multicolor spinels allowed them to sail under a foreign flag into the treasure chests of kings. The best known example of this is the fabled *Timur* ruby, as it is known, a ruby-red spinel weighing 361 carats, whose adventurous wanderings can be traced back to the fourteenth century. In spite of its name and contrary to the legend, it was never in the possession of the Mongolian conqueror. Another famous ruby-red spinel that created a place for itself in the annals was the *Black Prince's Ruby.* Its bloodthirsty past in no way prevented it from being included in Cromwell's inventory of the English crown jewels, where it was described as a large Balas ruby and its value recorded as a mere 4 pounds! Today, this magnificent ruby-red

Left: The only gemstone that can compete with the corundums is the spinel, since it is the only one to have a similarly wide color palette. It can also consider itself to be the precursor of the royal corundum dynasty. Long before the latter, that is, at a time when there was sufficient magnesia (MgO) available at the place of formation to crystallize with alumina (Al_2O_3). Photo: Erica and Harold Van Pelt, Los Angeles.

Right: The *Timur ruby* gets its name doubly wrong. It is not a ruby but a red spinel, and its incription "sahib keran" originates from Nadir Shah and in no way from Timur, the ruler of Eastern Iran in the fourteenth century. Timur's jewel collection never reached India. Tower of London.

109

spinel, set in a Maltese cross studded with diamonds, decorates the state crown and is admired by thousands of visitors who make their pilgrimage to the Tower of London each year.

The gemstone most likely originated in Myanmar; it was never cut and, on its longest side, measures approximately 5 centimeters. The largest spinel ever collected, a rolled crystal of 520 carats and an octahedron of likewise 520 carats, serves as a noteworthy exhibit in the mineralogy department of the British Museum. A third one, a colossus of almost 400 carats, is contained in the diamond treasury in Moscow.

The spinel has additional, especially distinctive virtues in addition to

Above: Pendant made of two unusually large, red spinels of 56 carats (top) and 100 carats (bottom), respectively. State Treasury of Russia (CIS).

its ideally esthetic values: its superb suitability for cutting and its power to withstand high heat without changing color. Its gamut of lively hues is based on its cheerful willingness to exchange foreign, color-effective elements for its hereditary ingredients. Thus, minute quantities of chromium – to the magnitude of 1 to 2 percent of its weight – can replace aluminum and cause its red color. The red spinel is, in fact, the only gemstone capable of holding a candle to the ruby. With unexpected variety, it goes through every section of the red scale and even flares up in a blood-red, tile-red, as well as a rose-red glow. As an impertinent outsider, there is the pale orange-colored fire spinel. In finely nuanced color gradations, the purple spinel makes the transition to the blue varieties of blue-green and ink-colored shades. These shades are caused by iron, titanium, or zinc (gahno spinel), which replace a few percent of magnesium in the body of the spinel. Violet spinels are numerous, clearly green ones in which iron has supplanted some of the aluminum, a rare dream, and yellow ones never occur.

What the individual spinel lacks in colorful perfection, it compensates for in its clear transparency and its brilliancy, which is often heightened by perfect purity. This does not mean that all spinels are endowed with total purity. On the contrary, many spinels contain typical inclusions as welcome identification features, which mainly consist of apatite crystals and rutile needles as well as of negative crystals filled by dolomite. The spinel even tries to compete with corundums in this aspect by occasionally transfusing its interior with a silkily fine web of rutile or titanite needles and thus tease with the magic of three- and six-rayed stars on its cabochon-cut surface.

The spinel is an exemplary contact mineral that is also a neighborly

Left: The spinels not only cover the entire color spectrum but the full range of tints and shadings. All these spinels come from Sri Lanka. Photo: Eduard Gübelin, Lucerne.

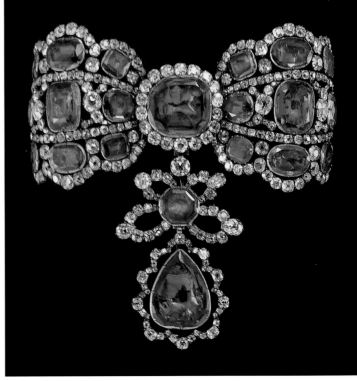

companion of the ruby in deposits. Like the latter, however, it was created in an earlier generation in the grainy dolomite and calcite marbles of Mogok in Myanmar and in the Hunza valley in Pakistan by means of contact metamorphism and was formed in the contact zones of the pegmatite layered within the crystalline schist (gneiss) on Sri Lanka. In Myanmar, spinel is associated with the ruby everywhere, and in Thailand, it is considered to be the pilot mineral for corundum. During weathering of these rocks, it was enriched in the young placer deposits and is found in conjunction with many other gemstones as a by-product of ruby and sapphire exploitation. Spinels are a compound of magnesia (MgO) and alumina (Al_2O_3) and is thus a magnesium aluminate ($MgAl_2O_4$). It crystallizes as clearly shaped octahedra. The spinel thus crystallized as a predecessor to the ruby as long as the magnesium dissolved from the dolomitic calcite was still present. Since magnesia and alumina were continuously processed during the course of crystallization that comprised several mineral generations, the magnesia finally became exhausted in the spinel.

Right: The bow brooch shown here was created by jeweler Leopold Pfisterer in April 1764. The large gems are spinels, the small ones white brilliant-cut diamonds. Eighteenth-century women wore jewelry of this type on a neckband made of velvet or lace or on the bodice. State Treasury of Russia (CIS).

SPODUMENE

PHOENIX
FROM
THE ASHES

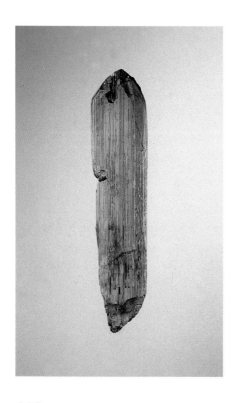

With spodumene, we are faced with a threefold jewel comparable to the triple-star constellation of the chrysoberyls. Collectors revel in the delightful colors that are the equal of those of beryls. Three different color-causing ions create three different varieties, although all three have the basic chemistry of a lithium-alumina silicate.

The Greek word *spodeios* (ashen) actually describes a cloudy to opaque, gray crystal that can achieve gigantic weights of up to 90 tons. However, this is only the common variety of spodumene. In close association with beryls, feldspars, quartzes, and tourmalines, spodumenes largely congregate in lithium-rich, granitic pegmatite dikes. There, they mature into remarkably giant crystals of considerable purity, attaining heights of up to 2 meters, as long as sufficient space is available in the pegmatite.

Together with diopside, jadeite, and other minerals, spodumene is assigned to the group of pyroxenes (*pyr* [fire] and *xenos* [foreign]), which means that it is not of plutonic origin. Due to this affiliation, it takes on monoclinic crystal symmetry. As is the case with beryls, the different colored varieties are attributable to various types of colorant metallic chromophores. The yellow, yellow-green, and green-yellow examples bear the joint name of spodumene and their colors are the result of bi- and trivalent iron. An exceptionally beautiful, golden yellow example weighing 327 carats can be admired at the Smithsonian Institution, Washington, D.C. (USA).

The best variety is hiddenite, discovered in 1879 in Alexander County near Stony Point in North Carolina (USA), and named after its discoverer, A. E. Hidden. Trivalent chromium gives it its luxurious emerald green color. Although primarily found in North Carolina as well as in Minas Novas, Brazil, and on Madagascar, hiddenite still remains the rarest spodumene. The Royal Ontario Museum in Toronto, Canada, houses a magnificent hiddenite weighing 1,804 carats.

Kunzite, the spodumene named after the gemologist, George Frederick Kunz, develops a palette of pink-colored tints ranging from bluish-violet to lilac and the purest of cyclamen reds thanks to the admixture of manganese. In 1902, the first and still operational deposits of gem-quality format were developed in the Pala mountains of San Diego County, California (USA). Other important occurrences are in the state of Maine (USA), on Madagascar, and in Brazil. One of the largest and finest examples of kunzite with a weight of 880 carats is part of the collection at the Smithsonian Institution in Washington, D.C. (USA).

Hiddenite and kunzite, with a hardness of not quite 7, both have good cleavage. This property, however, demands a certain amount of caution during the processing and wearing of this princely gemstone. Brilliant or step cut is mostly preferred, whereby the latter best corresponds to its crystal habit. If exposed to sunlight for longer periods of time, hiddenite and kunzite may gradually pale slightly; kunzite, though, is miraculously able to slowly regenerate itself. In comparison with the highly similar, identically colored beryls, spodumenes have a livelier brilliancy, stronger luster, and slightly more fire thanks to their higher refractive index and dispersion.

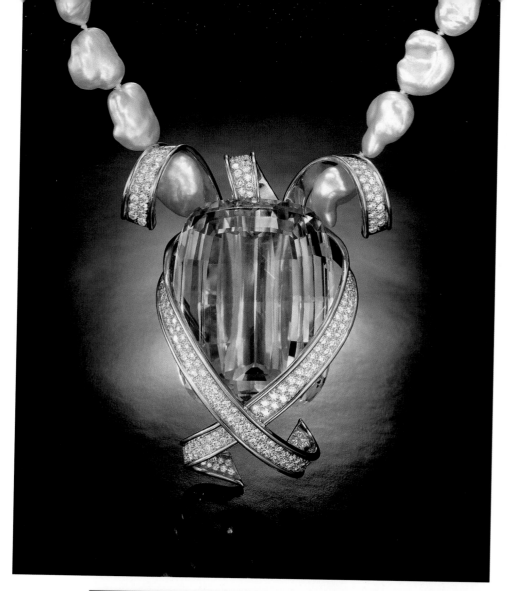

Spodumene, hiddenite, kunzite (also called triphane)

Chemistry: $LiAlSi_2O_6$ (mineral from the pyroxene group)

Crystal system: Monoclinic

Habit (form): Prismatic crystals; often with vertical striations.

Colors: Spodumene: colorless, yellow, light green-green
Hiddenite: emerald green thanks to chromium oxide
Kunzite: cyclamen pink thanks to manganese

Refractive index (R.I.): 1.65–1.679 (1.674)

Birefringence: +0.015

Pleochroism:
Spodumene: lighter and darker body colors
Hiddenite: bluish-green, grass green, yellowish-green
Kunzite: strong: colorless, rose-red, violet

Density: 3.17–3.23 (3.18)

Hardness (Mohs' scale): 6–7

Consistency: Good; cleavage parallel to the basal plane. Uneven, conchoidal fracture.

Occurrence: In lithium pegmatites and crystalline limestone.

Extraction: Usually from primary deposits.

Top: Kunzite is unique in its substantially more lively and pleasant, cyclamenlike lilac color. The picture shows it between ribbons set with brilliant-cut diamonds as a pendant on a necklace made of baroque pearls. Collection: Tiffany & Co., New York (USA). Photo: Erica and Harold Van Pelt, Los Angeles.

Left: Monoclinic kunzite crystal weighing 396.30 carats accompanied by a heart-shaped kunzite of 6.13 carats. This variety of spodumene is named in honor of its discoverer, F. G. Kunz, who was the first to discover and describe this gemstone in 1902. At that time, he was working as a gemstone expert for Tiffany's in New York. Collection: William Larson, Fallbrook, California (USA). Photo: Erica and Harold Van Pelt, Los Angeles.

Opposite: In the spodumene trio, the emerald green variety, called hiddenite, is the rarest and most precious. Its name comes from A. E. Hidden, who was the manager of the mine in North Carolina where hiddenite was discovered. Collection: William Larson, Fallbrook, California (USA). Photo: Erica and Harold Van Pelt, Los Angeles.

The storehouse of gemstones appears to be absolutely inexhaustible and new precious stones continue their triumphal march to the astonishment of the world. Occasionally, Mother Nature is pleased to offer previously unknown minerals – among these brasilianite, ekanite, painite, sinhalite, taaffeite – or produces hitherto unknown offspring such as the garnet varieties umbalite and tsavolite of long-established genealogies. Classic gemstones also continue to create surprises by the variety of their locations: thus the andradite grossular appears in Mali, the mandarine spessartite unexpectedly turns up in Kunene, Namibia, and

TANZANITE

BLUE PATRICIAN FROM BLACK AFRICA

Blue variety of zoisite

Chemistry: $Ca_2Al_3(SiO_4)_3(OH)$

Crystal system: Orthorhombic

Habit (form): Usually prismatic crystals, frequently with vertical striations.

Colors: Blue to violet (and brown)

Refractive index (R.I.): 1.691–1.72 (1.695)

Birefringence: +0.009

Pleochroism: Strong: blue, purple, brown

Density: 3.35–3.55

Hardness (Mohs' scale): 6.5–7

Consistency: Cleavage parallel to the base. Brittle. Conchoidal, uneven fracture.

Occurrence: In veins and fissures of graphite-containing gneiss and regional metamorphic rocks in the midst of the volcanoes surrounding Mount Kilimanjaro.

Extraction: Almost exclusively from primary deposits.

more recently near Josh in Nigeria, and opals honor Brazil and Tanzania with their presence. Long known as original rock, tanzanite first created a stir in 1967. This newly discovered, blue variety of zoisite is considered to be one of the finest blue gemstones and is only found in Tanzania. Zoisite, a family name like corundum, combines different minerals that tend to be classified as modest. Among these, the opaque, peach-colored thulite and the similarly opaque and lively green anyolite enjoy a certain amount of familiarity. This latter massive, grainy zoisite covers glowing red ruby crystals surprisingly as large as footballs within its green walls. Recently, another transparent zoisite variety was discovered, this time in a striking bright green. To this day, it does not have a name of its own but is traded under the name of *green zoisite*.

Of all the new gemstones that have conquered the hearts of people in the second half of the twentieth century, none has even approximated the success of tanzanite. Within a short period of time, it succeeded in achieving worldwide popularity and major acclaim. The triggering factors for this market success are the cardinal virtues incorporated in tanzanite. Not least among these is the compelling beauty of its suggestive color, which has an impressive similarity to top quality gemstones, its rarity and durability, as well as its availability. Together with the rare benitoite, tanzanite approximates the finest blue imaginable, the incar-

Opposite: These faceted gemstones are all members of the zoisite family. Only the blue ones bear the name of tanzanite, the others are called zoisite with the corresponding color designation, that is, yellow, brown and green zoisite. Tanzanite is one of the more recent gemstones, first found in 1965 in the Merelani Hills, southwest of Mount Kilimanjaro. Collection: William Larson, Fallbrook, California (USA). Photo: Erica and Harold Van Pelt, Los Angeles.

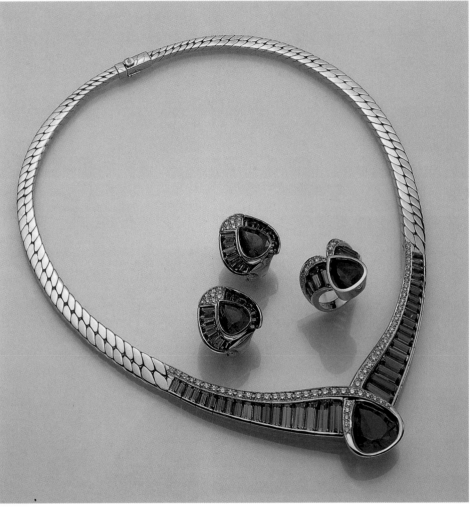

nation of a sapphire blue. Barely distinguishable at first glance from the precious ideal, tanzanite shares the fate of other famous simulators precisely because of this similarity. Just as red spinel competes closely with ruby, green zoisite and green tsavolite are forced to vie with emerald, yellow hessonite loses its own identity due to its flattering comparison with topaz, the mandarine spessartite emulates the padparadscha and a number of rivals lie in wait for the yellow diamond, among them yellow zircon, sphalerite, and scheelite, tanzanite also gains in importance and fame due to its similarity to sapphire. For all these emulators, it is a fact that they are frequently just as fine, to some extent harder and livelier, and, in any case, always more affordable than the originals. Though, tanzanite possesses a hardness of merely 6 1/2 – thus being close to

Left: Freshly broken from the rock, the tanzanite crystal has a not very popular mixed color of blue, violet, and brown, which can be transformed by heating into a magnificent blue very similar to that of sapphire. On the triangular-cut gemstone, only the brown-colored part has disappeared. Collection: M. M. Scott. Photo: Erica and Harold Van Pelt, Los Angeles.

Right: The breathtakingly beautiful, lively blue color of tanzanite very quickly and enduringly conquered the heart of gem collectors and lovers of fine jewelry. Tanzanite set comprised of necklace, ring, and earrings. Création Gübelin AG, Lucerne.

Right: Under the supervision of an overseer, a miner carefully applies a pneumatic drill in order to open up a suspected pocket of tanzanite. De Souza Mine, Merelani, Arusha, Tanzania.

Top: A skilled worker carefully taps open a block of gneiss in the hope that it will contain a tanzanite crystal worth cutting.

Above: As can be seen, the worker was not mistaken: in the center of the piece of gneiss is a large, blue tanzanite.
Photos: Eduard Gübelin, Lucerne.

demantoid and low zircon – its resistance to scratching and abrasion is surprisingly good.

The silicate of calcium and aluminum, zoisite, owes its name to Siegmund Freiherr Zois von Edelstein (1747–1819) who operated an iron mine in the Karawanken mountains in Kärnten (Austria) and encountered the foreign mineral on his own property. Centuries later, the discovery of a bright blue, transparent variety created some excitement in the specialist world, to which the special circumstances surrounding the find also made their contribution. The sensational discovery was made by a tailor named Manuel d'Souza in the region of the Merelani Hills near Mount Kilimanjaro, around 90 kilometers from his home town of Arusha. With few inclusions, the royal blue find was soon the focus of American and European publicity. However, a murderous attack put a swift end to exploitation of the mineral. A fake car accident in which d'Souza died, interrupted any follow-up supplies. As a result, supply was unable to keep up with demand during the following two years – imponderables of this kind are unfortunately no rarity in a trade that depends on prospectors, who still ply their trade in a buccaneering manner to some extent.

Although received at first with discomfort in specialist circles, the name *tanzanite* – borrowed from the country of origin – was given to this gemstone by Director Henry Platt of the leading jewelry dynasty of Tiffany. The aqueous calcium-aluminum silicate ($Ca_2Al_3Si_3O_{12}(OH)$) has strong pleochroism: Depending on direction, tanzanite is either violet-blue or an unmistakable amethyst color or simply brown. The undesirable brown and violet shades are only removed after professional heating and the radiant cornflower blue is brought to full expression. If this delicate process is only partially successful, a violet tint is left behind that is particularly visible under artificial light. No other gemstone possesses this unique ability to rid itself of two of its triple colors by means of heat treatment. If only one of its three colors, frequently the brown, is eliminated as a result of unprofessional heating, a color-changing tanzanite is created, similar to the color-changing sapphire or spinel: in daylight it looks blue, in artificial light it looks violet. Right from the very start, tanzanite set out to mislead experts. Initially, its delusive color behavior was attributed to a minute quantity of strontium. The author, however, considered it his task to get to the bottom of the real reason for the pleochroism and called on the services of Prof. Dr. Max Weibel at the Federal Institute of Technology (ETH) in Zurich for a chemical analysis. The findings of this early analysis could not have been more interesting: The exciting color behavior of tanzanite is attributable to vanadium.

In the rivalry between sapphire and tanzanite, the blue African was able to score an additional plus point for itself: the highly rare cat's eye with its countless fibrous inclusions arranged in parallel fashion in its interior. Tanzanite's tendency to large size is also undeniable. The heaviest step-cut jewel weighs 122.7 carats and is of exemplary transparency – one of tanzanite's most superb characteristics is to delight the eye with its limpid clarity and exquisite brilliancy.

Below: By nature, tanzanite is triple-colored, that is, blue, violet, and brown. After heating to around 320°C, it takes on a beautiful velvety blue. The larger tanzanite weighs 29.43 carats, the heart 5.41 carats. Collection: Karl Egon Wild, Kirschweiler.

Above: Precious tanzanite pendant, surrounded by diamonds. Collection: Karl Egon Wild, Kirschweiler.

TOPAZ

CHALICE OF GOLDEN CRYSTAL

Chemistry: $Al_2SiO_4(F,OH)_2$

Crystal system: Orthorhombic

Habit (form): Usually columnar prismatic crystals with well-formed terminal faces.

Colors: Usually in lighter tints and all shades of yellow, blue, brown, and red (= sky blue and rose red). Deep-blue topazes are artificially irradiated and heated.

Refractive index (R.I.): 1.606–1.638 (1.625)

Pleochroism: Weak: lighter and darker body colors.

Density: 3.50–3.60 (3.53)

Hardness (Mohs' scale): 8

Consistency: Good cleavage parallel to the basal face.

Occurrence: Widespread in pegmatites and hydrothermal veins and fissures as well as in granite and rhyolite.

Extraction: Mostly from primary deposits, sometimes from placers.

Sunlight flows into the golden-yellow chalice of the topaz to be forever imprisoned in this precious crystal vessel. The alluring sound of the name *topaz* resulted in its being given to all yellow- to gold-brown gemstones. This false designation was mainly given to citrine – a variety of quartz generally obtained by heating amethyst. Lacking both brilliancy and fire, citrine does not have the remotest chance of holding its own when directly confronted with the lively and brilliant topaz, radiant with its warm shades of gold. The glowing, fiery sparkle of topaz has always induced poets and esthetes to make enthusiastic comparisons with the fiery glow of a rare wine. Agreeing with the words of the poets, people only associated topaz with a superb, clear drop of gold; knowledge of other types, namely, the wide range of sky blue and delicate pink tones of topaz, which are equally of enchanting intensity and radiant luster, threatened to be lost, however. The variations of the glittering pink topazes easily cover the finest nuances of the pink scale to culminate in an unparalleled full and deep pink-red that even surpasses the ideal morganite of the beryl family in its flickering brilliancy. Just as a slight admixture of peach pink is imposed on the rich, sunny shade of the gold-colored topaz, the reddish versions let a barely perceptible neon blue shine through. The blue topaz delights the eye with its fresh, radiant azure blues without ever achieving the deep saturation of the aquamarine. With its perfect purity of color, without the slightest addition of green, it radiates its girlish grace in its transition into the gradually dwindling color of the colorless to pure white topaz. The colorless topaz was also well practiced in the art of involuntary subterfuge. The 1,680-carat *Braganza* diamond in the Portuguese state treasury is, in actual fact, a colorless topaz, while the opposite is true of a topaz in an ornament belonging to a Lower Rhine farming family in 1929, which was half the size of a pigeon's egg and was later identified as a yellow diamond.

Imperial topazes and pink topazes, particularly the ones left as nature created them, are very rare. In addition to the former alluvial deposits of the Sarnaka River in the Urals, Russia, the topaz hill near Katlang in Pakistan is the sole deposit still exploited today in which natural pink topazes are found. All other pink topazes owe their color to heat treatment. The rose-red tint of Pakistani topazes is so unique that a color-trained eye can recognize it immediately and distinguish it from those treated by heat. The most elegant pink tint of the topazes from Katlang has a slight lilac hue, and the best gems might be most accurately described as being cyclamen red. This distinct rarity value also applies to the pink topazes from Brazil. They are slightly paler and of the purest cherry-blossom pink. Most of the pink topazes in the gem trade have been heated to around 475°C and were originally yellow topazes. The stones selected for this process are those whose gold color is made up of an unfavorable mixture and that are therefore eminently suitable for upgrading.

The topaz crystallizes orthorhombically and develops columns with square or diamond-shaped basic planes as well as multisurfaced heads. Thanks to its excellent gemstone hardness, topaz lends itself to superb polishing. The clear smoothness of its surface even permits a diagnostic

statement: Topaz can be distinguished from similar looking gemstones not just by the play of light of its colors but also by its supersmooth slipperiness. In comparison to the upstart citrine, the far higher refractive index (n = 1.62) of topaz gives it the advantage of more intense brilliancy. As a flanking recognition measure, the gemologist can make use of the methylene iodide test. With a density of 3.33, this solution separates the arch rivals, with the lighter citrine (D = 2.65) floating on the surface and the heavier topaz (D = 3.53) sinking to the bottom. The perfection of topaz has an unmistakable disadvantage: It has easy basal cleavage that makes it react sensitively to sharp blows.

Brazil's leading position as a topaz source is incontestable. Even when grouped together, the Urals, Myanmar, Sri Lanka, the United States, and Pakistan cannot compete with the classic pegmatite source Ouro Preto in the gemstone-rich state of Minas Gerais, which is home to most of the top-quality and select topazes under its roof of weathered rock. Together with aquamarines, topazes are excavated either from their primary deposits or slightly downstream from the valley floors. Their extreme rarity is explained by fluorine, which is necessary for their existence and is one of those highly volatile components accumulated in the pegmatitic residual molten masses from which results the chemical compound $Al_2SiO_4(F,OH)_2$ of topaz. Since the residual molten masses do not travel far from their source – such as beryllium, boron, fluorine, and lithium, which are decisive for the creation of beryl, topaz, and tourmaline – their combinations are found almost exclusively in pegmatites.

However, not all topazes originated from pegmatitic mineral formation, since solutions containing fluorine also saturated the adjacent rock at a later date and dissolved existing minerals there if they became hot enough. This released silica and alumina that, together with fluorine, caused the creation of topazes. Such transformation processes mainly took place in cracks and cavities. For the gemstone market, only those topazes created in the pegmatitic-hydrothermal sources are of interest since this is where they received their desirable characteristics of beautiful color, hardness, and durability, which make them much sought after and highly appreciated precious stones. The diversity of their occurrences and their formation result in just as many different characteristics in the crystals. Each type of deposit thus possesses the topaz crystals that correspond to it. Collectors and connoisseurs can immediately recognize the type of formation from the appearance of a topaz crystal and, frequently, can even identify its place of origin. The druses that often contain topazes have contributed a great deal to the confusion of citrine and topaz since they often both develop there on and between the quartz crystals.

The trace element contents are normally so low in topaz that they are insufficient, with the exception of chromium oxide, to provide topaz with any color. The previous opinion that the color in the yellow, brown, and blue topazes was caused by the exclusive incorporation of iron, proved to be erroneous. Chromium appears to be a more essential color component with weight percents of between 0.03 and 0.1, depending on the richness of the color. In addition to these values, color centers definitely play a role, which is due to the fact that certain topazes bleach in daylight and regenerate themselves, and can also undergo color changes as a result of irradiation and heating.

Close parallels can be drawn between the colors of topazes and beryls. Given the fact that their prices are almost equally balanced, the higher refractive index and superior hardness of topazes, however, ought to ensure preferential favor by buyers due to their much more advantageous and ideal gemstone characteristics.

The origin of name *topaz* can only be speculated upon since it was also common in ancient times. Following the trail of Pliny the Elder, topaz is not the gemstone with the delicate touch of gold but a green jewel. *Topazion* (sought-found) was what peridot was called right from the start. In addition, peridot was also called *chrysolite* for a long time, which means gold stone – a designation that appears to be more logical for topaz.

The life cycle of topaz can be proven back into the eighteenth century when it was first discovered in the Schneckenstein in the Erz Mountains within the territories of Augustus the Strong of Poland.

The old continent was not just a little proud of its European gemstone. Schneckenstein was superseded by the unsuspected variety of colors and the additionally surprising size of some crystals from more recent deposits. Mineralogical museums in Florence, London, Paris, and Vienna house some select and unusually large topazes. Fairly recently, the Viennese Historical Museum acquired a giant topaz, which can boast of possessing all the superlatives. This topaz is among the finest, largest, and purest of all, with flames of yellow and peach. It weighs 117 kilograms or 585,000 carats.

Above: Superb crystallized pink topaz from the Ghundao Mine, near Katlang, Pakistan. The white parent rock (calcite-quartz) is easily recognized as is the gray adjacent rock of sedimentary limestone. Collection: William Larson, Fallbrook, California (USA). Photo: Erica and Harold Van Pelt, Los Angeles.

The tourmaline group includes a greater number of individual minerals with several interchangeable cations but with unchanged crystal structure. Each has its own name, for example, buergerite and povondraite (iron), liddicoatite, uvite and feruvite (calcium), olenite, elbaite (lithium), dravite, schorl and chromdravite (sodium tourmaline) as well as foitite (tourmaline without an alkali ion).

TOURMALINE

ALPHA
AND
OMEGA

Chemistry: $XY_3Z_6(BO_3)_3Si_6O_{18}(O,OH,F)$, whereby $X = Ca, K, Na$; $Y = Al, Fe^{2-}$ and trivalent, Li, Mg, Mn^{2+} and $Z = Al, Cr^{3+}, Fe^{3+}$ or V^{3+}, that is, the chemical composition of tourmaline is highly complex and many ions can be mutually exchanged (complex aluminum-boron silicate).

Crystal system: Trigonal (bipolar piezoelectric).

Habit (form): Short to long, columnar to fibrous prismatic crystals, usually with vertical striations. Three-faced bipolar ends.

Colors: Every imaginable color in all tints, shades, and mixtures, even colorless and black. The main colors have their own names.

Refractive index (R.I.): 1.616–1.652

Birefringence: -0.014 to -0.044 (–0.018)

Dichroism: Clear, depending on body color, light and dark yellow, green, brown, blue, red, or in the corresponding mixed colors.

Density: 3.00–3.15 (3.05)

Hardness (Mohs' scale): 7–7.5

Consistency: Good cleavage parallel to the basal plane. Brittle. Conchoidal, splintery fracture.

Occurrence: Usually in pegmatites and hydrothermal deposits.

Extraction: Mainly from primary deposits, occasionally from placers.

Origin and perfection: All the horizons of imaginable colors are united in this single gem. The name is derived from Sinhalese *turamali*, referring to gems of unknown identity since, despite being a familiar stone from as far back as the Middle Ages, it is still considered to be something of a stranger. There were times when its glowing red offspring were considered by our forefathers to be rubies of the highest order; another time at the end of the twentieth century it appeared in colors never before encountered in the gemstone kingdom. Discovered long ago, and appreciated since time immemorial, tourmaline still has not been thoroughly researched even today. Of all the gemstones, tourmaline undoubtedly possesses one of the widest color ranges, since it can reproduce every conceivable color of the universe without exception. Teamed with an oily sheen, it enchants and astonishes the eye with its wealth of hues – comparable to Aladdin's treasure in *1001 Nights*. In dynamic steps, it exploits all the complementary contrasts, spraying its color fountains heavenward in the finest of gradations, and paints every conceivable shade, transition, and mixture in the finest of nuances. A lifetime would not suffice to master the task of categorizing the tourmaline as a collector's item. Its specific specialty is mixed colors. With an average refractive index (n = 1.64), it dispenses with eye-catching brilliancy in favor of subdued restraint and contemplative peace. Its birefringence is sufficiently marked to permit the recognition of doubled facet edges in a cut gemstone with the aid of a magnifying glass. The gentle, delicate light of tourmaline incorporates the direction-dependent change of color and lightness in its masterfully strong dichroism. A dreamlike color symphony of intoxicating shades is played out in one single gemstone. Based on the alternating relationship between bi- and trivalent iron, the characteristic of absorbing ambient light to varying degrees, permits the lively alliance of divergent colors.

This gemstone family presents itself as a cornucopia overflowing with varied and contrasting hues, but it is also marked by other qualities. Trigonal (three-edged) crystallizing tourmaline, which develops three-sided columns often with very beautiful clear end faces, plays in one and the same piece with color modulations of quite contradictory nature – from the fleeting delicacy of a watercolor through to the darkest shades of night. At one end of the column, for example, the ruby-red rubellite sits in splendor, while at the other end the sapphire-blue indicolite rules supreme and, in and between, there is a wealth of color ranging from orange to brown to yellow to green. The yellow and brown elements in tourmaline are the result of the presence of iron, titanium, and/or manganese, whereas bi- and trivalent iron is responsible for blue tourmalines. Wherever magnesium displaces the iron, the shades become pale and light. Manganese causes pink to red coloration, whereas chromium and/or vanadium call the green shades into play – the spectrum reaches from almost emerald green sensuality through to powerful salad green and to the lacquerlike ponderousness of magnolia leaves.

Its hardness of 7.5 and density of 3.05 favor the extraction of tourmaline wherever it occurs, be it in Brazil, Namibia, Tanzania, Myanmar, on Sri Lanka, in the United States (Maine and California), in

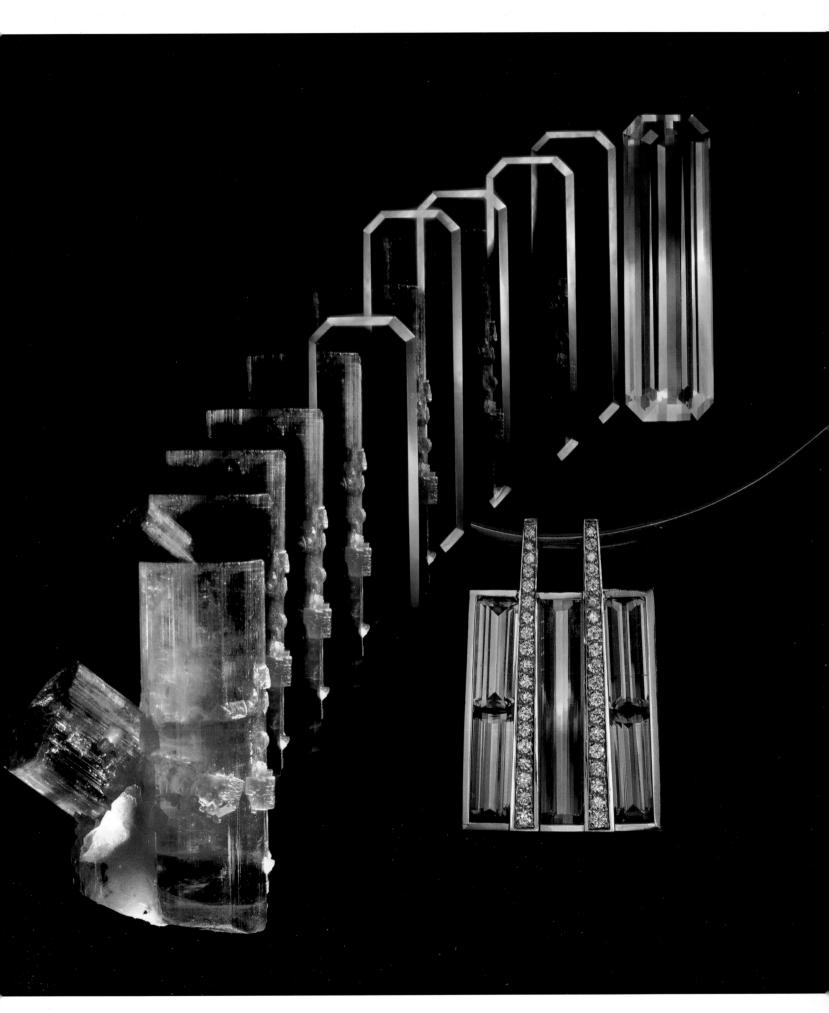

Page 123: Hardly any other picture can display the variety of tourmalines, their optical individuality, and the transition from crystal to polished gemstone in such a phenomenally eloquent way. The complex chemical composition of tourmalines results in the development of an inexhaustible range of mixed colors. Collection: William Larson, Fallbrook, California (USA). The tourmalines come from his Himalaya Mine, Mesa Grande, California (USA). Photo: Erica and Harold Van Pelt, Los Angeles.

1. It was a huge and pleasant surprise when completely new tourmaline colors were discovered in the San José Mine near Paraiba, Brazil, in the 1980s. They were immediately in high demand and found their

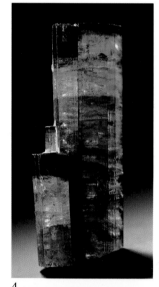

1

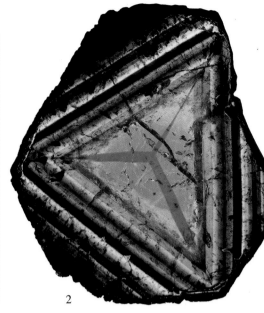

2

3

4

5

way into collections or were used for precious items of jewelry. Collection: Michael Scott. Photo: Erica and Harold Van Pelt, Los Angeles.

2. Typical cross-section through a so-called iddicoat-tourmaline from Madagascar. Collection: Julius Petsch, Idar-Oberstein.

3. Complicated preparation plant using numerous wash boxes and sluices below the immense pegmatite mine at Muiane near Alto Ligonha, Mozambique, from which tourmaline is excavated in every color. Photo: Eduard Gübelin, Lucerne.

4. Two blue tourmalines grown together in parallel. These indicolite tourmalines, as they are called, are among the great rarities, in particular, when they occur in sapphire blue. Brazil.

5. Scepter crystals are found more frequently among quartzes, but are an unusual rarity among tourmalines, particularly when they occur as a bi-color variety. Barro de Salinas, Brazil. Collection: William Larson, Fallbrook, California (USA). Photo: Erica and Harold Van Pelt, Los Angeles.

6. View of the entrance to the immense underground Golconda Mine in the state of Minas Gerais, Brazil. The parent rock of the tourmaline – white pegmatite – can be clearly seen. Photo: Eduard Gübelin, Lucerne.

Greenland, Bolivia, Mozambique, Nigeria, or on Madagascar. In Brazil, the economically most important location of tourmaline, this ubiquitous gemstone is found in all colors and not just separated according to colors and spread across the country, but frequently in a single pegmatite vein, even in a single crystal. As a complex boron silicate $(Na,Ca)(Mg,Fe,Li,Al)_3Al_6(BO_3)_3Si_6O_{18}(OH,O)_3(OH,F)$, tourmaline is a typical representative of rocks formed at great depth in which materials for its creation were substantially stored. Although only black tourmalines originate from the pegmatitic molten masses, other tourmalines worth cutting are more of hydrothermal origin. In Brazil, the tourmaline find of the century was made in 1989. The focus of this event was the unassuming village of São José da Batalha in the state of Paraiiba in northeastern Brazil. After many years of unsuccessful digging, Heitor

Left: The raspberry red color of this rubellite tourmaline, as it is called, apparently inspired the Indian artist to turn it into a fruit. This ornamental object can look back on a long history since it was mentioned as far back as the seventeenth century by Boetius de Boot, the Bohemian court jeweler. In the course of time, it frequently changed its princely owners until it finally was presented as a gift in 1777 by the Swedish King Gustav III to Empress Catherine II. The rubellite weighs 260.86 carat. State Treasury of Russia (CIS).

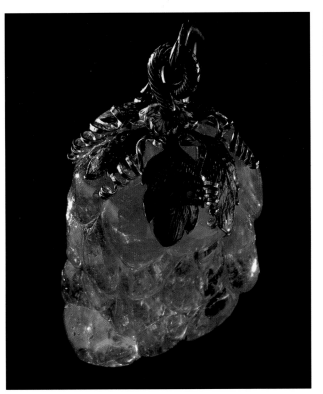

Dimas Barbosa, also called "Heitor the fool" because of the futility of his searching, finally found tourmalines of a color never before encountered in gemstones. These minute, transparent gems, colored by bivalent copper, created excitement because of the bright variety of their colors: flashlight blue turquoise, sugary candy pink in the style of American neon signs, busily flickering mint green – an incomprehensible expressiveness exaggerated into the realms of the artificial. And yet these Paraiiba tourmalines were natural gemstones, without any heat treatment and of such a pleasant array of colors that the prices for these stones of several carats soared astronomically. This winning streak lasted for only a brief period, however. Only four years later, in 1993, the mine was closed. It had been fully exploited. The "pockets," as they were called, in the pegmatite veins, miarolithic cavities the size of an orange were minutely small in comparison to others.

Right: Tourmalines form the most colorful and graduated gemstone family. Anyone unable to afford the expensive gemstones, for example, ruby, sapphire, or emerald, should find the requisite color among the tourmalines. Collection: Gustav Zang, Idar-Oberstein.
Historical records mention the tourmaline for the first time in 1703 in the Netherlands under the name of "Aschentrekker." This was because tourmalines become electrostatically charged under the influence of heat and attract ash and particles of dust so were thus eminently suitable for cleaning the meerschaum pipes popular at that time.

ZIRCON

DIZZYING QUICK-CHANGE ARTIST

Chemistry: $ZrSiO_4$ (zirconium silicate)

Crystal system: Tetragonal

Habit (form): Short and long prismatic crystals with square cross-section and dipyramidal end faces.

Colors: Mainly "warm" colors: yellow, brown, orange, rose red, and rose. Colorless and blue examples have been heated.

Refractive index (R.I.): 1.92–1.99 (green: 1.79–1.84)

Birefringence: +0.06 (green variety is isotropic [metamict])

Dichroism: Mostly weak: lighter and darker tints of the corresponding body color. Blue zircon clearly blue-gray.

Density: Very constant 4.69 (green zircon: 3.95–4.10)

Hardness (Mohs' scale): 7.5 (green zircon: 6.5)

Occurrence: Zircon is a resistant mineral that has survived many geologic events and thus occurs in many geologic formations.

Extraction: From primary as well as alluvial deposits.

The pure substance of zircon is noted for its colorlessness since, in its chemical compositions ($ZrSiO_4$), neither the zirconium silicate nor the silica have the slightest effect on color. In all likelihood, the zircon colors are not merely attributable to the usual chromophoric (colorant) elements but are largely the result of the admixture of the radioactive elements uranium and thorium, which are contained in zircon as trace elements in differing strengths. The incorporation of these radioactive atoms is also the reason for the zircon's ability to change color with the application of heat – the actual secret of its versatile color transitions. The most popular color varieties – the blue zircon, which rarely occurs in nature, and the colorless zircon, which of all the gemstones most closely resembles diamonds – are created by the fire of Hephaestus: the blue color is obtained if zircon is heated in a vacuum, whereas heating in a jet of oxygen removes all color and leaves behind a pure white glittering gemstone. The blue zircon was highly popular in the first half of the twentieth century as an eye-catching trompe l'oeil; in contrast, the colorless variety was used much earlier as a diamond imitation in jewelry because of its high refractive index and strong color dispersion. It almost seems as if the processed version occasionally resists an excess of human artistic improvement, since not all zircons treated are color-proof. Under ultraviolet light or in daylight, they frequently return to their original color.

As a master of confusion, zircon is less impressive for its richness of color, which is primarily limited to yellow, brown, red, green, and blue shades, than for its range of exquisite optical properties that mainly give brilliant-cut examples their high effectiveness. High adamantine luster and sparkling lively fire make zircon the close neighbor of diamonds. Its density (D = 4.0 – 4.69) is not achieved by any other transparent gemstone. Its high refractive index of 1.95 and the strong color dispersion of 0.038 endow it with fascinating aspects. This is increased by the remarkable circumstance of a certain amount of inconsistency in its value about whose laws there is now complete clarity. The ideally visible appearance of birefringence is manifested – looking from the sharp edges of the crown into the depth of the gem – by the blurred contours of its lower edges. Just as with zircon, many other gemstones possess this special ability of dividing penetrating light into two refracted rays along two different directions so that the objects presented to the eye are duplicated. No less complex is the life story of the tetragonal (fourfold) crystallizing zircon. Zircon, involved in the development of various gemstones, accompanies acidic deep rock partly as an accessory mineral, and appears partly in the wake of pegmatites (vein rocks) and certain crystalline schists. It is thus spread worldwide in rocks of all types. The most extensive exploitation – placer deposits without exception, from which zircon is panned as an accompanying material to rubies, sapphires, and many other gemstones – is carried out in the classic Asian gemstone countries such as Sri Lanka, Myanmar, Cambodia, Thailand, and Vietnam. Richly endowed with deposits, Sri Lanka not only provides a truly comprehensive color spectrum but also green zircon. Out of the glittering bouquet of colors, Myanmar mainly has cognac brown,

yellow, and red zircons as well as the rare blue examples. Vietnam has picked out mainly the yellow, brown, and red-brown examples for itself. Tanzania has new, hope-inspiring zircon deposits to offer. The purely sedimentary deposits are in the area around Songea and Tunduru.

Zircon was given the role of precursor when determining the age of gemstone locations ever since it was used to determine the age of a gemstone deposit for the first time. In zircons with high thorium and/or uranium content, the crystalline atomic structure can gradually dis-

integrate due to radioactivity into the amorphous state of an aggregate of zircon silicate and silica. Zircons become cloudy and green at the same time, the physical properties decline, the strong birefringence disappears, and part of the uranium and thorium is transformed into lead. The measurable proportions in terms of quantity between uranium and thorium on the one hand and the lead on the other now permit the age of the zircon to be determined and, in consequence, that of its deposit. The age of the locations on Sri Lanka was set at around 550 million years using this method. An additional check undertaken by the author using ekanite, a more recent radioactive gemstone also originating from Sri Lanka, confirmed these findings.

Last but not least, the name of this gemstone was not proof against change. *Hyacinth* was once a flowery reference that is presumably based on the Greek designation *hyakinthos* along a diversion via the Orient. Its more recent name of zircon is based on the Persian word *zargùn*, which means golden yellow and refers to the majority of stones of this type.

Opposite: Two women working at a zircon pit near Champasak, Cambodia, which is operated by a private family. In a depth of approximately 10 meters, the father digs the alluvial valley accretion containing zircons, while the daughter hauls the diggings to the surface. The mother is responsible for washing and careful sorting at the washing pit. Photo: Eduard Gübelin, Lucerne.

Left: The zircon crystals deposited in the alluvial valley floor on Sri Lanka have not traveled very far since their crystal forms are still clearly recognizable. Photo: Karl Hartmann, Sobernheim.

Top right: A gem cutter positions his dopstick correctly at his lapping bench in order to give a zircon crystal the right faceted cut. Photo: Eduard Gübelin, Lucerne.

Bottom right: Heavily rolled and broken zircon crystals from the alluvial deposits of Tunduru, Tanzania. Photo: Erica and Harold Van Pelt, Los Angeles.

The term *ornamental gem* covers two completely different areas. In everyday speech, it is a collective term for all gems that are used for ornamental purposes. In personal areas of application, this means rings, earrings, necklaces, and brooches. In the sphere of ornamental furnishings, this means cult and ceremonial decorations or objects such as dishes, statuettes, vases, and amphorae. In this connection, the term *ornamental gem* always indicates the use of valuable stones – in contrast to standard minerals.

For further terminological distinction, a differentiation is made between ornamental gems and gemstones. The term *gemstone* is, once again, an umbrella definition, this time as the general term for transparent minerals and precious, asset-maintaining rarities. The term ornamental gems, in contrast, refers to the mainly opaque gems that are either monomineral aggregates (agate, chrysoprase, jade, turquoise, etc.) or

PORTRAITS OF ORNAMENTAL GEMS

polymineral rocks (among these, lapis lazuli, maw-sit-sit).

There are several important exceptions in both groups. Among the gemstones, there are quite a number of opaque gems that are distinguished by their rare exquisiteness or eye-catching beauty such as starstones and opals. On the other hand, among the usually opaque ornamental gems there are also transparent ones that are all varieties of their opaque rock brothers: thus nature provides surprises such as clear rhodochrosites and rhodonites as well as transparent sodalites.

As regulated by the customs authorities, the trade made a distinction during the nineteenth century between gemstones and so-called semiprecious gems. Since no specific categorization and assignment of the gems to these two groups ever took place, however, the result was a hopeless confusion of terms among specialists and particularly among customers. At an international jewelers' congress (BIBOAH) in 1938 in Lucerne, Switzerland, an attempt was made to put an end to the confusion with the official discontinuation of the term semiprecious stone. Since then, this rather derogatory term has been despised in professional circles; unfortunately, it is still used unreservedly by art historians. Unofficially, the expression of *precious stone* is used several times in this book. This represents a collective term for the most precious of the gemstones – diamonds, rubies, sapphires, emeralds, alexandrites, and opals – to avoid having to list these individually in each case.

Opposite: The elegant figurine of a women is made of agate and the bowl is of rhodochrosite. These are only two examples of the degree to which the beauty of this material can inspire a gem lapidary to creative artistry. Collection: Eduard Gübelin. Photo: James G. Perret, Lucerne.

130

THE BEAUTY OF ORNAMENTAL GEMS

A highly illustrative comparison is preordained on the topic of ornamental gems: a host has a guest, and the latter gives the house a particular tone – futuristic paintings, charming drawings or meandering-shaped borders. It is not the typical harmonization of transparency, brilliancy, fire, and glowing colorful luster of gemstones or the will-o'-the-wisp effects that determine the popularity of ornamental gems. Their charm lies in the uniqueness of the picture content. Just as with phenomenon gems, ornamental gems can be explained by the term *inclusions*. Although the inclusions in phenomenon gems express themselves as wavering light features of mystic origin, they appear in macroscopic, that is, easily discernible for the eye, dimensions in numerous ornamental gems, particularly among the agates. Some examples of this are the glitter of a green fuchsite, which produces a glistening appearance in avanturine quartz or the red shimmer of hematite scales in sunstone. These inclusions can be a real feast for the eyes and raise the pulse rate of every collector. Depending on their type of formation, inclusions are frequently younger than the mineral surrounding them. They often penetrate fissures and cracks from outside as iron or manganese solutions and crystallize in there after drying as aqueous oxides of iron (brown iron) and manganese (psilomelane or pyrolusite), for example, in many ornamental agates and rhodonite. The growth of crystals was usually a rapid process, so that only the dendritic-shaped (mosslike or branchlike images) or other types of imaginative skeletal crystals were able to develop. The dendritic, mosquito, and landscape agates display picturesque images of filigree grace and surprising regularity, imitations of landscapes and hair-fine spun designs, all possessing a rare attraction.

All these gems are an invitation to introspective meditation. If thoughts are allowed to roam free, new miracles, even more abstract images are added. Mother Nature as the masterful artist shows herself in the ornamental gems in an even more extravagant way: multirayed fireworks unfold their radiance, fairy palaces and undulating hills form on the horizon like mirages, ancient plants seem to be recreated in stone for an eternity, oscillating needles draw trembling zigzags, and the most enchanting fact is that Mother Nature wrought all this freely and without a blueprint with a range of designs that are a testimony to an astonishing wealth of ideas.

Other ornamental gems have chosen an independent route in terms of color and shape: distinctive lines in the green-banded malachite; the rose-colored and marbled, blossomlike pattern in rhodochrosite; velvety-brown matrix veins in turquoise or the "gold speckles" in lapis lazuli, each of these having its own unique character. It is difficult to believe that the admixture of refining impurities can result in such enchanting images of nature's temperamental imagination.

Stone Age peoples used many of the ornamental gems to fashion tools and weapons as well as for cult and decorative objects.

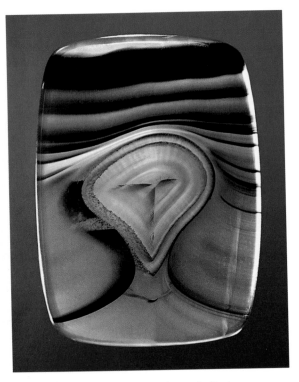

Opposite: In Russia, where malachite is found in the Urals, gem lapidaries make magnificent boxes and caskets from this ornamental gem. Manufacturer: Nicolai Medvedev. Photo: Erica and Harold Van Pelt, Los Angeles.

Above: Agate's general popularity is undoubtedly based on the boundless variety of imaginative designs that result from its varied coloration. Collection: Eduard Gübelin, Lucerne.

AGATE

FIRE
AND
FLAMES

CRYPTOCRYSTALLINE QUARTZES

Varieties:
- *Chalcedonies (fibrous aggregates): chalcedony, agate (banded), chrysoprase, heliotrope, and carnelian.*
- *Jasper (granular aggregates) – many varieties, colors and patterns: eye jasper, leopard jasper, band jasper, erongo jasper, and so forth.*
- *Silicified aggregates: Hawk's and tiger's eye, fossil wood as well as coral, shell, saurian bone quartz, and so forth.*

Chemistry: Basic mass SiO_2 (like opal)

Crystal system: Usually compact masses of fibrous or granular aggregates with botryoidal, kidney-shaped forms. Chalcedony has a radiating structure.

Habit (form): No crystal forms. Coarse, compact, massive.

Colors: All colors in every conceivable tint, shade, mix and pattern.

Refractive index (R.I.): Between 1.53 and 1.54.

Birefringence: +0.004–0.006.

Dichroism: Dependent on the aggregate structure (usually none).

Density: 2.58–2.64, usually 2.6.

Hardness (Mohs' scale): Almost 7.

Consistency: Brittle to tough. Conchoidal, uneven fracture. Porous, can therefore be dyed.

Occurrence: In numerous different rock formations as coarse masses, druses, geodes, amygdules.

Extraction: Depending on source, from the parent rock, from weathering grounds and alluvial sediments.

Versatile in its beauty, multicolored, multishaped, the text book description of agate can be continued endlessly thanks to its unparalleled wealth of abstract and figurative designs. While agates are unquestionably "spotted, clouded, banded, checked and flamed," they still cannot be precisely catalogued due to the great variety in their appearance. It was an accepted law that agates had a botryoidal shape until agates were found in Paraiiba in northern Brazil in the 1970s that had externally precisely delineated crystal faces. Only a decade previously, customers had been confronted with a hitherto unknown variety of agate. This was fire agate from the southwest United States and northern Mexico. Its versatile play of patterns made up of circles, curves, and vaults, which stand out in the liveliest of colors from a brown background, unite in its colorfulness to a color crescendo that can best be compared to a fanfare. This multicolored shimmering fire agate created excitement among collectors soon after its appearance. As colorful pebbles, collected from the Achates River on Sicily, agates were already known to the Greeks and Romans. The names given to its imaginative, figurative images – the miniature representations made up of tree, dendrite, landscape, moss, and mosquito agate – are only a modest selection from the limitless variety of possible forms of this gem. It would be a mistake to assume that these insubstantial pictures are attributable to fossilized plants or other organic remains. Instead, these are ramified inclusions of purely mineral substances, which have crystallized from iron, manganese, or chlorine-containing solutions. Growth must have been so precipitate that only the delicate skeleton crystals were able to develop. The ornamental gems are cryptocrystalline or fine crystalline mineral formations as they are called (the Greek word *cryptos* meaning hidden, secret), whose compact aggregates of microscopically fine minicrystals are individually undetectable to the human eye. It is all the more pleasurable for the eye to perceive the dreamlike images particularly in the tree, bush, branch, and plant style designs in the dendritic agates, which are unmatched in their charm.

The agates belong to the hierarchy of quartz, which rules over two subgroups, chalcedony and jasper. Like carnelian and chrysoprase, agate is assigned to the chalcedony group. Jasper, formerly known as hornstone, is an opaque, mostly finely grained quartz aggregate. The scope of color and variety depends widely on the type and quantity of the minerals interspersed between the microscopically fine grains. Jasper can be spotted, banded, striped, flowery, or even irregularly patterned and occurs almost everywhere in the world. The basic colors tend toward yellow, brown, red, white, black, and green shades. Jasper, which was highly popular in the Middle Ages for sacred objects and court decorations such as cups, canisters, and dishes, has been slumbering toward rediscovery. Agate is different as it has always managed to attract collectors. Its formation devolves from volcanic eruptions. In the boiling, flowing embers of lava, pea-sized to hundredweight drops of more or less pure silica (SiO_2) floated, with or without water content.

After the lava had solidified into melaphyre rocks, they crystallized as radially fibrous quartz masses of regular almond shapes. The speed of

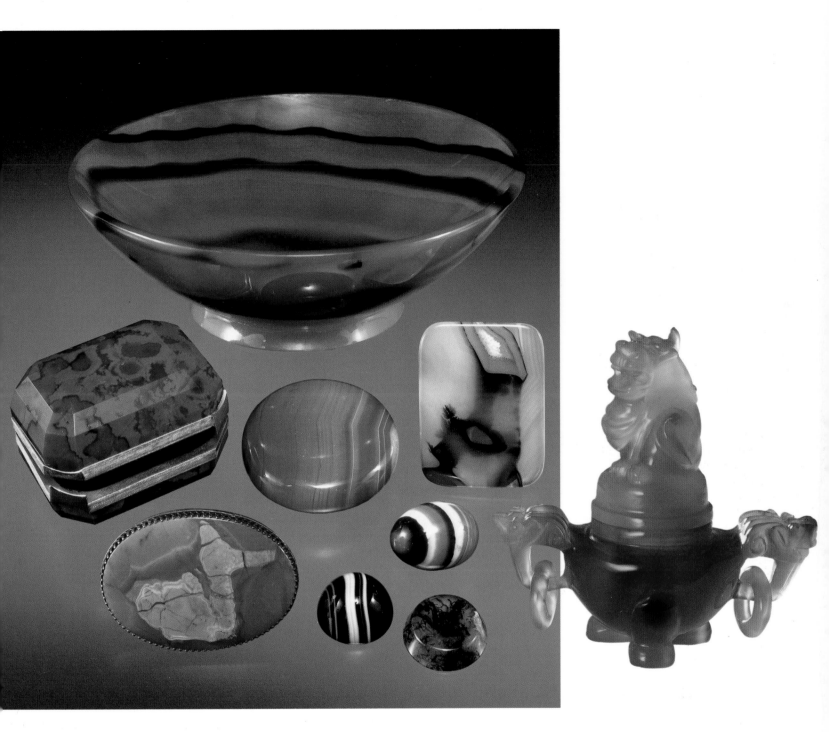

crystallization depended on the vagaries of cooling, which took place in irregular stages. In periodic layers, they thus formed either compact, finely fibrous, gray or porous, roughly stranded, white layers. White and gray-striped agates are mainly found in the southern Brazilian state of Rio Grande do Sul and in the area around Catalan in northern Uruguay. Agates from the United States and the melaphyre faults near Idar (Rhineland-Palatinate, Germany) are distinguished by their attractive rose-red to red and yellow to brown stripes. The white, porous agate layers can be dyed at will by staining and change names according to their colors, ranging from brown to red sard to red-brown carnelian and the banded stones as they are known. Along with marble, colored molten glass, and frequently mother-of-pearl, agates are a main component of mosaics, which retain their fresh and original sheen over a period of centuries.

Left: Agate's appeal and easy processing and, in particular, the wealth of imaginative patterns and designs, make it a popular raw material for countless ornaments, requisites, and decorative objects. Photo: Erica and Harold Van Pelt, Los Angeles.

Right: Incense container carved in Japan from local agate. Collection: Eduard Gübelin, Lucerne. Photo: James G. Perret, Lucerne.

CHAROITE

REED PIPES FROM THE RUSSIAN KARST

Charoite is a rock composed of the minerals charoite, aegirine, light quartz, and yellow tinaksite, and occasionally with inclusions of brownish ekanite.

Chemistry: $K(CaNa)_2Si_4O_{10}(OH,F) H_2O$

Crystal system: Monoclinic

Habit (form): Massive, compact.

Colors: The charoite mineral is violet, the ornamental gem named charoite is violet with black veins and yellow to brown patches. This results in a pretty pattern of restrained harmonizing colors.

Refractive index (R.I.): 1.55–1.56 depending on mineral content.

Birefringence: 0.009–0.01

Density: 2.54–2.7

Hardness (Mohs' scale): 5–6

Consistency: The mineral has cleavage in three directions. The rock is very tough.

Streak: White, chalky.

Occurrence: Along the Chara river, Aldan shield, Siberia. Accompanied by canasite and tinaksite in the contact zone of syenite and limestones.

Extraction: Open-cast and underground mining of primary deposits.

In its inhospitable and frozen rocky wastes, Siberia hides a contrapuntal kaleidoscope of promising, glowing, richly colored rocks. Charoite was the most recent chance find during extension work on the Trans-Siberian Railroad in 1976. During excavations for the new route along the Chara River in the Murun massif, northwest of Aldan, Yakut, the construction workers unwittingly came across an eye-catching colored rock, close to Lake Baikal, that fascinated them at once. Going by the name of charoite (Russian *charo* [beautiful]), the material soon gained entry into the studios of jewelry artisans all over the world. Its distin-

guishing features are its unusual structure and color. The opaque material is mainly marked by a lively lilac-purple to lavender and can have many or several sprinklings of aegirine/augite, which create a background shade of greenish-black. Individual pieces also incorporate weak greenish-gray microcline and are permeated with yellow- to orange-brown veins of tinaksite; the partially tea-brown, geometric patches are of ekanite. With their structure, the images created – white chrysanthemums on a violet background, waterfalls, leafy or needlelike ornamentation, flowing droplets – exploit the wealth of opportunities presented by a lively, natural imagination and frequently determine the purpose to which the stone is put. With its hardness of 5–6, charoite is eminently suitable for processing as cups and vases as well as in the shape of cabochons and, due to its pretty pictorial motifs, as chains and pendants, whereby the embracing gold gives it a softness and an aura of flattering luxury.

JADE
METAPHOR
FOR
LUCK

Jade is a collective term covering two similar-looking minerals, JADEITE AND NEPHRITE, which are completely different mineralogically.

Jadeite:
Chemistry: $NaAlSi_2O_6$ (sodium-aluminum silicate)

Crystal system: Monoclinic

Habit (form): Rare as a monocrystal, usually long prismatic to granular interlocking, rock-forming crystals.

Colors: As a result of iron: yellow, green, brown; as a result of manganese: pink to lavender and violet: as a result of chromium: emerald green; white (mutton-fat jade).

Refractive index (R.I.): 1.65–1.67

Birefringence: +0.013

Density: 3.3–3.5

Hardness (Mohs' scale): 6.5–7

Consistency: Tough, thanks to close interlocking of the grains. Splintery fracture.

Occurrence: As lentils, veins, and massive lumps in metamorphic albitite.

Extraction: From the parent rock as well as conglomerates and alluvial deposits in northern Myanmar.

As a companion of humans, jade can look back on a long and important past. It was processed into jewelry and, in the form of amulets, met the need for protection. In the early Stone Age, jade was also used as a tool for hammering, splitting, and cutting. Although jade is only of average hardness (H = 6.5–7), it is of unyielding toughness, even exceeding that of steel. For this reason, it was used as a weapon in the fight for survival against the rawness of nature – and later elevated to the status of a supreme cult gem in gratitude to the gods. In particular, excavations in Mexico have revealed ritual items that bear witness to a high level of artistic skills. These allow the conclusion to be drawn that the *chalchihuitl* (green stone) was respected deeply among the superior Indian cultures of Central America.

In the gemstone trade, jade is the collective term for two different minerals, namely, the inexpensive nephrite and precious jadeite. The ornamental gem nephrite is an intercalation in serpentine rocks and similar crystalline schists that resulted from eruptive rocks low in silica; the same applies to jadeite from Myanmar. In this case, an acidic, granitic magma suffered desilication as a result of penetration into existing ultrabasic serpentine, with the consequence that quartz was separated and a major proportion of the albite ($NaAlSi_3O_8$) was transformed into jadeite ($NaAlSi_2O_6$). Wherever chromium was present by chance, the result was a highly appreciated emerald green "imperial jade." This valuable, translucent material is also known in a variety of delicate shades. It is common in a pale white ("mutton-fat" jade) with a barely perceptible pastel tint and is frequently veined and speckled in emerald green due to traces of chromium oxide; a stronger chromium concentration is marked by richer green shades, the finest emerald green tint of which achieves enormous sums in the Far East. As a result of coloration by iron, jadeite becomes apple green-yellowish to orange or brown, but turns lavender blue to violet if manganese is present.

Maw-sit-sit is an exceptionally pleasant version of jadelike ornamental gems. This Burmese designation, which has generally become the accepted term even in the gemstone trade, refers to a gem composed of different minerals. Two of its mineral components provide it with its glowing green color of freshly sown rice: symplektite as well as the chromium-rich jadeite kosmochlor. Together with other minerals, they are embedded in random distribution in a basic mass made up of pale mineral accessories. The kosmochlor forms the irregular speckles and veins that contribute to the beauty of this ornamental gem. Nowadays, maw-sit-sit is an exceptionally popular gem for ornamental use and is increasingly being chosen for use in men's jewelry since its fresh color looks sophisticated, distinguished, and elegant.

Asia continues to supply astonishing examples for the constant and incomparably high values put on jade. In one of the devotional sites behind thick, protective panes of glass in the Po Lin Monastery on Lantau Island near Hong Kong, which is famous for the largest sitting Buddha in the world, there is a Buddha statue weighing several kilograms. It was carved from a single white "mutton-fat" block of jade.

The jade necklace that was known under the name of the *Mdivani*

Above: An exceptionally fine and much-prized variety of the jadelike ornamental gems is the maw-sit-sit, which owes its glowing green color and black veins to irregular inclusions of chromium-rich jadeite (Kosmochlor).

necklace and belonged to the millionaire heiress Barbara Hutton also acquired a legendary character. Made by Cartier in Europe from twenty-seven beads with circumferences between 15.2 millimeters and 19.2 millimeters, this necklace was presented as a gift by Barbara Hutton to her sister-in-law Princess Nina Mdivani. At the end of the 1980s, it changed hands in Geneva for the spectacular sum of over $2 million. Adventurous theories have been proposed about the origins of the intensively emerald green beads of almost semitransparent composition. One particularly imaginative theory dates the original purchase as being made during the period prior to World War II. The necklace is said to have been obtained from a dealer in Beijing who is supposed to have created four similar necklaces for four American socialites from a long court chain originating from the imperial palace. When this same necklace was again up for auction half a dozen years later at Christie's, the auctioneers in Hong Kong, it achieved the incredibly high price of $4.27 million.

Nevertheless, jade is not an exceptionally rare material in the variety of its color shades. Nephrite deposits are encountered in many parts of the world. The most commercially abundant ones are in Canada and New Zealand. Myanmar is home to the most productive jade mines in

Left: With his sunscreen, a jade dealer checks the quality of a large block of jade that has just been brought from Hpakan, where it was extracted from the Uyu River, to Mogaung, the trading center in northern Myanmar.
Right: In the courtyard of a jade dealer in Mogaung, jade blocks wait for further transportation to the jade auction in Yangon. They are sawed in half to assess the quality of the interior of the jade pieces.

Photos: Eduard Gübelin, Lucerne.

the northern part of the country around Tawmaw and in the craggy hillsides along the Uru River. Between crumbling rocks, the conglomerate masses as they are known, jade is found relatively close to the surface in the deposits of the river that are young in terms of the earth's history. The workers toil during the six-month dry period from October to April with pry-bars, picks, and patient care to separate the rare blocks of jade from the barren rock. From Mogaung, where the state controller submits them to scrutiny under the sun for the purpose of determining color and transparency and then estimates their value, most of the gems travel down the Ayeyarwaddy River from Yangon overseas, across the sea to the east. Their destination is Hong Kong and there the small workshops in the crooked alleyways where, under the steady rhythm of treadling feet, the masters of jade art carve their figurines on grinding wheels coated with the finest of diamond dust. Thousands of years of experience have culminated in their expertise.

In classical Chinese art, the precious gem *Yu* is the earthly embodiment of the cosmic principle that governs mental, ethical, and social life in the Middle Kingdom. With reverential awe, the purity, immortality, virtue, and power that find expression in the "jewel of heaven" are given a shape subordinate to the natural material: the harmony of color and structure. Similarly, any irregularities are incorporated into the design. Guided by nothing more than intuition and with a distinct sensitivity for the nature of each gem, the carver first draws the miniature picture designed in his or her mind's eye onto the smooth gemstone creating an objet d'art after many weeks of work. With borrowed motifs, the living tradition of the forefathers is continued into the present-day. The precious and almost prohibitively expensive imperial jade is a challenge for a large number of frauds. The victims are the many tourists on the lookout for bargains.

Left: Jade in different color variations as well as decorative objects made of jade are shown here. The magnificent figure in lavender jade with its green hem is particularly noteworthy. Collection: Eduard Gübelin, Lucerne. Photo: Fotoatelier Fruttig, Säriswil.

Right: In a jade-cutting workshop in Hong Kong, a young woman draws a figure on a piece of raw jade for the gem cutter to work from. Photo: Eduard Gübelin, Lucerne.

LAPIS LAZULI

INCARNATION OF THE STARRY FIRMAMENT

Compact, granular aggregate (rock) composed of the blue minerals hyaune, nosean, lazurite, and sodalite.

Chemistry: Chemical composition of the minerals listed above.

Crystal system: All the above-listed minerals are cubic; usually compact, granular aggregate.

Habit (form): Coarse, formless masses.

Colors: Dark blue, azure blue (best color), royal blue, violet blue to greenish blue. Usually rich in gold-colored pyrite insets or permeated by white calcite veins.

Refractive index (R.I.): 1.5 (isotropic)

Density: 2.7–2.9 (without pyrite 2.5)

Hardness (Mohs' scale): 5–5.5

Consistency: Brittle to tough. Uneven, conchoidal fracture with finely grained surface.

Streak: Pale blue

Occurrence: As contact metamorphic aggregate in metamorphic limestones and marbles with magmatic intrusions.

Extraction: Directly from the parent rock.

The Roman Pliny the Elder already used this metaphor to describe the gold-speckled, deep blue lapis lazuli, which is not, in contrast to all ornamental gems, a mineral but a rock. Emerged from a pneumatolytic transformation of a contact metamorphic limestone, it is composed of varying quantities of several minerals. The gemstone's unrivaled midnight blue is just as unique as its chemical composition. Even the ancient Egyptians inlaid their magnificent goldsmith artifacts with the blue "heaven's stone" since it combines ascetic purity with esthetic spirituality like no other. The name lapis lazuli is derived from the Latin *lapis* (stone) and the Arabic word *azul* or *al-lazward*, which, as well as the sky, describes all shades of blue. Ancient writings testify to the fact that this "stone of blue" has been used preferentially for at least five thousand years in the land of the Nile for the decoration of bracelets, chain pendants, daggers and cuirasses, and the production of signet rings, sculptures, and scarabs. The Egyptian artisans probably used material obtained from Afghanistan, since even today the most valuable lapis is to be found in the Firgamu mines in the Badakhshan area of the Hindu Kush mountain range. The rock is blasted out of the mountain by heating it up and then cooling with cold water. The quality is an intense ultramarine blue, uniformly colored and flecked with minute, metallic gold glittering pyrite crystals. White calcite is less sought after as inclusion mineral, whereas pyrite – which nonexperts often take to be pure gold – is highly popular. In contrast to Afghanistan, the other occurrences, southern Siberia on Lake Baikal, Myanmar, North America, and the extravagantly endowed Chilean Andes, supply less uniformly blue, lighter, and less valuable examples in terms of composition. They usually have calcite veins and white patches. The thoroughly pleasant, warm blue is attributable to the incorporation of the ultramarine molecule from the minerals sodalite, lazurite, and hauyne. As a result of its dense, barely perceivable red-tinged shade, pulverized lapis lazuli was a much sought after paint in the Middle Ages, remaining permanent to this day. Similarly, in the Middle Ages, a pinch of lapis was considered to be a remedy against fever and frailty. A comparison of the prices of goods offered for sale in the drugstore of Brückner, Lampe & Co. in 1757 demonstrates the high value placed on this blue stone: a medicinal pound of emerald cost 5 groschen, while the same quantity of lapis cost 5 thaler (or ten times as much). With its velvety blue, lapis lazuli has been highly prized since time immemorial in the production of breathtakingly beautiful engraving and inlay work, as well as for sumptuous objects such as the globe fashioned out of single block above the grave of Saint Ignatius in Rome or for those royal wall panels that can be admired in one of the chambers of the small palace town of Zarskoje Selo, or Pushkin, as it is called nowadays.

Due to its soulful, harmonious color, lapis lazuli used to be made into sophisticated chains and transformed into small boxes and carved statuettes due to its patches and shades – and in all these objects the lively blue of the lapis is revealed to the heart's eye as an interplay of music and poetry. Ancient cultures appreciated the royal blue of lapis lazuli and created many delicate objets d'art from it.

MALACHITE
MASTER OF THE GREEN SHADES

Above: The exquisite patterning of the green shades of malachite and its low level of hardness make it the ideal material for the creation of charming decorative objects. Collection: Eduard Gübelin, Lucerne. Photo: James G. Perret, Lucerne.

Opposite: Raw gem and string of beads made of malachite. Malachite cat's-eyes were first found in the large copper mine of Mednorudyansky near Nizhny-Tagil in Siberia. Photo: Michael Hügi, Muri, Canton Berne, Switzerland.

The decorative appeal of malachite may be ascribed to its unique gradations of green shades that are unique in the kingdom of gemstones. The effect of the mottled veins is not due to their colorfulness but to the stratification of the wide range of alternating dark and light shades of green. This peculiarity attracted many enthusiastic fans. Its name is derived from the Greek adjective *malakos* (soft, delicate, charming, sweet), which are very true of its gently flattering green tones. The atmospheric interplay of light and shaded parts makes it an inexhaustible source of rounded, bent, and twisted through to perfectly circular and concentric lines, curves, stripes, waves, and serpentines – an illustrated carpet as if seen with a bird's-eye view flying over endless jungle-covered areas of its current main supplier, Zaire. The undulating green rivers and their confluence in varied surge patterns are caused by the particular origins of malachite. Under the influence of meteoric water, it was a superficial weathering product from lower-lying copper ore deposits. It is an aqueous copper carbonate $Cu_2(Co_3)(OH)_2$ and thus one of the few stones to be idiochromatically colored by copper. Malachite is found everywhere in the upper areas of copper ore deposits and occurs as thick, opaque masses composed of small monoclinic crystals. Although malachite is a frequently occurring mineral, suitable nodules for processing – with their roundish, kidney-shaped, clustered, twisted, turned, and cone-shaped surface forms, which clearly indicate that the rock must have bubbled and boiled before solidification – have become very rare. With the help of an artistic cut, these interesting tectonics disclose an exquisite harmony of shapes. The unique pictorial language of malachite is the result of the colors that cover the entire green scale from emerald green, spinach green, dark leek green, to black green as well as in the alternating light and dark layering of the concentric shell formation. The highly contrasting movements of these pictures are optically underscored by the lively silky luster that the gemstone adopts during polishing and with its pearly sheen that arouses the desire to touch it. Since the Urals has extensive occurrences of large malachite nodules and slabs, the stone was put to generous decorative use in czarist Russia. The pillars of the iconostases in the world-famous Saint Isaac's Cathedral in St. Petersburg are fully clad with malachite and lapis lazuli; the same is true of the walls and ceiling of the malachite room in the Hermitage, the winter palace of the czars, where countless artifacts, table surfaces, huge vases, and amphorae also await visitors. As a result of its relatively low degree of hardness (H = 3.5–4) this ornamental gem is also particularly suitable for carving. The finest and most detailed artistic creations are known from China, in particular. Looking as if it were endowed with energetic inlaid spirals, the material is also popular for intaglio work and attractive stone necklaces. The formerly flourishing mines in the Urals have nowadays been mainly replaced by malachite deposits with less and constantly decreasing supplies from Katanga (Zaire), Zimbabwe, southwest Africa and Australia. This fresh green stone with the exclusive shell patterning has recently gained a brother with cat's-eye effect (chatoyancy).

Malachite forms radiating nodules of needles, less frequently of fibers, that are radiolitic reniform and botryoidal, with light to dark green banded texture. Frequently intergrown with blue azurite.

Chemistry: $Cu_2(CO_3)(OH)_2$ (aqueous copper carbonate)

Crystal system: Monoclinic

Habit (form): Small, mostly needlelike to fibrous crystals. Short to long prismatic. Usually twinned.

Colors: Light and/or dark green to black-green, frequently concentrically banded and permeated with blue as a result of intergrowth with azurite.

Refractive index (R.I.): 1.65–1.9

Birefringence: 0.25

Pleochroism: Intensely colorless and green.

Density: 3.5–4 / Hardness (Mohs' scale): 3.5–4

Consistency: Perfect cleavage, uneven, scaly fracture.

Streak: Light green

Occurrence: Worldwide as a secondary mineral in the oxidation zone of copper deposits; in close connection with blue azurite. Mainly from the Urals, Russia, and Katanga, Zaire. Intergrown with turquoise and chrysocolla as "eilatite" near Eilat, Israel.

Extraction: In open-cast mines from the surface layers of formation.

145

RHODO-CHROSITE AND RHODONITE

With its delicate colors, rhodochrosite looks as if it has stepped straight out of the fairy tale of Snow White and Rose Red. As malachite brandishes its bands, rhodochrosite, from the Greek *rhodon* (rose); *chros* (skin color), repeats its rings, meanderings, crinkled peaks, and dainty watercolor lines in pink loveliness. With never-ending fantasy and delicate grace, it also owes its pictorial designs characterized by light and dark pink contrasts to its weathering origin. In this case, it is from calcareous rock containing manganese. Rhodochrosite is a manganese carbonate $MnCO_3$ in nodular form or tube-shaped aggregates whose individual microscopically tiny and sparry crystals have trigonal symmetry and the good cleavage of all carbonates. Only becoming known after the Second World War, rhodochrosite has proved to be less suitable for daily wear and tear as jewelry due to its low hardness. In contrast, it can show off its charms to the full in the form of handcrafted ornaments. Its distinct marbled and layered structure in a variety of gradations from pure white to pinkish white, gleaming raspberry red to dark pink provides charming, airy color and shapes on the larger surfaces of slabs, dishes, or paperweights. Top quality material is obtained from San Luis (Argentina) from a silver mine proved to have been closed down by the Incas in the thirteenth century and where stalagmitic rhodochrosite has been developing ever since. This corroborates that it cannot be more than seven hundred years old. Recently, magnificent, clearly transparent crystals have also been found in the United States. The latest occurrences in South Africa have provided rhodochrosite in a brownish-red color.

The glowing red of sun-flamed peaches is the trademark of rhodonite, which is very similar in appearance to rhodochrosite. Occasionally having a darker wine red color, it is a silicate of manganese [(Mn, Fe, Ca, Mg) SiO_3 manganese silicate] with a low iron and calcium content. The cryptocrystalline aggregates whose individual crystals crystallize triclinically form dense masses with prismatic cleavage. Formerly, rhodonite originated from the Urals and was highly respected both as an ornamental gem and as Easter eggs – red and red-brown eggs were given as tokens of affection. Currently, Sweden, Australia, and in the United States, California and Massachusetts are the most important suppliers of this fine material. Together with its black veining due to the oxidation of manganese, the fine gradations of deep rose red to blue red shades create those richly structured scenes that arouse the enthusiasm of innovative people for the beauty of the gemstones. Drawn as if with a delicate india ink pen on the rose-colored background, the black streams of manganese create pictures that adorn decorative items of all types made of rhodonite. The first encounter with transparent rhodonite crystals occurred two centuries ago – these glowing red gemstone crystals with their flickering fire color with which no other red gemstones can compete. They were discovered at Broken Hill in Australia in a lead/zinc deposit. Rhodonite crystals of value to collectors had also been previously found in Ärmland in Sweden and Franklin, New Jersey (USA), but the Australian rhodonite crystals with their select quality were the first to earn respect from the gemstone world and are traded as precious rarities.

Opposite: Peach-blossom colored rhodochrosite *(left)* permeated with white bands and silver veins and rhododendron-red rhodonite *(right)* similarly permeated with black veins enjoy wide-scale popularity and are superbly suited to the creation of a wide variety of decorative objects.
Left: Collection: Michael M. Scott. Photo: Erica and Harold Van Pelt, Los Angeles.
Right: Collection: Eduard Gübelin, Lucerne. Photo: James G. Perret, Lucerne.

RHODOCHROSITE

Massive light to deep rose-red aggregates. Light and dark bands in angular pattern. Often permeated by manganese oxide, pyrite, or silver. Recently, magnificent, raspberry red crystals have been mined in Colorado (USA), and brown-red ones in South Africa.

RHODONITE

Compact rose-red to red, polycrystalline aggregate, frequently permeated by black branches of manganese oxide. However, it is also found as magnificent, transparent, large crystals, usually embedded in lead glance in Broken Hill, New South Wales, Australia.

Chemistry: $MnCO_3$ (Manganese carbonate)

Crystal system: Trigonal

Habit (form): Thickly tabular, rhombohedral, scalenohedral, rarely prismatic.

Colors: Pale rose-red to deep raspberry red, frequently with white stripes. The compact aggregates have concentric zigzag stripes; the transparent monocrystals are usually homogeneous in color.

Refractive index (R.I.): 1.60–1.82

Birefringence: 0.22

Dichroism: None

Density: 3.4–3.6 (Monocrystals: 3.7)

Hardness (Mohs' scale): 3.5–4

Consistency: Perfect cleavage; uneven, conchoidal fracture.

Streak: White

Occurrence: As a vein mineral in hydrothermal druses in very hot, contact metasomatic deposits and as a secondary mineral in manganese-rich deposits. As stalagmites and stalactites in the abandoned silver mines of the Incas near San Luis, east of Mendoza, Argentina.

Extraction: In open-cast and underground mines in the primary deposits.

Chemistry: $MnSiO_3$ (manganese silicate)

Crystal system: Triclinic

Habit (form): The crystals are usually tabular. The massive aggregates are mostly coarse, granular, nodule masses.

Colors: Rose-red, red to dark red, as well as brown-red with black dendritic insets of manganese oxide, which frequently form attractive patterns.

Refractive index (R.I.): 1.71–1.75 (usually 1.73)

Birefringence: 0.02

Dichroism: Yellow red, rose-red, red-yellow

Density: 3.6–3.8

Hardness (Mohs' scale): 5.5–6.5

Consistency: Perfect cleavage. Uneven, conchoidal fracture.

Streak: White

Occurrence: Mostly in manganese-bearing rocks. From metasomatic or hydrothermal processes as well as sedimentary deposits resulting from metamorphism. Fine crystals from New Jersey (USA), and Broken Hill, New South Wales, Australia.

Extraction: Open-cast and underground mining of primary deposits.

SUGILITE
BUDDING
MALLOW SPUR

Fairly homogeneously violet, massive aggregate of more or less angular grains, frequently with sprinkles and patches.

Chemistry: $KNa_2(Fe,Mn,Al)_2Li_3Si_{12}O_{30}$

Crystal system: Hexagonal

Habit (form): Unknown as a monocrystal, but only as a compact, granular, massive aggregate.

Colors: Usually uniformly violet, often with white stripes and bands or patches that result in pretty designs.

Refractive index (R.I.): 1.607–1.610

Birefringence: -0.003

Dichroism: Barely perceptible.

Density: 2.74–2.80

Hardness (Mohs' scale): 6–6.5

Consistency: Good with weak cleavage. Uneven, splintery fracture.

Streak: Very pale lilac.

Occurrence: In pegmatites in the Wessels Mine near Hotazel, Kalahari Desert, South Africa, with the accompanying minerals braunite and chalcedony.

Extraction: Directly from the pegmatite from which manganese was mainly mined until the discovery of sugilite. The deposit is estimated at 12–15 tons of sugilite.

Comment: The Wessels Mine also contains sogdianite, which is identical in appearance to sugilite but contains zirconium in its chemical composition.

Sugilite shared the fate of a newly discovered stone: it is only after two or three attempts that a stone can become established among goldsmiths and dealers. This is due less to the lack of acceptance of the newcomer than generally to its great rarity as a result of the sparseness of the occurrence. The first involuntary encounter with sugilite took place in Japan, a country of no special importance on the gemstone world map. While taking a walk on the island of Iwagi in the southwest of the island country, Japanese Professor Ken-ichi Sugi picked up a stone as a souvenir. This occurred sometime in the middle of the twentieth century. The professor investigated and described this stone. No connections with other stone families could be established and thus the stone was named after its discoverer. The samples tracked down were small, unassuming, and neither sufficiently attractive nor interestingly colored for jewelry production. At this point, the story ends as it does for many other finds. It was continued many years later in central India. A reconnoitering party took up the trail of sugilite for a second time. Again, specialist circles sat up and took notice, only to learn that the yield was again unsuited to the demanding jewelry market. Although no attention was paid to the stone over the ensuing decades, the jewelry trade reacted with great attention when new finds of sugilite were reported from South Africa at the beginning of the 1980s. At first, several small deposits in South Africa's Cape Province stirred up an anticipatory mood. Soon after, a sugilite vein of substantial size was uncovered in the Kalahari Desert. From one day to another, twelve to fifteen tons of an unusually attractive material, never previously used as a gemstone, was at the disposal of a business branch that had an attentive eye open for anything new. The deposit is in the area of the Wessels mine where manganese is extracted. Manganese is also primarily responsible for the restrained to intense blue-red-violet coloring. The color palette ranges from bright pink to dark violet with similarity to the color of amethysts. Tiny white eyes seem to blink impudently from the semitranslucent to opaque stone, which makes a fascinating challenge in the search for design and processing ideas for the sugilite. Despite its individuality, the stone has a look-alike discovered at approximately the same time and in the same region. In its verifiable gemological characteristics, the extremely rare sogdianite corresponds completely to sugilite, with only one exception: sogdianite contains zirconium, whereas sugilite does not. Chemical analysis is therefore always necessary to distinguish between these apparent twins. Since the discovery of the deposit in the Wessels mine, no further finds have been announced. It is therefore not inconceivable that sugilite, after its meteoric rise, may once again just as abruptly retire from public life due to a lack of supply. It would thus share the fate of many other minerals. Today, sugilite is mined in blocks and turned into slabs, dishes, figurines, and cut into cabochons and balls for rings and chains. Accompanying minerals such as braunite and chalcedony often give it a speckled and spotted appearance, which increases its liveliness and predestines it for fashion jewelry.

TURQUOISE

MORNING
FRESH BLOOM
OF
HEAVEN

Turquoise is found as compact masses of cryptocrystalline nodular, botryoidal aggregates in crevices of copper-bearing rocks.

Chemistry: $CuAl_6(PO_4)_4(OH)_8\,5H_2O$ (aqueous aluminum-copper phosphate).

Crystal system: Triclinic

Habit (form): Crystals are rare, mostly small, and prismatic.

Colors: Light blue, sky blue, bluish-green, greenish-blue. Often with light or dark veining of brown limonite or black psilomelane.

Refractive index (R.I.): 1.61–1.65

Birefringence: 0.04

Pleochroism: Weak, lighter and darker tints.

Density: 2.7–2.9

Hardness (Mohs' scale): 5–6

Consistency: Good. Uneven, conchoidal fracture.

Streak: White to pale bluish or pale greenish.

Occurrence: As a secondary mineral in crevices and cavities of trachytic rocks. Locations: in the Kuh-i-Binalud Mountains near Nishapur in eastern Iran, also in Afghanistan, Australia, Israel (near Eilat: "eilatite"), Tanzania, Tibet, and in Arizona (USA).

Extraction: Mainly from primary deposits, occasionally also from secondary embankments.

With its presence and uninterrupted popularity, turquoise has created a bridge across the centuries like no other gemstone. Four thousand years before the Christian era, the pharaohs of Egypt worshipped the sensuous beauty of its glowing blue to greenish-blue color. Egyptians first excavated the unattractive raw material for their elaborate jewelry on the Sinai peninsula. During later epochs, turquoise was found in many countries, even in Germany. Today, only Iran, Australia, and the southwestern United States still have stocks of turquoise of commercial value. However, Iran still remains in key position, where turquoise of unparalleled quality has been mined for more than two thousand years in the remote deposits of Maaden in the Kuh-i-Binalud mountains in Chorassan province, northwest of Nishapur in northeastern Iran. These old mines still exude their romantic charm and are still producing the finest of pale blue and forget-me-not blue turquoises with their pearly waxen luster for worldwide trade. The older sedimentary rock in these deposits are intercalated and partially metamorphosed by younger volcanic rocks consisting of porphyric trachytes and felsite porphyries, so that turquoise precipitated as filling material in fissures and cavities in the brecciated trachyte and spreading as a densely ramifying network of narrow veins ranging in thickness from 2 millimeters to 20 millimeters. Simultaneously, it was completely or partly enveloped by older limonite and intergrown with reticulated patterns, thus creating the matrix motifs so highly prized in the West. As a result of the hydrothermal solution strength of the rising surface and rain water, feldspar minerals decomposed, important components were released from the adjacent rock, and, thanks to their circulation, were compiled for the new formation of turquoise. Similar to malachite, turquoise is a secondary mineral that mainly developed in magmatic rocks close to the earth's surface under the dissolving influence of transforming meteoric water.

The majestic, powerful sky blue is attributable to a bonded copper content of less than 10 percent; turquoise thus belongs to the group of idiochromatic ornamental gems. If traces of iron occur instead of copper, the coloring takes on a less attractive green tinge.

Depending on composition, the following gradations are used to differentiate Iranian turquoise: Angushtary is a sky-blue to Prussian blue turquoise of even color distributed over the entire stone without the matrix marking; Barkhaneh is a sky-blue to greenish-blue stone, occasionally interlaced with fine matrix veins; Arabi are paler stones with patchy color or with a much darker matrix. The noble material with its alluring sky blue is not only extracted from primary deposits in the earth but is found just as frequently in weathering masses, talus debris, and alluvial deposits. Pliny's finding that the *Kallait* or *Kallelith*, from the ancient Greek designation *kalos lithos* (beautiful stone), could be attacked by oils, ointments, and wine still applies today. Impregnation processes are used to counteract its porosity and sensitivity to external substances. Turquoise only received its current name at a later point in time when it found its way to Europe via Turkey, and the French welcomed it under the name of *Pierre Turquoise*, whence the English word turquoise was derived.

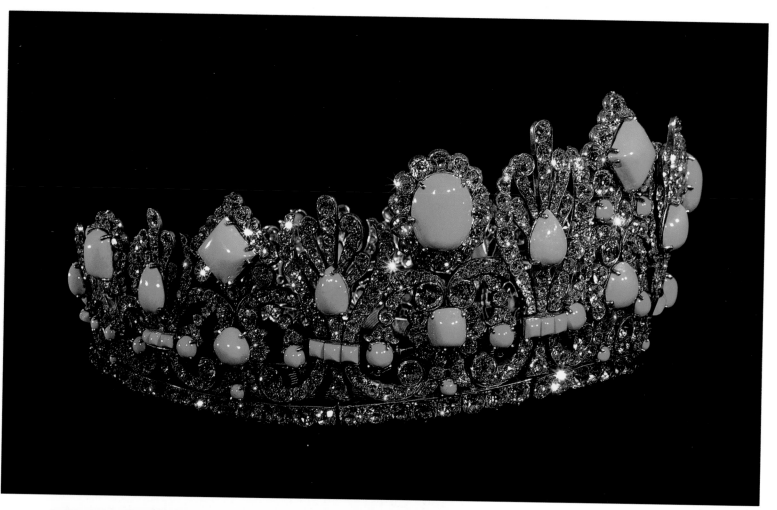

Above: Diamond diadem set with turquoises. Smithsonian Institution, Washington, D.C. (USA). Photo: Erica and Harold Van Pelt, Los Angeles.

Left: The convex botryoidal form of the turquoise mass at the top of the picture indicates that it is of sedimentary origin. It consists of minute turquoise crystals.
In the foreground, a top-quality turquoise with cabochon cut and weighing 108.7 carats from the Abdurreza Mine in the Kuh-i-Binalud Mountains near Nishapur, eastern Iran. Collection: William Larson, Fallbrook, California (USA). Photo: Erica and Harold Van Pelt, Los Angeles.

Page 149: Due to its violet color, sugilite is very similar to charoite and is just as suitable for processing into jewelry or decorative items such as the one shown here. However, since sugilite is a monomineralic aggregate, it is therefore more compact. Collection: Herbert Klein, Idar-Oberstein. Photo: Erica and Harold Van Pelt, Los Angeles.

Crowns are symbols of the authority and power of rulers. They are also highlights of goldsmiths' artistry in the Western world. In all their variations, they are sumptuous head coverings – symbols of wealth as well as a sense of beauty. As jewel-studded *hats* they are also reminiscent of an ancient symbol of law, of the hat of the sovereign *(dominus terrae)* that, as the great Swiss historian Johannes von Müller (1752–1809) conjectured – in a footnote! – provoked the irritation and indignation of the free people of the Swiss canton Uri ("Tell"!) in the shape of Gessler's hat. The hat on the stick meant, in the case of canton Uri: "The land under this hat is under the sovereignty of the counts of Hapsburg," which could not possibly apply to the free canton of Uri.

GEMSTONES: SYMBOLS OF AUTHORITY AND POWER

The cap worn by the Doge of Venice – an original piece of head wear made of precious silk – is also the "hat of the sovereign," the ruler of the lagoon city state, the ruler of the seas. Although the Roman Caesars, the predecessors of the rulers of the Middle Ages, wore a *corona*, this was not a crown. Their symbol of sovereignty was a leafy wreath that encircled the ruler's head. Oak leaves were reserved for the emperor. The wreath could be made of gold, with stylized leaves, and was sometimes placed in the grave of a dead ruler.

Crowns and Coronation

In their earliest creations, the actual crowns were bands, either smooth or decorated with gemstones, that, made of gold, silver, or iron and decorated with leaf ornamentation, adorned the wearer's head. Spanning the crowns with one or several hoops created some of the world's most important crowns: for example, the Imperial Crown, various royal crowns, as well as the crowns of dukes, princes, and counts that, in turn, represented more understated, but sometimes also imaginative, variations of the "major crowns." The pope wore a triple crown, the papal tiara.

However, crowns always enjoyed their important function during

Above: The heavenly crowning of the Virgin Mary found its symbolic analogy in the sets of insignia for the Mother of God and the Child Jesus. In German cultural areas, the Madonna with Child wore the highest-ranking crowns in accordance with the interweaving of state and religion in former times (e.g., the emperor's crown with an ecclesiastical miter in the middle. The set of insignia shown here for a carved and lost Madonna group originates from Augsburg (goldsmith Joh. Jos. Anton Reidler, 1763). The crowns are of beaten silver and gilded in places. The scepters are of brass with silver applications. Collection: Abeler Crown and Insignia Collection, Wuppertal.

coronations: By placing the crown on the anointed head, sovereign power was transferred to the crown-bearer before the eyes of the onlookers. The highest rank was bestowed upon the wearer of the Imperial Crown. Western Imperialism started on December 24 of the year 800 with the crowning of Charlemagne in Rome: Pope Leo III probably crowned him, however, with a crown that belonged to the Vatican and which was originally the property of Emperor Constantine the Great. An "Imperial Crown" did not exist at that time. He thus transferred West Roman emperorship to the ruler he had anointed with the title of *Imperator augustus* (majestic sovereign). There definitely was a crown for Emperor Charles at a later date. Imperial status, however, did not confer any particular rights on the emperor, which nevertheless went beyond the rights of a German king. Charlemagne therefore saw the coronation in Rome as a particularly religious act; nor did he take the title of "Emperor of the Romans." As emperor, he held an unshareable position and was additionally the German king. In 813, he elevated his son, Ludwig, to be co-regent. In the laws of succession of the Frankish king, the German king alone held the right to imperial status. To obtain this, however, he required anointment and coronation by the pope.

Charlemagne's Crown–"Crown of France"?

"Charlemagne's Imperial Crown" was a crown of the early Middle Ages, which is said to have been kept at the Abbey of Saint-Denis until the time of the French Revolution. During the revolutionary confusion it was destroyed there by an incensed crowd. However, Saint-Denis had also once housed the French royal crown: *La couronne royale – dite de Charlemagne*. A successful attempt was made to reconstruct the appearance of this precious crown jewel from the monastery treasures by researching inventories and historical descriptions. (cf., Bernard Morel, *La couronne royale de France – dite de Charlemagne*, 1974). The most precious parts of the crown were the three Balas rubies (spinels), among these the "egg of Naples" (241 carats) and the spinel *Côte de Bretagne* (206 carats).

The Saint-Denis monastery housed a series of French crowns. Since the time when King Philipp I (1060–1108) expressed the wish that, on his death, his crown should be consigned to the care of the abbot of Saint-Denis, many of his royal successors – the first of these being Louis VI (1108–1137) – have followed this last will. Louis VI decreed that, in future, all the insignia of deceased French rulers were to be presented to Saint Dionysius.

For coronations, the necessary insignia were brought from the treasury at Saint-Denis to Reims, where the coronations took place. However, since each ruler, even after the coronation, wanted to wear a crown at ceremonial events, he had to have a new crown made that he then bequeathed to Saint Dionysius on his death. So, over time, the treasure store of crowns multiplied at the Saint-Denis monastery. However, there was never an actual French royal crown with the status of the Imperial crown. A Charlemagne crown–*Couronne de Charlemagne* – also admittedly existed at the Saint-Denis monastery until the time of

Above: Miter of gold brocade with pearls and gemstones dating from the fifteenth century. This miter belonged to Abbot Rupert who ruled the Benedictine Abbey of St. Peter in Salzburg from 1466 until 1495. St. Peter's Abbey, Salzburg.

Left: The royal crown of King Louis XV of France. The large gemstones in this jewel created by L. and C. Rondé were replaced by imitations over the course of history. The famous *Sancy* diamond, for example, once adorned the top of the crown and the *Regent* diamond was above the band. Both gemstones can currently be admired as solitaires in the Louvre.

Above: A successful reconstruction of a precious jewel of a crown in the treasure chamber of the Abbey of Saint-Denis: *La couronne royale – dite de Charlemagne.* The most precious parts of the crown were large Balas rubies (spinels), among these the "egg of Naples" and *Côte de Bretagne.*

the French Revolution, but it definitely did not originate from Charlemagne. This was a crown from the early Middle Ages as the sketch of the reconstruction confirms.

While the king of France required a crown, it did not need to be a specific one. In times of political unrest or emergency, it was not rare for royal crowns to be melted down or pawned. The crown of Charles V (he reigned from 1364 until 1380) was taken apart on the instructions of his son in order to "exploit" the gemstones; in other words, to meet his debts with the revenue from the gemstones.

In the case of Charlemagne's crown, this was a "plaque" crown. The individual plaques were richly ornamented with sapphires, emeralds, and rubies and attached to each other with hinges. They also bore the so-called fleur-de-lis attachments that were directed outward. Hoops were missing, however. This crown of Charlemagne is probably goldsmith work from Ottonian times (cf., Heinz Biehn, *Die Kronen Europas*).

Albrecht Dürer (1471–1528) painted this likeness of Charlemagne. It is easy to imagine the spiritual father of Europe in this pose. The script at the emperor's eye level states: "Charlemagne ruled for 14 years." The picture also reproduces the German eagle coat of arms on one side and, on the other side, the fleur-de-lis of France. The picture was painted on basswood (215 cm × 115.3 cm) and is now in the German National Museum in Nuremberg.

The "Reichskrone"

Known as the "German Imperial Crown," the Imperial Crown in the Secular Treasury of the Viennese Hofburg is world renowned and much admired. It is the crown of the emperor of the "Holy Roman Empire of the German nation" and embodies (together with the imperial orb, imperial sword, and the imperial cross) the so-called imperial insignia. (Since these played a significant role at coronations, we will also include these in conjunction with the imperial crown.)

The imperial crown was originally considered to be the crown of Emperor Charlemagne. Albrecht Dürer reproduced it in his famous portrait of *Charlemagne* (dating from 1514) on the emperor's head. The imperial crown was incontestably the most venerable of all crowns. The Hohenstaufen chancellor and archbishop of Cologne, Rainald von Dassel (1120–1167) thus observed that the rulers of France and England were only "small kings in comparison with the wearer of the imperial crown, the Emperor." A profound imperial mysticism developed in Europe.

The creation of the imperial crown is dated in the second half of the tenth century or early in the eleventh century. Gold, gold filigree, gemstones (as was then the custom – smoothed sapphires, rubies, emeralds, amethysts, topazes, and aquamarines) as well as pearls and gold enamel were the elements that made up this famous jewel. The design of the crown is said to be "based on a clearly-defined spiritual program" (H. Biehn, q.v., above-mentioned book) so that the precious item would represent "an image of heavenly Jerusalem" as a result of a numbering system, gem positioning, color scale, and number of pearls.

The imperial crown was probably made for the coronation of Otto I (962). It would be called the "imperial crown" because only the one who was crowned with it in Aachen (later in Frankfurt), where the archbishop of Mainz (sometimes also the archbishop of Cologne) had the right to crown the German king, was truly the king of the empire.

Image of Universal Sovereign Claim

The imperial crown was rarely used for the coronation of emperors by the pope in Rome, although it represented the universal sovereign claim of the emperor on the basis of its symbolism.

Three things basically set this crown apart: the eight crown plaques, the crown cross, and the crown's hoop. Two bands of iron, which were inserted into the crown at an indeterminate time, gave the crown the shape of an almost regular octagon. The four main plaques over the brow, nape, and temples are completely covered with gemstones and gold filigree decoration. The four slightly lower enamel plaques represent in *cloisonné* technique "the almighty (pantocrator), Kings David and Solomon and the scene in which the prophet Isiah announced God's decision to the sick King Hezekiah to extend his life by fifteen years" (cf., Hermann Fillitz, *Die Weltliche Schatzkammer in Wien [The Secular Treasury in Vienna]*).

Based on an inscription on the crown's hoop, the imperial crown was

GEMSTONE
Beauty
As old as the Earth:
With a precious cut
Freed to the light
Glows and glistens
And honors the creator
Just like creation.
Not just decor, not just a jewel
Set in gold by an artist's hand
Attainable happiness –
and eternity.

Franz-Xaver Erni (1988)
for Walter Fleischmann

commissioned before the time of Emperor Conrad II (who reigned from 1024 until 1039). (The imperial cross dates from the second decade of the eleventh century, during the reign of Emperor Conrad.)

A woodcut from 1260 shows a page carrying the imperial crown and the imperial sword. The large stone inset under the cross that bore the name of "the wise one" and was the "sovereign's guiding stone" can be seen in the crown. This stone is no longer present; it was mentioned for the last time in 1350. The greatest scholar of the Middle Ages, the Dominican monk Albertus Magnus (Count Bollstädt, 1200–1280) called the stone the *Orphanus*. It was possibly a huge, magnificent opal.

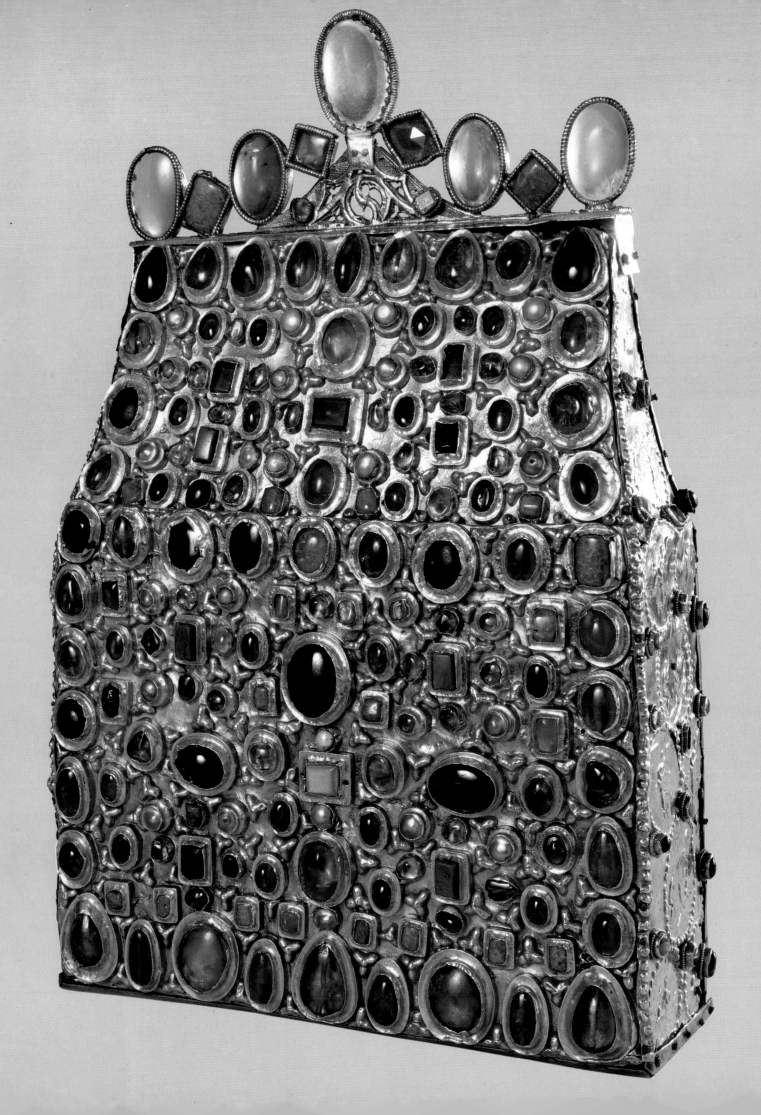

Walther von der Vogelweide (1170–1230) also knew of this "light" or guiding star. In his political lyrics, he dedicated these lines to it:

"whoever now is on the wrong path where the king is concerned
should look to whom the wise one stands above his neck:
the stone is the guiding star of all princes."

The guiding star adorns the upper edge of the brow plaque as the dominant jewel. Today, its place is taken by a sapphire set in a mount that is far too big for it with fine wire.

The crown and the cross on top of it are made of 21-carat gold, the hoop of 19-carat gold. The red velvet cap in the crown's interior dates from the eighteenth century. In the Middle Ages, the emperor would wear, as a symbol of his position, a bishop's miter inside the crown (cf., the so-called "Rudolph crown").

Imperial Treasures

Along with the imperial crown, the imperial insignia also include the imperial orb, the imperial sword, the imperial cross, and the coronation robe. In addition, there are several mementos of Charlemagne: Emperor Otto III is supposed to have found them in Charlemagne's grave. These items are known collectively as the *Zimelien* or treasures: the Stephansbursa, a type of bag set with gemstones, the imperial gospel, and Charlemagne's sword. These treasures were moved from the treasury at Aachen Cathedral to the treasury in Vienna in 1801.

The imperial orb is made of gold, gold filigree, resin beads, gemstones, and pearls. This jewel was crafted in Cologne in the last quarter of the twelfth century. The imperial cross is of western German manufacture from the time around 1024 (Emperor Conrad). Gold and partially gilded silver surround a wooden core. Gold filigree, gemstones, and pearls represent a precious adornment for the contents, which were far more costly in the early days of the empire: After removing the front of the cross, the relics of the empire – the large particle from the true cross of Christ and the "Holy lance"–could be inserted.

The coronation robe is a textile treasure: red silk fabric is richly embroidered with gold and blue silk. On its two halves, the robe displays, separated by a tree of life, a lion triumphing over a camel. Gold enamel trimmings, pearls, and gemstones emphasize the importance of the imperial robe. An inscription in script (the rectangular monumental form of Arabic script) on the edge of the robe permits its precise dating: 1133/1134 (Palermo, royal workshop). Frederick II used the robe at his coronation (1220).

The imperial sword resides in an olive-wood sheath plated with gold. Gold enamel and garnets are used for decoration. The sword itself is made of steel. The pommel and parry guard are gilded, the handle is wound with silver wire. The sword was added to an older, even more precious sheath. The inscriptions on the guard are taken from the *Laudes* (hymns of hommage to the crowned monarch). They glorify the triumph of Christ. The imperial sword dates from the period between 1198 and 1218.

Opposite: Among the imperial treasures is the *Stephansbursa* (height: 32 cm), which is a container (pilgrim's bag) named after the arch-martyr Stephanus and that is said to have contained earth saturated with the blood of the martyr. The *Bursa* was made in the first third of the ninth century at the court of Charlemagne or in Reims. A wooden core is covered with gold plate and set with convex gemstones. History of Art Museum, Secular Treasury, Vienna.

Above: The Secular Treasury in Vienna also houses the imperial orb (height: 21 cm). It dates from the end of the twelfth century or from the early thirteenth century. A resin ball is surrounded by gold and decorated with pearls and gemstones. The row of pearls on the equatorial band have been lost. On one side of the two identically designed sides of the cross, where the bars intersect, is a late classical Byzantine seal stone: a sapphire with a cross-shaped monogram. As a symbol of imperial power, the orb has been recorded pictorially since the time of the Carolingians. It was first mentioned as part of the coronation ceremony in 1191.

The Crown of the Philosopher

After the imperial crown, the finest crown in the Viennese Secular Treasury is probably the "Rudolph crown," which was commissioned by Emperor Rudolph II, the philosopher and patron of the arts and science.

Emperor Rudolph not only gathered scholars around him (among these, the astronomers Tycho Brahe and Johannes Kepler), but also artists from all spheres of art. He did not reside in Vienna but in Prague: The imperial workshop at the Hradcany Castle thus created the crown that bears the ruler's name in 1602. Rectangular tablet stones, rubies, and pearls as well as a large, pear-shaped sapphire are the prominent elements of the jewel along with gold and gold enamel. Visible inside the crown and made from gold, the miter depicts in relief the coronation of Rudolph II as emperor and the ride to the Pressburg Königshügel (part of the coronation ceremony for the king of Hungary) as well as the ceremonial procession at Hradcany with the bast shoes of Premysl (part of the coronation ceremony for the Bohemian king).

Rudolph's crown is a band with four large fleur-de-lis attachments angled outward and four small ones. The borders of the crown band set with tablet stones are lined with rows of pearls. The four large fleur-de-lis attachments each have a ruby at their center surrounded at each side, top, and bottom with a diamond. The four smaller fleur-de-lis attachments each have a base of three rubies side by side supporting a vertical band of rubies that decrease in size toward the top. The tips of the fleurs-de-lis are crowned with superb pearls. Over the large rounded ruby at the front of the crown there is an imposing, pear-shaped pearl.

At the peak of the hoop, there is a small gold cross with clover-shaped ends and a diamond at their intersection. The small cross is itself crowned by a large, convex sapphire.

Emperor Rudolph II wore his crown for official duties. After his death, it was also used by all his successors from the house of Hapsburg. In 1804, Emperor Francis II proclaimed Austria to be an empire in order to keep pace with Napoleon. Two years later, he renounced the title of German emperor and reigned from that time as Emperor Francis I of Austria. The Rudolph crown thus became the Austrian imperial crown.

The Crown of a Rebel

The crown of the prince of Transylvania, Istvan Bocskay (1557–1606), was given to him as a gift by the ruler of the Ottoman Empire, Sultan Achmed I, and presented to him by the Grand Vizir Mohammed Pascha in 1605. This was in recognition of Bocskay's reign, which he had achieved in an uprising against Emperor Rudolph II. Bocskay had been the leader of the Hungarian Protestants, who were striving for religious freedom.

This crown is in the style of a helmet, made of gold and niello and richly set with rubies, emeralds, turquoises and pearls. The jewel was made in a Turkish workshop. It is made up of two parts: a broad coronet band and the hood, which is crowned by pearls and an emerald.

Opposite: The crown of the philosopher on the Roman-German imperial throne – the private crown of the patron of the arts, Emperor Rudolph II–was made in 1602 in the court workshop in Prague. When Emperor Francis II founded the hereditary empire of Austria in 1804 and, after renouncing the title of Roman-German emperor (1806), took the name of Emperor Francis I, the Rudolph crown became the Austrian imperial crown (until 1918). It is in the Secular Treasury, Vienna.

THE UNPAID CROWN
In Vienna, an old man, Professor M., looks at the Rudolph crown fairly regularly. The loyal friend of the Austrian imperial crown is a direct descendant of the Prague goldsmith who was commissioned to create the crown by Emperor Rudolph II. "The crown actually belongs to me," says the professor, "Emperor Rudolph never paid for it at the time, and his successor Emperor Matthew refused to pay ..."

Above: The crown of the prince of Transylvania, Istvan Bocskay (1557–1606). It was a gift from the Ottoman ruler, Sultan Achmed I, in recognition of Bocskay's uprising against Emperor Rudolph II. Secular Treasury, Vienna.

The Crown of Kunigunde: Symbolic Power of Gemstones

In the Treasure Chamber of the in Munich Residency, there is a famous woman's crown: the crown of Empress Kunigunde, the wife of Emperor Henry II, the Holy. She died in 1033 at the Kaufungen convent, which she founded.

Her crown is reminiscent of the "wreath" or "coronet" (corona) of antiquity. A wide coronet made up of five curved plaques is similar to the "Iron Crown" of Monza (dating from the second half of the ninth century). In the opinion of all authoritative specialists, Empress Kunigunde's crown originated from a workshop in Lorraine and was prob-

Dumb jewels often
in their silent kind
More than quick words do move
a woman's mind.

Shakespeare, *Two Gentlemen of Verona*
Act III, Scene I, Valentine

The Kunigunde crown was created around 1010 to 1020. It belonged to Empress Kunigunde, the spouse of Emperor Henry II, who was elected King of Germany in 1002. It is reminiscent of the antique style of crown – the "corona" or "wreath." The crown, richly decorated with gemstones, adorned the head-shaped reliquary of the empress in Bamberg Cathedral on special feast days after the death in 1033 of Empress Kunigunde, who was elevated to sainthood, as was her husband. The crown is currently kept at the Treasure Chamber of the Munich Residency.

ably produced between 1010 and 1020. It came into the possession of the chapter of Bamberg Cathedral at an early date and was put on display on special feast days on the head-shaped reliquary of the empress who was elevated to sainthood in the year 1200. The coronet was increased in height, according to Herbert Brunner (in *Die Schatzkammer der Residenz München*), in the fourteenth century with a second coronet. The two crowns were only separated again in the 1930s. The crown from Metz is adorned with valuable gemstones: sapphires, topazes, peridots, carnelians as well as amethysts and pearls. In addition, there are various colorful glass flows. The front plaque of the Kunigunde crown is decorated with a large oval sapphire in convex shape. As may be assumed on the basis of tradition, it is the symbol of the wisdom of God, while the amethysts on the crown – according to ancient opinion – symbolize the begetting of Christ.

162

Preciousness Instead of Symbolism?

In 1805, Bavaria became a kingdom. Together with the royal insignia, the Bavarian royal crown is the work of the Parisian goldsmith Martin-Guillaume Biennais. As Herbert Brunner notes, not without reason, the relatively new crown has almost nothing of the symbolic power of Queen Kunigunde's crown. Instead, it seems to show "a purely esthetically effective, complementary change" of precious rubies and emeralds and a large number of diamonds. However, it lacks any symbolic meaning. In the sapphire in the peak of the crown, connoisseurs can see a reminder of the old "ruler's stone" of godly wisdom, such as the former *Orphanus that* adorned the German Imperial crown. A large sapphire blazes out and enlightens, perhaps, the wearer of the crown, too. However, no Bavarian king ever wore this superb crown: A coronation never took place in the Kingdom of Bavaria – the crown was thus merely a symbol on a sumptuous cushion, but a never-ending symbol of the excellent artistry of the Parisian goldsmith Biennais. It is probably only a delightful legend that the blue sapphire is said to have changed places with the "blue diamond" on special occasions.

Has the symbolic power of the crowns and their gemstones truly declined with the increased use of precious diamonds? This might be a fair assumption in view of the fact that, for example, the English state crown (The Imperial State Crown) of Queen Victoria (1819–1901) boasts 3,000 diamonds along with 5 rubies, 11 emeralds, 18 sapphires, and 277 pearls. In addition, it has three unique large stones: the second *Star of Africa* (the first one was found in South Africa in 1869 and weighs 83.5 carats), the *Black Prince* ruby as well as the *Stuart* sapphire at the nape. *Embarras de richesse* one might say, but the English state crown is the crown of a former empire and is thus of truly imperial caliber.

Before we take a closer look at this crown and its jewels, a word about the crowns of old England is in order. The crown jewels, which are currently kept in the Tower of London – three rulers' crowns, five women's crowns, and the crown of the Prince of Wales – all date from centuries in the post-Middle Ages. In 1649, Oliver Cromwell decreed after the violent end of King Charles I that "the crown jewels will be dismantled and the individual pieces, as symbols of former tyranny, will be broken up – the value of the jewels will be disposed of" (Heinz Biehn). At that time, five crowns were destroyed (among these, the crowns of Alfred the Great, who died in 899, and his wife, Edith; as well as the crown reputedly found in the grave of Edward the Confessor, 1003 to 1066). Legend has it that all the later kings of England were crowned with Edward's crown. In actual fact, there was never a single royal crown that was repeatedly used. After the Norman conquest, the French tradition of using two crowns at a coronation was more prevalent. The heavier coronation crown for the actual coronation act and then a second, lighter crown, which was subsequently called the state crown. The coronation ritual with two crowns has been documented since the twelfth century. Henry VIII (died in 1547), Mary Queen of Scots (died in 1587), and Elizabeth I (died in 1603) even used three crowns at their coronations.

Below: On New Year's Day 1806, Bavaria became a kingdom. King Maximilian I Joseph had crowns made for himself and his wife in Paris. The king's crown has a band set with color gems. The hoops are flat bands, each with five gems – in each case three emeralds and two rubies in alternation. The crown is at the Treasure Chamber of the Munich Residency.

Following page: The Imperial State Crown, the British state crown, is admirable for its 3,000 diamonds and large historic gemstones. At the front, the *Second Star of Africa* (weight: 317 carats, also called *Cullinan II* because it was split from the largest diamond in the world, the *Cullinan*). The *Cullinan II* replaced the *Stuart Sapphire*, as it is called, which is now over the nape of the crown. In the cross at the front is the admirable ruby, which the "Black Prince" received from Dom Pedro, King of Aragon in 1367. The sapphire in the cross above the orb is said to have come from the coronation ring of Edward the Confessor. The crown jewels are kept in the Tower of London.

163

Triumph of Pomp

Two crowns have been used at the coronations of English kings and queens during the past three centuries, including the coronation crown of Charles II, "Edward's crown." It is made of gold and silver with sapphires, emeralds, rubies, and diamonds. Altogether, it has a total of 440 gemstones.

Edward's crown was used as the coronation crown until the time of George III (1738–1820). For the coronation of Queen Victoria's son, King Edward VII (1902), the tradition was to be revived. However, since the king had only recently recovered from an illness, the heavy crown was dispensed with and it was only used in the coronation procession. The tradition was revived with Edward's son and successor, King George V (he reigned from 1910 to 1936). King George VI (died in 1952) and his daughter, Queen Elizabeth II, were also crowned with both crowns.

The history of the Imperial State Crown starts with Queen Victoria, who reigned from 1837 to 1901. She requested the manufacture of a new coronation crown as she disliked all the women's crowns available. Gemstones from older crowns were removed to adorn her new crown – the state crown. The famous sapphire of Edward the Confessor is therefore the central gem adorning the cross on the crown's peak. During the entire coronation ceremony, Victoria wore only this new crown. The extravagant ornamentation of this jewel with its many gemstones, pearls, and diamonds forms the right setting for the select main gemstones of this exceptional symbol of power.

In 1905, a huge diamond of 3,106 carats was found in South Africa and named *Cullinan* after the head of the English diamond company. General L. Botha and the South African statesman, J. C. Smuts, were endeavoring at the time to establish the Union of South Africa. They succeeded in exerting sufficient influence on the government of Transvaal for the government to send the *Cullinan* to the English King Edward VII (who reigned from 1901 to 1910) on the occasion of his birthday, November 9, 1907). This gift to the king was combined with a hope: The gem was to "represent a greater Africa" that in accordance with the importance of the diamond, wished to become "an important member" of the British crown. The *Cullinan* had a value at that time of 150,000 pounds sterling.

However, since the *Cullinan* was irregular in shape, it had to be broken down before polishing. This task was assigned to the famous gem cutter, Joseph Asscher, in Amsterdam in 1908. When the stone split apart as anticipated, Asscher fainted with joy. Nine large gems and 96 smaller diamonds were formed. The largest – *Cullinan I* (530 carats) also called the *Star of Africa* today decorates the Royal Sceptre; *Cullinan II* (317 carats) is set in the rim at the front of the Imperial State Crown; *Cullinan III* (95 carats) and *Cullinan IV* (64 carats) were used in the crown of Queen Mary, the wife of King George V. The state crown also holds the *Black Prince's* ruby and, at the back, the *Stuart* sapphire.

The royal scepter with the *Cullinan I* diamond, also called the *First Star of Africa*. This giant, weighing 530 carat is the largest cut diamond in the world. Tower of London.

165

Top: The legendary *Koh-i-noor* diamond adorns the crown of Queen Elizabeth, the Queen Mother. Tower of London. Photo: HMSO, Norwich.

Above: Necklace set with gold and diamonds with the *Timur* and two other rubies. Tower of London. Photo: HMSO, Norwich.

The Black Prince's Ruby

The Maltese cross set with diamonds above the front rim of the crown, has a drop-shaped red stone in the center. The Black Prince, the oldest son of King Edward III of England (1327–1377), is said to have received this red gem – not actually a ruby, but a spinel – as a gift from Don Pedro the Cruel (king of Castile in the fourteenth century). Don Pedro had learned that Abu Said, the Moorish ruler of the kingdom of Granada, owned an exceptionally beautiful ruby. The king of Castile wanted this stone badly. He therefore invited Abu Said to his court in Castile. The ruler of Granada accepted this invitation and arrived with great pomp before King Pedro, who had him killed, together with all his court. Pedro only enjoyed this bloodstained jewel for a short time: Defeated by his half-brother, Henry of Transtamar, in combat, Pedro lost his kingdom and fled to Bordeaux where the Black Prince ruled as Duke of Aquitaine. The refugee King Pedro of Castile successfully won over the Black Prince to help in his struggle against his half-brother. After the victory near Najera (1367), he thanked the Black Prince by presenting him with the magnificent gem. After the death of the regent of Aquitaine, the red jewel came into the possession of Richard II and finally, into the hands of Bolingbroke, who ascended the English throne as Henry IV. At the Battle of Agincourt, the *Black Prince's* ruby decorated the helmet of King Henry V. In Cromwell's inventory of the crown jewels (cf., above), this stone was listed as a "large balas-ruby" and was valued at the ridiculous sum of 4 pounds.

Timur and Koh-i-noor

Another story in which a superb spinel was mistaken for a wondrous ruby is that of the best-known spinel of all, the so-called *Timur* ruby. Timur or Tamerlane (1336–1405), the Turkish Mongolian conqueror and ruler in Samarkand, had stolen the jewel in Delhi. Together with the *Mountain of Light*, the large Indian *Koh-i-noor* diamond, the *Timur* spinel enjoyed an eventful and varied fate. Since 1612, the *Timur* and *Koh-i-noor* were owned by the same person. The two stones were together in India, Persia, and also in Afghanistan. Around 1850, the *Timur* passed from the King of Lahore to the East India Company. The latter presented the red gem, together with the *Koh-i-noor* to Queen Victoria. Since then, the *Timur*, accompanied by two rubies has made up the superb centerpiece of a diamond-studded necklace and the *Koh-i-noor* soon adorned a woman's crown. Today, it is set in the crown of Queen Elizabeth, the Queen Mother (Queen "Mum"), the wife of King George VI, who was born in 1900. The *Koh-i-noor* was removed from Queen Mary's crown (grandmother of the current queen) and traditionally decorates the front of the cross above the rim. The rim itself bears the *Star of Africa*. The cross above the diamond-studded monde, mounted on the top of the crown, has a 22-carat diamond from Lahore at its center.

Crowns from the "Third Rome"

Was there perhaps an increase in extravagant crown pomp or are the crowns of the British monarchy simply unparalleled? With all caution, there was an increase: It took place in a country that, like the British Empire, was a "continent of jewels," namely, in Russia.

The Russian czarism felt it was the legitimate heir to the East Roman Empire: Russian Grand Princes, for example, Saint Vladimir (956–1015) and Ivan III (1440–1505), had, in addition, both married princesses from Byzantium. An independent czarism gradually developed "which, after the fall of Constantinople" (H. Biehn) thought of itself as the "third Rome": the protector of all Orthodox believers.

On February 4, 1498, Ivan III enthroned his grandson Dimitri as his successor in the Cathedral of the Assumption in Moscow by placing around him a so-called "Barmen," a collar decorated with enamel medallions, as a sign of inherited succession. In addition, Dimitri was allowed to wear the Monomachus cap. No real coronation took place before that of Ivan IV, the Terrible, on January 16, 1547. The czar now called himself "by God's grace, sole ruler of all Russia." The legend was also laid down, in an official document, that the Monomachus cap (Monomachus's reign: 1113–1125) had previously been Vladimir II's crown. This cap was used by all the czars until the coronation of Peter the Great. However, other crowns or caps reminiscent of the Monomachus cap were made, such as the cap of Kazan, the cap of Astrakhan, and the cap of Atabasnaya, which got its name from the precious gold fabric used.

The oldest czar crown is the "crown of Monomachus," the Monomachus cap richly set with gemstones, pearls, gold, and filigree. According to legend, this imperial head covering is a gift from Emperor Constantine Monomachus of Byzantium to his grandson, Prince Vladimir Monomachus of Kiev. The crown cap dates from around the turn of the thirteenth century to the fourteenth century. The tip with its cross and fur trimming were added at a later date. The current appearance of the Monomachus crown was already attested in the seventeenth century.

The cap of Kazan was made on the orders of Ivan IV (1530–1584) for the last czar of Kazan, Ediger. It is made of gold, set with turquoises, rubies, almandines, and pearls and decorated in niello technique. The helmetlike skullcap is made up of eight triangular, rounded plaques. Filigree lacing covers the seams. Three rows of tiny shieldlike attachments cover the skullcap like a diadem. These are held at the back by silver hoops. Arabesque ornamentation covers the surfaces of the shieldlike attachments that are also set with round or oval rubies, almandine garnets, and turquoises. The gemstones in the middle row of little shields are set particularly high in imitation of a Byzantine stone arrangement. The dome-shaped attachment above the skullcap is decorated with a swirling ornament: the four curved, sweeping arms of the swirl are made of convex rubies and turquoises. All the gemstones are in bezel settings with some being held by claws. A yellow corundum crowns the dome, set between two large pearls.

Top: Czar Nicholas II places the small empress crown on the head of his wife during the coronation ceremony (1896). From the coronation book of 1899.

Above: The state insignia of czarist Russia: crown, orb, czarina's crown, and scepter (with the large Indian *Orloff* diamond). State Museums of the Kremlin, Moscow.

During the sixteenth century, Russia developed into a powerful, centralist empire with worldwide relations. Court ceremonies were therefore of increasing importance, particularly coronations.

Peter I, the Great, proclaimed the foundation of the Russian Empire. The coronation of the czars was replaced by an even more pompous imperial coronation. A new ruler's crown was used instead of the simple crown. The Barmen was succeeded by a precious robe of gold brocade lined with ermine. The first coronation of this type took place in the Cathedral of the Assumption in the Kremlin. The ceremony, determined by Czar Peter himself, was a mixture of Western European and Byzantine coronation rites. For the coronation of the first Russian empress, Catherine I, a crown was made consisting of two parts (halves, hemispheres) intended to represent, in the style of the Byzantine imperial crown, the unity between the Western and the Eastern parts of the Roman Empire. Only the carcass of this crown remains, without any gemstones. (These were used in 1730 for the crown made in St. Petersburg for Empress Anna Ivanovna.)

The large imperial crown is considered to be the zenith of creative goldsmith work and jewelry artistry. It was made in 1762 for the coronation of Catherine II. The creator of this masterpiece was the court jeweler Jérémie Pauzié, assisted by outstanding goldsmiths, Ivan Liebmann and Ivan Yevstifeyev. The crown took only two months to make.

This crown jewel is made up of two silver halves, depicting five-lobed leaves and laurel boughs. A garland of oak leaves rises between the two halves of the crown, with the entire garland as well as the acorns – they count as symbols of the well-established and consolidated power of the state – being made of diamonds. A large 56-carat diamond sits at the base of the garland. This jewel was a gift from the Russian tradesmen's guild to Empress Elizabeth Petrovna (1754) because the empress had granted the tradesmen customs and tax relief. The perfect harmony and balance of this work of art is attributable to the differing facets of the gems achieved by the crown's creators. Two rows of pearls with a delicate luster, which increase in size toward the peak, emphasize the perfection of the crown. Almost 5,000 diamonds of varying sizes (a total of 2,858 carats), shapes, and shades, 75 pearls, as well as a large, irregular, polished spinel (398.72 carats) at the top of the garland and crowned with a cross of diamonds relieve this masterpiece of all its earthly heaviness. The beauty of this symbol of sovereignty is so overwhelming that the word *splendor* can barely be applied to it. This is truly a world-class work of art.

The emperor's crown is also accompanied by the small empress's crown, the scepter, and the orb. The empress's crown is really small: The diameter of the lower band is only 12 centimeters. The small crown created around 1801 by the Duval brothers is made of gold, silver, and diamonds. The coronation book of 1899 has a picture showing (in 1896) Emperor Nicholas II placing the small empress crown on his wife's head. The scepter should also be mentioned at this point: it bears the famous Indian Orloff diamond (189.62 carats), which is described as the "eye of the Hindu god Sri Ranga."

Opposite: The large Russian imperial crown was created in 1762 for Empress Catherine. Along with pearls and spinels, 4,936 brilliant-cut diamonds (a total of 2,858 carats) decorate the 18.75 centimeter crown. The crown jewels are kept at the Kremlin Treasury, Moscow.

Above: Portrait of Empress Catherine by S. Torelli. The empress is wearing her coronation robe with the crown and "Barmen" (collar around the shoulders set with pearls), the large chain of the Order of St. Andrew, and the scepter. Russian State Museum, St. Petersburg.

Memories of "Teheran" and "Persepolis"

Muhammad Reza Shah, the emperor of Iran, and his third wife, Farah Diba, were like the "dream couple of the Western world," although they lived and ruled in an Eastern country. Power, beauty, and immense wealth turned the ruling couple into important figures in the gossip columns. Who would ever have thought that this fairy tale magnificence would come to an end? However, looking back on the history of the Pahlevi dynasty, there is nothing unusual in its outcome. The father of Emperor Muhammad Reza, Reza Khan (1878–1944), started out as a simple soldier and later became the commanding officer of a Cossack brigade. In 1921, he marched on Teheran with his troops and overthrew the ruling government. He became minister of war and commander-in-chief of the armed forces. Between 1921 and 1923, he reinstated the authority of the central government. On October 30, 1925, he deposed the Qajar dynasty represented by Ahmed Shah and had himself named shah by the national assembly. This was the start of the Pahlevi dynasty. When the allied troops occupied Iran in 1941, they forced Reza Shah to abdicate – he was considered a sympathizer of the axis powers – and exiled him to the Union of South Africa.

Muhammad Reza, his son, then joined the government. He was a friend of the West, but also wanted to get along with the Communists. The shah's three wives–"the most beautiful women in the world" at that time, Princess Farida (sister of King Farouk), Soraya Esfandiari, and Farah Diba – adorned the magazines of the Western world, frequently decked out in jewels. Before the Pahlevi family, the Persian rulers acquired the finest gems and precious jewelry for their beautiful women.

The Persian crown of the Pahlevi dynasty was ordered by Reza Khan Shah at the time of his coronation (1926). It was modeled on the "crowns of the great epochs of the Sasanid dynasty" (224 to 651 A.D.) with the stepped merlon shape also serving as the design principle for the Pahlevi crown. The "four tympanums are set with rayed haloes formed by diamonds, against a red velvet background" (Jürgen Abeler). At the front, they are grouped around a pale yellow diamond of 60 carats. A Sasanidic motif (crossed curved lines: stylized lotus blossoms) is repeated twelve times to decorate the band and four times on the cap. Based on an emerald surrounded by diamonds, this ornament serves as the fixation point for the white feather aigrette at the peak of the crown (cf., V. B. Meen and A. Tushingham, *Crown Jewels of Iran*, 1968).

This crown was also used in 1941 for the coronation of Muhammad Reza Shah. The shah had a new crown made for his wife Farah. At his request, select rubies and emeralds were removed from the Persian crown jewels and recut for use in the new crown. Large diamonds and oriental pearls completed the jewel ensemble. The Parisian jeweler, Pierre Arpel, was commissioned to design the crown. It has a carcass of platinum and a dark emerald green velvet cap. While the front of the crown is decorated with two dark green emeralds cut in cabochon form

Opposite: The Russian scepter, dating from around 1770: gold, silver, brilliant-cut diamonds, and the 189.62-carat *Orloff* diamond.

In 1926, Reza Khan, the father of Shah Reza, commissioned the "Pahlevi crown" for the dynasty he founded. Reproduction from the Abeler Crown and Insignia Collection, Wuppertal.

171

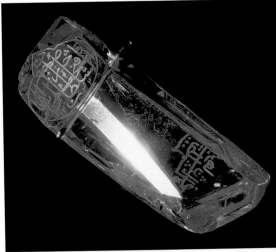

(91.32 carats and 66.35 carats), two large spinels in oval shape are positioned at the sides (each approximately 83 carats). A further spinel of around 17 carats is above the nape. The crown of the empress is also adorned with numerous other gems: 32 emeralds, 33 spinels and rubies, 105 large pearls, and 1,469 diamonds.

Among the many treasures of the Persian throne, mention should be made of a diadem created by the renowned New York jeweler, Harry Winston, for the wedding of Empress Farah in 1959. Along with numerous yellow, pink, and colorless diamonds, it contains the largest pink diamond in the world as its central stone: the 60-carat Nur Ul-Ain, the *light of the eye.* Together with the Darya-i-Nur, it is possible that this gem had once formed the unique Great Table diamond that was formerly in the possession of the gemstone dealer Tavernier.

In 1971, the world experienced the high spot of imperial power: Muhammad Reza Shah hosted a fairy tale gala in Persepolis. Twenty-five hundred guests, provided with luxury tents for their comfort, celebrated the 2,500th anniversary of the Persian kingdom with the ruler. The renowned gastronome, Felix Real, from Vaduz, Liechtenstein, prepared an exquisite gala dinner for the event and, as the master chef himself, cooked it with staff from the Maxime in Paris. A party of the century? A party of the millennium? A swan song of beauty? "All good things come to an end." The shah died in exile.

Two Female Crowns: Myth upon Myth

The *Iron Crown*, as it is known, is kept in the Church of St. John, in Monza. It is made of a gold band comprised of six movable plaques held together with gold wire. Convex gems – rubies, sapphires and amethysts – decorate the outside of the gold band, while the inside has an iron ring. Hence the name *Iron Crown*. According to a legend handed down from the late sixteenth century, the iron band is said to have been cast "from a nail in Christ's cross." This legend, however, is only one of many that surround this understated yet perfect crown. The *Iron Crown* is probably Upper Italian in origin dating from the second half of the ninth century.

Contrary to the opinion that the *Iron Crown* is the "Italian royal crown," very few kings of Italy were actually crowned with this banded crown: Emperor Charles V (on February 22, 1530), Napoleon (on May 26, 1805), and Emperor Ferdinand I of Austria (September 6, 1838). Since 1866, the crown has served as the Italian crown, but kings from the House of Savoy were not crowned with it. It was only put to use for the obsequies of King Victor Emanuel II (1878) and King Humbert I (1900).

But who actually wore this simple and yet princely crown? Once again, only a myth can provide further help as there is no documentary evidence. It is thought to be a woman's crown, created for Gisela, the daughter of Louis the Pious and wife of Eberhard of Friuli. This couple's son, King Berengar I, is said to have donated the crown to the treasury in the Church of St. John in Monza. The crown is still with us.

A crown of a special nature is the so-called *Eagle's Crown* of the last French empress, Eugénie (1826–1920). For the coronation (1853), Emperor Napoleon II had commissioned two crowns: one for himself and a smaller one for his wife. Since his own crown was paid for out of the coffers of the state, it was robbed of its gemstones and melted down in 1870 after the proclamation of the republic. In its day, the crown of the empress had been paid for out of the imperial privy purse. For this reason, it escaped destruction. Taking the *Eagle's Crown* of the empress as a model, which had been put on show a short while before in the Louvre in Paris, the former crown of the emperor could be reconstructed. The goldsmith and jeweler Jürgen Abeler, who has reconstructed over sixty famous crowns, was also able to recreate the *Eagle's Crown* of Napoleon III. The hoops of the *Eagle Crown* are gold palm leaves set with diamonds that alternate with imperial eagles. These eagles – made of gold – have wings raised to the peak of the crown. A diamond-studded monde, which is encircled by a horizontal band of emeralds, is crowned with a cross made up of diamonds. Diamonds and emeralds are also present on the crown's band, which is bordered top and bottom by a row of diamonds.

Where can this unique crown be seen? It is "privately owned," perhaps in a bank vault, where the anonymous owner possibly inspects it occasionally. The crown has become a myth. The empress died on July 11, 1920 in Seville.

Top: The *Eagle's Crown*, as it is known, for the wife of Emperor Napoleon III of France. Worn at the coronation in 1858, the design of the crown is impressive: set with brilliant-cut diamonds, gold palm leaves alternate with imperial eagles to serve as hoops. Louvre, Paris.

Above: The *Iron Crown of Monza* from the Church of St. John in Monza. Convex gemstones (rubies, sapphires and amethysts) decorate the outside of the crown, which probably dates from the second half of the ninth century.

EXQUISITE TREASURES

Crowns serve sovereigns as symbols of their greatness and power. But the gemstones – even those in crowns – always embody their own values: values in themselves. In the second chapter of our brief cultural history of gems, we would also like to highlight these special values: The luster of noble minerals does not illuminate an earthly ruler and his power, but praiseworthy attitudes and ideas. Perhaps in the case of people who practice chivalrous virtue and uphold their faith (Order of the Golden Fleece). However, when it is also a matter of paying due respect to the Word of God, to the Holy Scriptures (the precious bindings on the books of the Gospels). Last but not least, gems represent the trust in God that the people of the Middle Ages had, in the "divine idea": represented by the votive offerings, the litanies to the Virgin Mary, and the grace of God becoming reality – at the Virgin Mary's intercession (votive crowns). However, gemstones are always eternal witnesses to the Creation and to eternal beauty.

Albrecht Dürer, the inspired artist of fine and eternally valid art, once wrote: "I am not aware of what beauty is." (from the *Schriftlicher Nachlass*). Dürer was actually too closely involved with the essence of beauty to have been able to put a name to it. The poet August Graf von Platen (1796–1835), a Bavarian nobleman, found an astonishing formula in a sonnet *Ew'ge Schönheit ist das ewig Neue* (Eternal beauty is what is eternally new). Gemstones, millions of years old, are the valid proof of this for all time. Although they are ancient, they continue to delight us anew.

The Golden Fleece: The Order of the Hapsburg Family

The Golden Fleece is the Hapsburg family order, but the order's founder was Philip the Good, Duke of Burgundy. The order of Knights of the Golden Fleece, founded in 1430 (although some authors give 1429 as the year of its foundation), was intended to "gather the noblest men in Christianity around the duke at magnificent ceremonies" (Walter Pohl and Karl Vocelka *Die Habsburger*, 1992). The golden fleece of the classical Greek saga (flight of Phrixos and Helle on the golden ram to Kolchis, collection of the golden fleece by the Argonauts, under the leadership of Jason), and the Biblical references to the ram's fleece of the Hebrew judge Gideon were, on the basis of their symbolism, also intended to support the right of the Duke of Burgundy to lead a planned crusade against the Turks.

On January 5, 1477, Charles the Bold, Duke of Burgundy, fell at the battle of Nancy "piteously hit in the head" (Jakob Unrest). His daughter, Mary of Burgundy (1457–1482), inherited his great wealth and rich lands and enjoyed the attentions of many suitors. On April 21, 1477, the marriage was arranged in Bruges, by proxy, between Mary and Maximilian, the son of Emperor Frederick III. (Charles the Bold had already been negotiating a possible marriage between Mary and Max-

Above: The Order of the Golden Fleece (period: 1760–1770). A red almandine garnet of rare purity in the center of the order is accompanied by rubies and almandines. The Golden Fleece (height 15.7 cm; width 7.1 cm) is decorated with brilliant-cut diamonds on the horns and hooves. Treasure Chamber of the Munich Residency.

imilian in 1473!) On August 19, 1477, the day after the bridegroom from Vienna had arrived in Ghent, the wedding ceremony of the two royal children was conducted by the papal legate.

One year after his marriage (1478), Maximilian became head of the Order of the Golden Fleece. Since this time, a Hapsburg family member, as the Duke of Burgundy, has always been the grand master of the order. "In the order of succession, the current head of the Spanish branch of the Habsburg family had precedence over the Austrian branch." (Pohl and Vocelka, as above). The members of this highly respected order of knights were renowned, weapon-bearing noblemen "without blemish or blame." They took a vow of unswerving loyalty to their leader. They also vowed to wear the order's insignia on display, a golden order chain (Collane) set with flints, with its impressive golden fleece as a pendant.

The treasure belonging to the Order of the Golden Fleece was transferred from Brussels to Vienna in 1794, where it currently comprises five groups in the Viennese Secular Treasury. Since the sovereignty of the order, according to its statutes, was indivisibly connected with the Duke of Burgundy, the immeasurable wealth of the court of Burgundy could always be relied on for any festivities of the order. "This is why the small number of precious objects in the treasure belonging to the Order of the Golden Fleece is immediately evident." (Herman Fillitz, as previously referred to). What can be admired in the Viennese treasury dates, both in the goldsmith work as well as its textiles, from a time when court artistry in Burgundy had reached its zenith. Not all the objects in the treasure were made for the order, however. For example, the cross on which the knights swore their oath of allegiance was once the property of the most important collector of the late Middle Ages, Duke Jean de Berry.

One artifact that was certainly made for the order is the *Potence*, the *Collane* of the order's herald who wore this chain at ceremonial events. The *Collane* is decorated with the coats of arms of the order members. Two escutcheons are reserved for the sovereign, Emperor Charles V. The herald's *Collane* is a work originating from the Netherlands (gold and enamel) and dating from 1517. It replaced an earlier chain, which bore only thirty-two small coats of arms. The chain under the collar decorated with coats of arms is the actual chain of the order worn by order members.

However, the treasure of the golden fleece also contains mementos of members of the Duchy of Burgundy, for example, the "Ainkhürn sword," which belonged to Duke Charles the Bold, a valuable brooch, and what must be the finest rock crystal goblet of the late Middle Ages, once owned by the order's founder, Philip the Good, and named the *Burgundian court beaker*. This unique, 46-centimeter high goblet (rock crystal, gold, partly enameled, with diamonds, rubies and pearls) dates from the second quarter of the fifteenth century.

Crowned heads, in particular, received golden fleeces from the House of Hapsburg. For example, the *"Grünes Gewölbe"* (Green Vault) in Dresden contains two jewel sets (an emerald set and a carnelian set) that were probably connected with the elevation in rank of the electors of

The *Burgundian court beaker* is the finest rock crystal goblet of the late Middle Ages (height 46 cm). Decorated with gold, diamonds, rubies and pearls, this drinking vessel was once owned by Duke Charles of Burgundy, the founder of the Order of the Golden Fleece. Secular Treasury, Vienna.

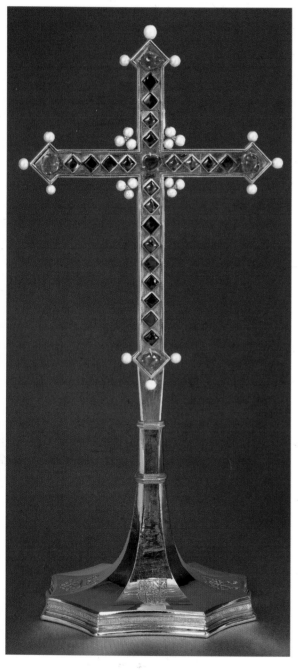

Above: The cross for swearing the oath of allegiance in the Order of the Golden Fleece is of French craftsmanship dating from around 1400. Pearls, rubies, and sapphires decorate the cross, which also serves as a vessel for a splinter of the "true Cross of Christ." Secular Treasury, Vienna.

Saxony: they were also Kings of Poland between 1697 and 1763 (cf., Joachim Menzhausen, *Das Grüne Gewölbe in Dresden/Schatzkammern Europas*). They therefore had to document their increase in power appropriately. In the emerald set, there is also an example of the Order of the Golden Fleece with three emeralds and seventy-two diamonds (1732/1733). The carnelian set (hunting set of King Augustus the Strong) similarly contains an Order of the Golden Fleece with carnelians and 135 diamonds (post-1719).

The fact that personages of the elevated aristocracy frequently incorporated their own original ideas into the design of the order pendant is proved by one of the order pendants of the House of Hapsburg housed in the Treasure Chamber of the Munich Residency. The two-part *coulant* depicts a lyre in its upper part and is also closely set with diamonds in its lower half. The setting is of gold and gilded silver. Some of the diamonds (these are older gems already present in the Treasure Chamber) have a layer of pink-colored foil under them. The golden fleece is also richly set with cut diamonds. This work of jeweled art was commissioned by Elector Max III Joseph. The jeweler who carried out the work was Johann Staff in Munich (1765). The order pendant was placed in the Treasure Chamber before 1774 and is in the possession of the *Wittelsbacher Ausgleichsfonds* (Wittelsbacher Compensation Fund) (cf., Herbert Brunner, *Die Schatzkammer der Residenz München*). Golden fleeces were still awarded even after the end of the monarchy by the pretenders to the throne. In 1953, the Republic of Austria recognized the Order of the Golden Fleeces as a "legal entity with foreign rights."

Orders from the Czarist Realm

Orders were unknown in old Russia. When, however, a well-deserving Boyar (members of the upper class) or noble at court was to be honored, this was in the form of tangible goods (payment in kind). They were presented with a silver or gold *Bratina* (a brotherhood dish). This was not actually a dish, but a lidded goblet that was crowned with, perhaps, a white, enameled, Polish eagle. This was crowned in turn with a Siberian rubellite. Sometimes, however, the honoree would also receive a valuable item of property of the czars, such as a fur coat. Czar Peter the Great (1672–1725), the reviver of Russian czarism, introduced orders during his rule. These were intended for members of his court and were therefore of great pomp.

The highest honor in czarist Russia, until the end of czarist rule, was the Order of Saint Andrew "Pervosvanny." The added name was intended to indicate that Andrew, the brother of Simon Peter, was "called first" by Jesus. *Pervosvanny* means "the first called." It was undoubtedly Czar Peter's thought when creating this order that Saint Andrew was the patron saint of the Russian church. He is supposed to have been the first to erect the cross on the bank of the Dnieper. According to an unsupported report (cf., reports by O. W. Goreva, I. F. Polynina, A. Raimann), the first holder of this order was Field Marshal F. A. Golovin (1698).

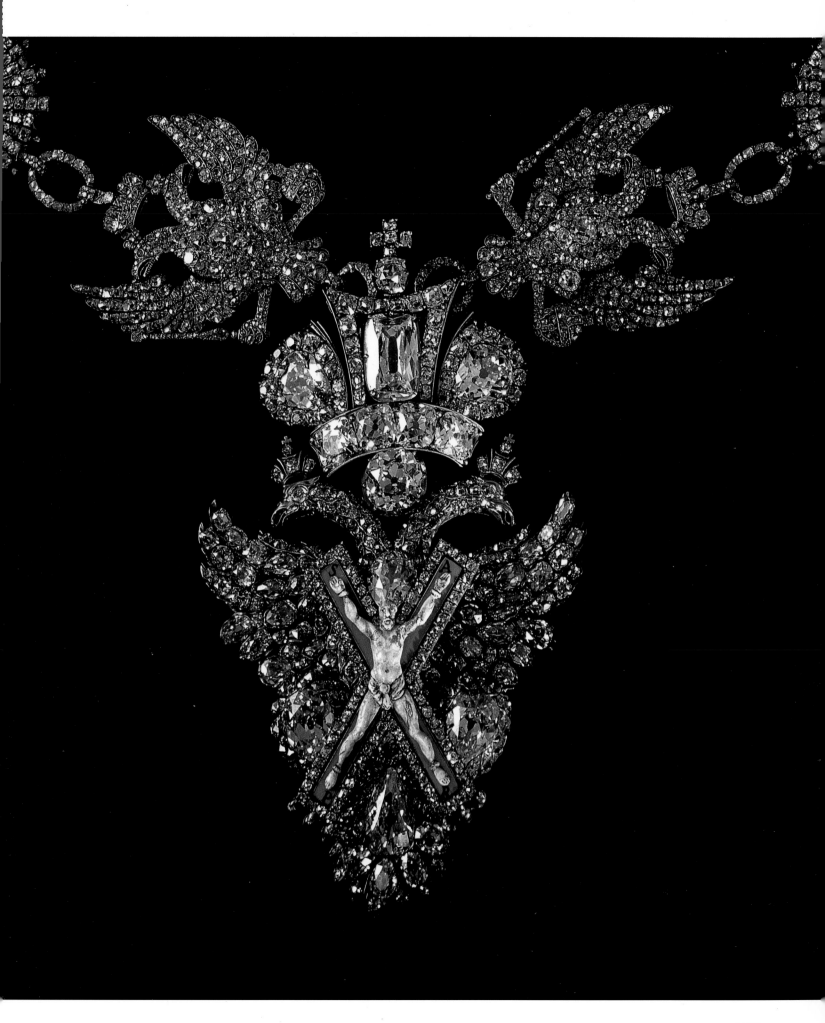

Four famous orders from the Kremlin Treasury in Moscow:

1. Star of the Order of Saint Andrew Pervosvanny (14.25 cm × 14.25 cm; gold, silver, brilliant-cut diamonds, enamel; dates from 1795–1800).

2: Jewel of the Order of Saint Catherine (8.4 cm × 5 cm; gold, silver, brilliant-cut diamonds, enamel; dates from 1770–1780).

3. Order of the Golden Fleece (6.2 cm × 6.2 cm: gold, silver, brilliant-cut diamonds, topazes; mid-nineteenth century).

4. Emblem of the Order of St. Anna (5.0 cm × 3.5 cm; gold, silver, brilliant-cut diamonds, rubies, enamel; end of the eighteenth century).

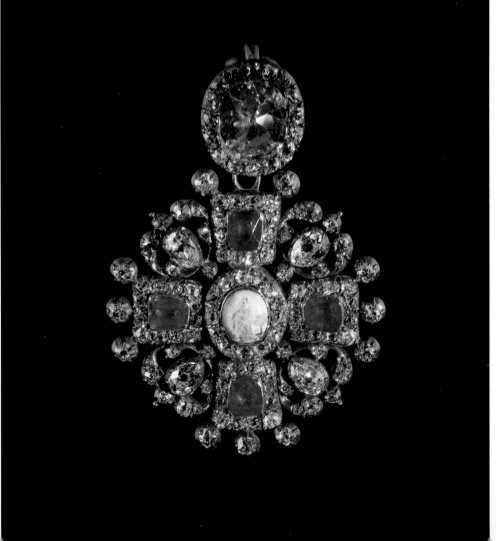

The oldest remaining Andrew Pervosvanny order in one of the finest precious collections in the world, in the so-called diamond fund in Moscow, dates from the early eighteenth century. The cross of Saint Andrew is worked in enamel and surrounded by diamonds faceted in the old style, deeply encased in gold. At the four ends of the cross of Saint Andrew, four letters are discernible: "SAPR" (*Sanctus Andreas Patronus Russiae:* Saint Andrew, Patron of Russia). As the authors quoted above assumed, this order was the one awarded to Czar Peter himself in 1703 for an act of heroism that he rendered as an artillery captain on the Neva estuary. The Cross of Saint Andrew was attached to a light blue sash worn across the right shoulder. The Andrew Pervosvanny order was also worn as an eight-pointed star (gold, silver, diamonds, pearls, and enamel). A central medallion, surrounded by particularly large diamonds, depicts the two-headed Russian eagle on a brownish-yellow enamel background together with the order's motto: "To loyalty and faith."

The miniature portraits of the sovereign, which were called *Parsunen* (persons!), were also a special order. The czar always awarded these personally as a special token of his favor. These *Parsunen* were made in series and had precious settings.

Peter the Great also founded the only order for women in Russia in 1714: this was dedicated to Saint Catherine, in memory of the favorable campaign on the Prut (1711). The Order of Saint Catherine is a miniature enamel portrait of the martyr Saint Catherine. Made of gold, silver, and enamel and richly set with diamonds, it was worn on a pink sash. The order also included a semicircular disk decorated with precious diamonds and rubies and surmounted by a cross also set with diamonds. This semicircle was then attached to the order hat.

Under the motto of "To him who loves truth, honor and loyalty," the Order of Saint Anna was an honor awarded for special services on behalf of the country and for the promotion of general good. This order originated in Holstein, where it was founded in 1735. It was first recognized as a Russian order in 1797.

There were four categories in the Order of Saint Anna, which affected how it was worn: on a sash over the shoulder, around the neck, in a buttonhole, or on the handle of the parade weapon. The example housed at the diamond fund dates from around 1760. The central gold medallion with melted enamel shows the standing figure of Saint Anna. On the ring surrounding the medallion, which is set with diamonds, there are four large rubies as arms of the cross and between them equally large diamonds. An exquisite solitaire diamond crowns the order and also serves to cover its means of attachment.

We began our look at order treasures with the Order of the Golden Fleece. It is hardly surprising that Moscow's diamond fund also contains a golden fleece! It is a captivating piece with its heated, pink-violet topazes from Brazil. These are arranged as a bow. At the lower edge of the largest topaz, the golden fleece is closely covered with small diamonds. The order in Moscow dates from the nineteenth century. It was presented to a Russian ruler by the emperor in Vienna. This golden fleece is an extremely valuable example of the Austrian family order.

Jewel with a likeness of Czar Peter I (8.0 cm × 4.5 cm) made of gold, silver and enamel with a precious setting. Such miniature portraits of the sovereign, called *Parsunen*, were awarded by the czar personally as a special token of his favor. Kremlin Treasury, Moscow.

179

NOBLE GEMS FOR THE WORD OF GOD

The people of the Middle Ages focused on life after death. They not only hoped for the end of all earthly ills but, above all, for a new life in Paradise – eternal life in the presence of God, which God had promised them. In accordance with the promising meaning that the word of God had for the Middle Ages, great attention was not only paid to the holy book, the Bible, and in particular, the Gospels of the New Testament, they were also revered. They were decorated in the finest leather, with precious metals, with gemstones and ivory reliefs, and many other precious decorations. God's word was worthy of the highest honor.

These ornate religious volumes of the early Middle Ages received scant scientific attention for a long time. However, no attention was paid to matters of shape or style. Nor was much thought given to the "individual laws of decoration based on the function of the book" (Frauke Steenbock, *Der kirchliche Prachteinband im frühen Mittelalter* [The Ornate Religious Volume in the Early Middle Ages]). Modern research into these ornate religious volumes is now taking pains to coordinate criteria gained from volume research using methods from the history of art. It became evident, as Frauke Steenbock says "that the design of a cover, i.e., the structure and arrangement of its decorative elements, can reflect specific contents." The contents are related to the manuscript enclosed and to the liturgical use of the corresponding book.

The Uta Book Box from Regensburg

The Uta book box (44.3 × 32.5 × 8.9 cm), which has been in the Bavarian State Library in Munich since the beginning of the nineteenth century, is a work dating from the first quarter of the eleventh and thirteenth centuries. The manuscript (Gospels) was completed on the instructions of Uta, the abbess of the Niedermünster Benedictine convent in Regensburg. The manuscript is richly ornamented and illuminated: pictures of the crucifixion, depictions of Saint Erhard (patron of the Niedermünster abbey, pictures of the Virgin Mary with the donor as well as the Evangelists. The Uta manuscript is a major work of the Regensburg school.

The wooden core of the book box is covered with gold plating on its front. Christ is enthroned in the center as the judge of the world. His feet rest on a footstool. His left hand holds the book decorated with gemstones and filigree, while gemstones and pearls adorn the front edges of the throne and the footstool. A richly ornamented nimbus (halo) – enamel platelets, gemstones, pearls, and gold filigree – surround his head. The four corners of the central part have square plates with stamped replicas of the Evangelist's symbols. This decoration is an addition from the beginning of the thirteenth century. The book cover rises slightly toward the frame. This sloping surface is covered with a wooden strip and set with small square pictures in enamel at irregular intervals: "vegetable patterning." Stamped-out metal plates are nailed between these patterns – a work of more recent date. Originally, the

Opposite: The Uta repository (44.3 × 32.5 × 8.9 cm) has been in the Bavarian State Library in Munich since the beginning of the nineteenth century. It was created in Regensburg between 1002 and 1025 when Uta was the abbess of the Niedermünster Benedictine convent. Decorated with superb gemstones, the repository depicts Christ in the center as judge over the world. A richly ornamented halo (enamel platelets, gemstones, pearls, and gold filigree) surrounds the Lord's head.

Christ as judge over the world is seated in a stern position facing the observer. This type of depiction, as well as the throne and footstool, are reminiscent of pictures of the Pantocrator in the Eastern Church. According to Frauke Steenbock, this was mainly "adopted by the carvers of miniatures and ivory of the Carolingian Ada school" and further developed. While the figure of Christ looks monumental (it extends beyond its frame at the top and bottom), the angled strip set into the frame lifts it above the figure of the judge over the world and disturbs the harmony of figure and background. This duality caused H. Schitzler (in *Forschungen und Kunstgeschichte der christlichen Archäologie, [Research and History of Art in Christian Archeology]* volume 2, Baden-Baden, 1953) to presume that the repository was modified in the first half of the thirteenth century.

frame was decorated with evenly arranged, large gemstones. Smaller noble minerals were grouped around these gems. Closely worked carved filigree covered the free areas.

The individual plates surrounded by filigree "are mostly damaged" (Frauke Steenbock, as mentioned) but show traces of restoration. Just as with the small ornamental enamels, which are inserted somewhat unsystematically, the two round disks on the frame do not belong to the original work. They are attached in position rather roughly with nails. The disk to the right of the judge of the world (on the left-hand edge of the book) depicts a medallion of Christ surrounded by eight half-circles with blossom ornamentation. To Christ's left, on the right-hand edge of the book, a larger disk shows his mother. The lid of the Uta book box is a superb example of goldsmith work from Ottonian times.

The Codex of Bishop Godehard

This codex (37 × 26 cm) is housed in Trier Cathedral treasury and dates from the last quarter of the twelfth century. According to an entry made in the fourteenth century, the manuscript is supposed to represent the Gospels from St. Godehard in Hildesheim (Germany). The codex became part of the cathedral treasury in Trier in 1799 when it came from the collection of the canon of Paderborn Cathedral, Christoph, Graf von Kesselstatt. The lid decoration is mounted on an oak base and, apart from a few missing gems, is well preserved.

The codex lid is striking for its broad, decorated frame, in which an enamel plate is set. The latter depicts, in three sections, scenes from the life of the Son of God. The upper section shows the appearance of the Lord to Mary Magdalene (John 20,17). The center section shows Christ on the cross between Ecclesia and Synagogue, Mary and John (John 19, 16–30). The lower section shows the three Marys at the Lord's empty tomb (Mark 16, 1–8) on which the angel is sitting. Two Latin inscriptions on narrow bands separate the individual sections and refer to the two lower pictures. The gems are in toothed settings, surrounded by filigree (upright notched wire), whereby the ends of the tendrils bear small orbs. Eight plates with small walrus tooth reliefs decorate the frame. The reliefs in the four corners depict the four symbols of the Evangelists (with empty designation bands), Mary and a bishop, probably St. Godehard. Along the sides, the symbolic figures of Ecclesia (with flag and shield) and Synagogue (with the sacrificial sword) are shown. In the crucifixion scene that forms the center, the figures of Ecclesia and Synagogue indicate the change brought about by the Son of God.

The way in which the decoration of the frame is designed harmonizes with the design of a second book cover also belonging to the cathedral treasury in Trier. The gemstones set into it and the filigree are again carried out in the style of Hildesheim goldsmith work. Both volumes would appear to have originated from the same workshop. "On the basis of their advanced style," the date of their creation is thus sometime in the 1170s.

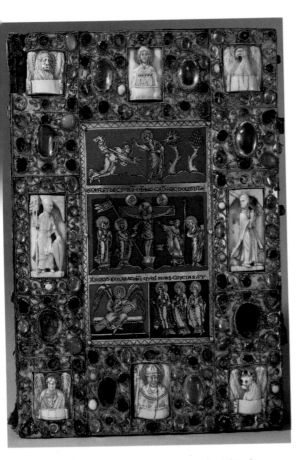

The lid of the Codex of Bishop Godehard (37 cm × 26 cm; in Trier Cathedral treasury) is conspicuous for its frame, which is richly decorated with gemstones. In the middle, three sections depict scenes from the life of Jesus (appearance to Mary Magdalene; Christ on the cross between Ecclesia and Synagogue, the three Marys outside the empty tomb).

The Imperial Gospels

In the Vienna Secular Treasury the Imperial Gospels are one of the traditional witnesses to great history. The texts appear in gold on dyed purple parchment (32.4 × 24.9 cm). The headings and marginalia are in silver. Sixteen canon plates, four pictures of the Evangelists, and four initial pages go back to the time of Charlemagne, for the manuscript was written and illuminated at his court in Aachen toward the end of the eighth century. The current volume of the Gospels is made of gilded silver and was created by Hans von Reutlingen (Aachen, from around 1500). God the Father is enthroned in the center of the book's cover. The symbols of the Evangelists are depicted in four round medallions, one at each corner. The annunciation to Mary is shown alongside the figure of God the Father. So as not to distract from the figurative decoration, only a few gemstones were used. They were inserted in the outermost corners of the volume and under the figure of God on the throne as well as at the feet of those in the annunciation scene (cf., Hermann Filliz, *Die Weltliche Schatzkammer in Wien/Schatzkammern Europas*).

Famous Reliquaries

Relic is the term used for the ashes or bones of saints. In addition, articles that the saints once used are also elevated to the rank of relics. One example is the "Holy Robe" of Trier.

The veneration of relics is only ecclesiastically possible if the authenticity of the bones to be venerated or the items connected with the saintly person are guaranteed by documents. This had to be done either by a cardinal, a bishop, or clerics who made special statements about the objects in question and gave reasons to back up their statements. Any purely magic interpretation in connection with relics is wrongful use.

The cult of relics was already attested to at the time of death of the martyr Polycarp (156). In later times, churches were erected over the graves of martyrs (sarcophagi), which became centers of Christian piety. From this, the tradition developed of also enclosing relics in altars. The veneration of relics was also of major importance in the Eastern church in particular. The mortal remains of saints were kept in reliquaries. This resulted in arm, head, and foot reliquaries, for example.

Shrines are special highlights in the design of reliquaries. For example, as a "Golden House," in basilica or cupola style, "which represented heaven in small format" (Erich Stephany, *Wunderwelt der Schreine*" Frankfurt am Main, 1959).

The reliquaries holding particles of the cross also hold a high position, corresponding to the fact that the Cross of Christ and the crucifixion represent the redemption, the zenith of God's earthly existence. Reliquaries are among some of the most precious works made by goldsmiths and jewelers: precious metals, gemstones, pearls and enamels, embossed and cast figures complement and enhance them to the level of unique works of art.

The lid of the Imperial Gospels in the Secular Treasury in Vienna. These Gospels are one of the great witnesses to history. This volume of the Gospels is made of gilded silver. It is a work of Hans von Reutlingen (Aachen, around 1500). God the Father is enthroned in the center.

The Staurothek in Limburg

St. George's Cathedral in Limburg on the River Lahn (Germany) possesses the artistically most superb and also the largest preserved cross reliquary from Byzantine times: the Limburg Staurothek. This term is derived from the Old Greek word for a "cross post" *(stauros)*. The Staurothek is a panel reliquary for particles of the cross, relics of the Lord, of the Virgin Mary, and John the Baptist. It is comprised of a flattened panel in the form of a tall rectangle with a protruding frame and a sliding lid to cover the drawer thus formed. It is 48 centimeters high, 34 centimeters wide, and has a depth of 6 centimeters. The cross relic is encased in a cross with a double crossbeam and arms framed in gold. This relic cross is set into a container of the same dimensions that is cut into the base of the rectangular interior. The relic remains visible from the front and, on the reverse, an embossed inscription states that emperors Konstantinos and Romanos commissioned the work of mounting the relic. "Konstantinos" refers to Emperor Konstantinos VII "Porphyrogennetes" (905–959). "Romanos," the second emperor, was one of the "co-emperors" of Konstantinos VII–either his father-in-law, Romanos I "Lakapenos" (870–948) or his son, Romanos II (945–963).

Twenty gold enamel plates surround the recess for the relic in the drawer. The "heavenly hierarchy" is depicted on the plates. The archangels venerate the cross "in five rows, arranged in pairs." Eight four-winged cherubim and twelve six-winged seraphim flank them. On the lid, in the recessed center section, nine gold enamel plates are arranged in three rows. In the center, there is a large "Deesis": an enthroned Christ is accompanied by the Virgin Mary and John the Baptist as well as by the archangels Michael and Gabriel. The sections above and below each depict six standing apostles, grouped in twos. Between filigree strips, square gold enamel plates show the busts of four soldiers and four bishops who became saints. Crosswise strips with rosettes of gemstones (including almandine) and pearls are attached above and below them. These rosettes possibly originate from an earlier modification. They perhaps replaced reproductions of the donors or of saints (cf., A. Boeckler, *Zur Wiederherstellung der Staurothek von Limburg, Kunstchronik 4/ 1951*). The embossed inscription on the raised frame of the drawer indicates that Basileios Proedros commissioned the decoration for the cross relic – possibly around 964–965 (cf., M. Ross, Basil the Proedros. Patron of the Arts, *Archaeology*, 11, 1958). This Basileios had been the Proedros (chairman) of the senate. He was an illegitimate son of the Emperor Romanos I. Until his fall in 989, Basileios was the most powerful and influential man at the Byzantine court. During the fourth crusade (cf., the section on votive crowns "The crown of the Mother of God with the crystal grotto") in 1204, the Staurothek came into the possession of the knight Heinrich von Uelmen as a trophy of war. In turn, he donated it in 1208 to the Augustinian convent of nuns in Stuben on the River Mosel. The reliquary remained there until 1789. Finally, it came to Koblenz and, in 1827, to Limburg Cathedral. Heinrich von Uelmen also donated a splinter of the cross to the abbey of St. Eucharius in Trier.

In terms of art, the Staurothek in Limburg is the most important Cross reliquary preserved from Byzantine times. A rectangular panel with a protruding frame and a sliding lid closes the reliquary containing the relic of the Cross. The latter is enclosed in a double cross, alongside other relics in the decorated transverse rectangles. Treasury of St. George's Cathedral in Limburg on the River Lahn (Germany).

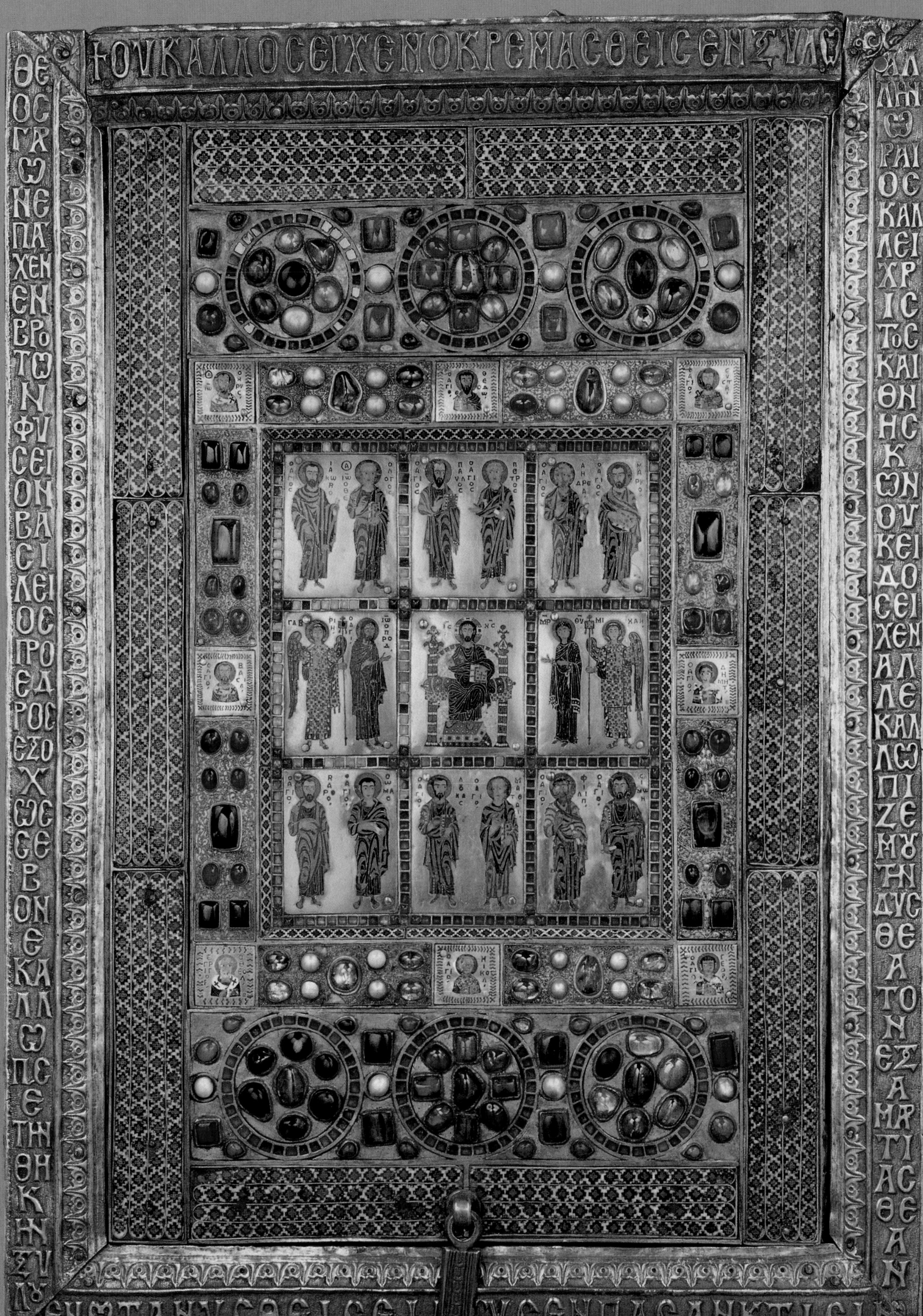

The Bust Reliquary of Charlemagne

The bust of Charlemagne, created in 1350 and contained in the treasury of Aachen Cathedral, was made to hold the cranium (calotte) of the great emperor and keep it in dignified style. The bust, which has been carried in the Corpus Christi procession since 1367 was, according to Heinz Biehn (q.v., reference), probably a donation by Emperor Charles IV (rule 1346–1378). From 1350, the bust of Charlemagne was crowned with a silver crown, which had, however, already been made in 1300. In the opinion of some historians, this crown, which is actually gilded silver, is identical to the one that King Richard of Cornwallis (1257–1272) "left in perpetuity" in Aachen Cathedral to prevent his successors from being crowned since they would thus not have a crown. However, it is also quite possible that the crown on the head of the bust reliquary is also a donation by Charles IV.

The crown on the reliquary is richly ornamented with gemstones, pearls, and a glass flow. The crown's lower edge is encircled by a ring of pearls. The crown as well as the four fleurs-de-lis protruding on all four sides is made up of two silver plates riveted together. The crown's band and top are decorated with gemstones, some of which are intaglios and cameos, as well as with pearls: They are positioned on high, cylindrically shaped "often small, funnel-shaped, tapering tubes" (H. Biehn) in a box setting. Claws were used to fix the gems more firmly. There are three large pearls, fifteen cut, and fifty-five convex gemstones (amethysts, rubies, sapphires, emeralds, and a colorful glass flow). Above the front fleur-de-lis and connected with the hoop is a cross that is reminiscent of a Maltese cross. The band at the lower edge is made up of 149 pearls. This dates from the nineteenth century. The bust reliquary stands 86 centimeters high. The bust itself, which depicts eagles within lozenge shapes, is richly set with gemstones.

The Shrine of the Three Magi

Cologne's cathedral houses a reliquary that uniquely reflects the title of the important work by Erich Stephany, *Wunderwelt der Schreine (Wonderworld of Shrines)*. Started in 1180, this shrine was finally completed after 1220. It measures 118 centimeters in length, 130 centimeters in width, and stands 170 centimeters high.

This magnificent work of art was created for the bones of the "three Wise Men from the East"–for the relics of the Magi. These relics were housed in Milan until 1264. Reinald von Dassel then brought them to Cologne. The upper part of the shrine contains the bones of the martyrs Felix and Nabor, which were likewise transferred from Milan to the banks of the River Rhine. From the time of its creation, the Magi shrine was "the largest and finest of all shrines from the Hohenstaufen period" (E. Stephany). The front end of the Cologne reliquary depicts Christ at the top as a judge. He holds an open book of life and is accompanied by two angels. The latter symbolically hold the gifts brought by the Three Wise Men from the East. In the lower part, the Mother of God is en-

The bust reliquary of Charlemagne from the treasury of Aachen Cathedral. This reliquary was created in 1350 in Aachen. The crown on Charlemagne's head is Bohemian (second quarter of the fourteenth century).

throned, with the Magi approaching with their gifts. The Magi are accompanied by Otto IV. The ruler of the Holy Roman Empire of the German nation is a companion to the Magi. With his donations, Otto enabled this side of the shrine to be made of pure gold. At the rear, there is a depiction of Reinald von Dassel, the archbishop of Cologne and the chancellor of Emperor Friedrich Barbarossa.

The depictions of the prophets and apostles in the arcades of the upper and lower longitudinal sides of the Magi shrine are also of major importance. According to Erich Stephany, "Gestures, body positions and facial expressions give an individual look to each one. The influence of French sculpture and a knowledge of ancient depictions are unmistakable."

The Cologne Magi shrine is noteworthy for its wealth of antique cameos and intaglios. Albertus Magnus, who once taught in Cologne, remarked on these gemstones. On the trapezoid central plate of the front end, there is a particularly fine example of the antique art of gem cutting: a very large cameo, representing Mars and Venus.

The shrine of the three Magi in Cologne Cathedral, "the largest and finest of all shrines from the Hohenstaufen period" (E. Stephany), contains among other things the relics of the Magi, brought from Milan to Cologne. The front end of the shrine depicts Christ as the judge over the world holding the "book of life." The arcades of the upper and lower longitudinal sides depict the figures of prophets and apostles.

VOTIVE AND CONSECRATION CROWNS

The sovereigns, kings, and emperors of the Middle Ages frequently donated their crowns to a church or a convent (cf., also *Edle Steine*, 1991 edition). In connection with the *Iron Crown* of Monza, we have already pointed out that King Berengar I donated this crown to the Church of St. John. Crowned sovereigns made donations of this type mostly in the belief that Christ was the "true King of Kings": *Rex Regnum*. Early consecration crowns (votive crowns), that is, crowns given, with this intention, to a religious institution as a gift, include, for example, the crowns from the Treasure of Guarrazar in Spain.

The Treasure of Guarrazar

In 711, the kingdom of the Western Goths in Spain was conquered by the Saracens. The last of the Goths therefore buried the treasure of their kings. More than eleven hundred years later (1858), the buried Goth treasure was found by chance near Fuente de Guarrazar, close to Toledo. Along with church jewels, twelve gold consecration crowns were found, two of which bear the name of the donors. Gold letters, hanging from the lower edge of the crowns' rims, named the West Goth kings Svinthila (reigned 621–631) and Reccesvinth (reigned 649–672). Nine of the crowns found went to the Musée Cluny in Paris. During the Second World War, this museum had to return these crowns to Spain on the orders of the German occupation force. There, they were united in an archaeological museum with another crown found near Guarrazar and a crown fragment. Three of the crowns were subsequently returned to the Musée Cluny, which had originally bought the crowns.

The crown of King Svinthila was lost in 1921 (theft) and is now even thought to have been destroyed. The treasure of Guarrazar is divided up into five groups "according to ornamentation and shape" (H. Biehn, as before). The consecration crowns of King Reccesvinth and the lost crown of King Svinthila belong in the first group. Both crowns were made of gold and richly set with gemstones and pendant letters. The second group contains a crown with three rows of colored gems on a smooth background. The third group is made up of a crown with one row of gems and embossed ornaments. Group four contains three crowns with embossed ornamentation and no gems. The fifth group has four crowns "which are comprised of baluster hangings in the form of a network" (H. Biehn, as above).

The Crown of King Reccesvinth

After the loss of King Svinthilas's crown, the most important piece is the crown of King Reccesvinth. Gold, gemstones (including almandines), and pearls decorate the crown's band, which is composed of two superimposed gold plaques and can be opened by means of hinges. The edges of the crown band are each bordered top and bottom by a narrow strip

The consecration crown of West Goth King Reccesvinth from the treasure of Guarrazar. The gold crown is decorated with thirty pearls and thirty sapphires and attached to four chains. National Archeological Museum, Madrid.

containing almandines and glass flows encased in cell form. Circular shapes contain lozenges with these, in turn, having alternate green and red inserts, while the circles are set with almandines. The triangles between the circles again alternate in red and green. Between the narrow edging strips, the crown band has three rows, each of ten sapphires and pearls. These jewels are arranged so that beneath a pearl, a sapphire is positioned in the next row and, underneath this, another pearl. The gold base for the jewels has a slight outward curve in the middle row that, with the addition of incisions, gives the impression of stylized, leafy branches. The individual leaves are underlaid with almandines. Twenty-two uppercase letters hang on chains from the lower edge of the crown (each 3.4 cm in length). Composed of zigzag gold cells, they are decorated with almandines. In addition, a rectangular glass flow hangs on each letter in a box setting, with a droplet-shaped sapphire as the final gem. The letters give the inscription RECCESVINTHUS REX OFFERET. This inscription allows the crown to be accurately dated as originating from the time of King Reccesvinth's rule, that is, 649 to 672.

The crown has four loops on its upper edge for the attachment of four gold chains. Votive crowns used to be hung in churches for ceremonial occasions, for example, above the sovereign's throne.

The crown of King Svinthila was similar to that of King Reccesvinth. When Svinthila's crown was found (near Fuente de Guarrazar), it did not have all its uppercase letters. The complete set of letters would have read: SVINTZILANUS REX OFFERET (King Svinthila is offering this crown, "donating it").

The Crown of Theodelinde

The crown of the Lombard queen Theodelinde (died in 627) is also a votive crown of a special kind. It is contained in the treasury of the Church of St. John in Monza.

Theodelinde was the daughter of the Bavarian Duke Garibald I and the wife of King Authari. On his death, she became the wife of Agilulf. She paved the way for the transition of her people from their belief in Arianism to Catholicism. Her consecration crown is made of sheet gold and is decorated with blue gems and star coral around the outside of the crown's band. A punched filigree wire edges the crown band at the top and bottom. Three eyelets on the upper edge of the crown served for the attachment of three gold suspension chains that join together in a ring.

Hanging from this ring, a gold chain goes through the middle of the crown. Attached to it is a cross, set with pearls and gemstones, that is supposed to have once belonged to the votive crown of King Agilulf. "Probably the crown donated by Queen Theodelinde also possessed such a cross" (H. Biehn). The diameter of the cross is 18.8 centimeters and it is 4.9 centimeters in height.

The Agilulf crown arrived at the Bibliothèque Nationale in Paris in 1797. It was stolen from there in 1804 and melted down. An inscription on it referred to "Agilulfus." This Latin inscription was the reason for researcher R. Elze to consider the lost Agilulf crown to be a fake.

Gold cross of King Reccesvinth with pearls and ornamental stones, mid-seventh century from the treasure of Guarrazar. Musée de Cluny, Paris.

189

The Crown of the Mother of God with the Crystal Grotto

Votive and commemorative crowns were also known from the late Byzantine period, for example, the votive crown of the Byzantine emperor Leo VI, the Wise, who reigned from 886 to 912. This unique work of art was a crown dedicated to the Mother of God. The top of the crown was formed by a "Grotto of the Holy Virgin" carved out of a large, absolutely pure rock crystal. A gold statue of the Madonna stands with hands outstretched in prayer in front of the hollowed-out, hemisphere-shaped crystal, a masterpiece from ancient times. The crown's band is set with medallions surrounded by pearls. In colorful *cloisonné* work, they depict the "pious and wise Emperor Leo VI" accompanied by saints. The fact that this unique "grotto crown" still exists is the result of a raid. Doge Dandolo of Venice, who was over ninety years of age, exhorted the knights of the fourth crusade "to attack and plunder rich Constantinople." This happened in 1204. Since then, the *Crown with the Madonna Grotto* has been one of the finest and most valuable objects in the treasury of San Marco in Venice. Doge Dandolo and the knights he encouraged to commit outrageous deeds in actual fact saved this wonderful crown from the Orient. After the capture of Constantinople by the Turks (1453), it would undoubtedly have been lost.

Crown of the Andes: The Emerald Wonder of Popayán

The *Crown of the Andes* is perhaps the most beautiful of all crowns ever created. However, it has never adorned a mortal's head. It was created for Mary, the Mother of God, as thanks for sparing the town of Popayán from the plague.

Popayán is an old Inca town the ruins of which were discovered by the Spanish invaders in 1535. "Taken by the beautiful scenery and the mild climate in the Andes," the conquerors settled there and built houses and churches and cultivated the land. Popayán was finally elevated by the pope to the status of cathedral town and so a cathedral was built. Then plague broke out in Quito, the capital of the viceroyalty. The purpose of rogation services was to ask Mary, the Mother of God, for intercession with her son so that he would spare the town of Popayán and the land around it. "Daily, for weeks and months" the fervent prayers beseeched the Queen of Heaven. The prayers and pleas helped: the plague subsided. Popayán was spared.

How could the Mother of God be thanked? The bishop had the inspired idea of donating a crown "more beautiful and exquisite than all earthly crowns." The crown was to be made of the purest gold and adorned with the finest emeralds. The nobles in the town of Popayán thus had experienced goldsmiths and experienced gem cutters sent from Spain. Twenty-four artisans worked for six years to transform a large solid lump of gold weighing approximately 100 pounds into an exceptionally fine and richly decorated crown since "fire was not to touch the magnificent object."

The most enchanting feature of the unique Virgin Mary crown, how-

The crown of the Mother of God with the crystal grotto ("Le trésor de Saint-Marie de Venise) is a consecration crown of the Byzantine Emperor Leo VI, the Wise, who reigned from 886 to 912. The top of the crown was formed by a *Grotto of the Holy Virgin* carved out of a large, absolutely pure rock crystal. Since the period of office of the Venetian Doge Dandolo (since 1204), the crown has been one of the most valuable objects in the treasury of San Marco in Venice. Our pictures show the crown of the Mother of God from the front *(opposite)* and from the side *(above)*. Treasury of San Marco, Venice.

Above: Detail from one of the hoops of the *Crown of the Andes* with valuable Colombian emeralds.

ever, is undoubtedly the gemstones: 447 exquisite emeralds, the largest, named "Atahualpa" with a weight of 45 carats, decorate this work of art. All the gems originated from Inca possession. The largest was personally taken from the Inca prince Atahualpa on the occasion of his imprisonment in 1532 by the Spanish conqueror Pizarro. Seventeen imposing, droplet-shaped gems were once suspended from the hoop of the crown. (One droplet has since been replaced with glass.) Together, the emeralds have a total weight of 1,524 carats. The incomparable votive offering was conducted on December 8, 1599, on the feast day of the Immaculate Conception, with great pomp, on the head of a gigantic statue of the Virgin Mary to the cathedral in Popayán.

However, objects of high value also attract thieves. In Popayán among the faithful offering up their prayers in the cathedral were "bandits and desperados." Several times the crown had to be rapidly taken to safety. It was then hidden in the cellar vaults, buried in gardens, or concealed in highly inaccessible caves. But then it finally happened. Around 1650, the "crown of our beloved Lady of the Andes" fell into the hands of armed robbers. The young men of Popayán followed the thieves, however, and were able to win back the crown after a hard fight.

But other, serious crises lay ahead. In the battles for independence in the nineteenth century, the crown was dismantled into its six parts and each part was buried separately in a secret place. When times started to become more settled again, the individual parts were removed from their hiding places and the magnificent work of art was reassembled. But fate was not kind to the cathedral town of Popayán: It became increasingly poor and soon was in acute need. In 1909 the Holy See (Pope Pius X) allowed the sale of the commemorative crown so that the town could finance social institutions (orphanages, hospitals) with the proceeds. In a letter dating from 1914, papal authorization for the sale of the crown was confirmed once again. Czar Nicholas II of Russia, the last czar, was supposed to have been very interested in acquiring the crown. Around the mid-1930s the Andes crown arrived in America. It became the property of an American foundation. In 1968, on the occasion of Germany's Gemstone Day, it was put on display in Frankfurt am Main. Mab Wilson, the important American gemology publisher, was among the admirers of the unique work of art. She wrote: "The crown is as beautiful as ever, the gold gleams so softly as only pure gold can, the emeralds sparkle at the beholder like green lance tips – but there are cracks here and there .... "

In Europe, in the United States, and in South America, the *Crown of the Andes* was such a legendary treasure that many people thought it was just a symbol, a sort of mythical jewel, as was the Holy Grail or the philosopher's stone – an abstract concept rather than a reality made of gold and gemstones. According to Mab Wilson, "When you looked at it (the Andes crown) in its noble gleam, you sensed something of that atmosphere of belief and pious trust" that surrounded the crown in devout centuries. A piece of heaven in the midst of earthly misery. A fragment of hope of deliverance.

FAMOUS JEWELS AND THEIR HISTORIES

BEAUTY, MAGIC, AND MEDICINE

This chapter takes a look at special jeweled works of art as well as at people's relationships with gemstones, both in the past and in the present. Magic and esotericism will also get their due.

The publisher of an anthology of important lyrics spoke in his foreword about the difficulty of giving the major poets their due. It was extremely difficult, he wrote, with such a choice – in view of the high quality of the texts – not to overlook a poet's most typical and finest verses and, by doing so, rob him of his linguistic jewels. Beyond the wealth of world-famous goldsmith artistry set with superb gemstones, it is so easy to get carried away that there is a danger of overlooking exceptions in the art of jewelry because new highlights repeatedly inspire and entice. We would like to avoid this danger.

St. George, the "Dragon-slayer"

The Treasure Chamber at the Munich Residency houses a statuette of the knight St. George. He is sitting on his horse, in monument pose, on a high pedestal containing relics. Total height of the statuette is 50 centimeters, width is approximately 30 centimeters, and depth is approximately 20 centimeters. The knight has just felled the dragon – the broken tip of the lance is still sticking in the throat of the monster – and he has now drawn his sword out of its sheath for the decisive coup de grâce. The blade of the sword is made of rock crystal. The statuette of cast gold and embossed work in gold is richly set with exceptionally fine gemstones. Table-cut diamonds can be seen on an enameled, ornamented background or, on the edges of the shabracks (saddlecloths), rubies in the form of drops. Parts of the horse (head, legs, tail) are stone cut in agate and chalcedony. The plume on the dragon-slayer's helmet and the two plumes on his mount bear large pearls. Another one hangs from the neck of the noble charger. The dragon is embossed with gold and is similarly extravagantly trimmed with fine emeralds and rubies. The pedestal of the statuette is decorated with the Bavarian lozenge-patterned coat of arms.

The creators of this unparalleled work of art – it was made sometime between 1586 and 1597 – are unknown. However, it is thought to be the work of artisans in Augsburg and Munich: the master goldsmiths Hans Schwanenburg, Hans Schleich, Ulrich Schwegler, and Andreas Athemstett; the enamelers Hans Reimer and Abraham Lotter the Elder; the gem cutters Zacharias Peltzer and Valentin Drausch (details from Herbert Brunner, *Die Schatzkammer der Residenz in München*). The work of art was completed for the enthronement of Maximilian I, the "Duke of both Bavarias and Elector of the Holy Roman Empire (according to an inscription on the statuette's pedestal). St. George is the patron saint of the Wittelsbachers who still own the dragon-slayer (*Wittelsbacher Ausgleichsfonds*: Wittelsbacher Compensation Fund).

Opposite: One of the most magnificent jeweled artifacts in the world, the statuette of the knight St. George is richly decorated with gemstones and pearls and housed in the Treasure Chamber of the Munich Residency. The three-dimensional depiction captures the moment in which "St. George delivers the decisive coup de grâce to the still rearing dragon." The statuette (height 50cm) was commissioned by Duke William V in 1590 as a repository for a relic of the saint.

The Mirror of Marie de Médicis

Of all the major collectors of gemstones and goldsmith work, the French King Louis XIV (1638–1715) was one of the most outstanding. In the lower floors of the long gallery in the Louvre (cf., Pierre Verlet, *Die Galerie d'Apollon des Louvre in Paris*), he employed numerous artists who worked solely for him – for the enrichment of his collections and for the embellishment of his palaces. In 1684, Louis XIV acquired a mirror (height 40 cm) from a dealer named Le Brun, which had probably been owned by Marie de Médicis (1573–1642). She was the daughter of Francesco I de Médicis, Grand Duke of Tuscany, and, in 1600, she was married to King Henry IV of France. After King Henry IV was murdered in 1610, she assumed the regency of the country.

The gable-shaped top of the mirror "is worked in agate-onyx, the two pillars are of gray jasper. At the side of the pillars, there are two heads made of garnet, which are decorated with enameled gold and rest on two large emeralds" (as listed in Louis XIV's inventory). The gable area has a very fine emerald, surrounded by rubies and a cameo (likeness of a woman) surrounded by emeralds. A further cameo depicting a woman is centered in the mirror's base.

The Jeweled Bouquet of an Empress

In 1723, at the age of 15, Franz Stephan, Duke of Lorraine (1708–1765) arrived in Vienna. Franzl–"a nice lad," as a contemporary report noted – delighted the daughter of Emperor Charles VI in particular. Princess Maria Theresa (1717–1780, empress from 1740 to 1780) was as pretty as a picture and the heiress to a large empire. Her father kept a very close eye on which suitor he would accept for his "Resl": many a high-ranking nobleman had already been shown the door. But Maria Theresa really wanted to marry the young man from Lorraine and finally "the last Hapsburg" agreed. Since Charles VI had no sons, the Luxembourg crown and kingdom would take over, strictly speaking, after his death.

The suitor was successful. His bride also gave him a gift. Maria Theresa knew that Franz Stephan was a connoisseur and collector of gemstones. So she had the court jeweler Johann Michael Grosser create a jeweled bouquet for her Franzl "decoratively made up of many gemstones." Franz was delighted with Maria Theresa's gift. This gemstone bouquet set the seal on his betrothal to the emperor's daughter. It was the start of a happy, thirty-year marriage that produced sixteen children.

The betrothal gift of the empress, as she later became, is undoubtedly one of the finest jeweled works of art ever. From a vase made of a piece of rock crystal, a bouquet of gemstones with delicate blossoms and tendrils rises to a height of 49 centimeters. The gemstone flowers are fantasies with blossoms made up of sapphire, ruby, topaz, garnet, amethyst, hyacinth, and turquoise as well as agate moonstone, peridot, and other rich minerals. Delicate silver stems carry the colorful blooms toward the light. An enthusiastic observer described the precious object thusly: "The diamond sparkles, the topaz, shaped into small sun-

The Louvre in Paris contains an exquisite mirror (height 40 cm) decorated with jewels that probably belonged to Marie de Medicis (1573–1642). She married the King Henry IV of France in 1600. The mirror has a gable-shaped top of agate-onyx, the two pillars on either side are of gray jasper. Two heads made of garnet, decorated with enameled gold, rest on large emeralds.

flowers, radiates a golden shimmer like a sunset, the emerald shines between them, green as an Alpine stream, the dark lilac amethyst is transformed into a modest violet ...." The admirer goes on to compare the turquoises in the bouquet – forget-me-nots – with the "Resl's bright, sky-blue eyes." In his interpretation, the garnets and rubies take on the role of "roses of love" from which this bouquet arose.

However, the goldsmith and court jeweler Johann Michael Grosser had the major problem of how to design the leaves at that time. What material could be used? He thought silver foil would be "too hard and too stiff." He therefore cut delicate pinnate leaves from white parchment. What appears, at first glance, to be a stylistic incongruity – precious minerals, precious metal, and paper! – turned out to be, after enlivening the brittle material with multiple pleatings and shaping, a true stroke of genius: what colors and light were able to provide the gemstones with as an illusion of reality was underscored and perfected with the leaves and panicles in their apparently static motion. But Grosser the artist was still not satisfied. He enlivened his masterpiece still further with all sorts of insects that were positioned between the leaves and flowers. From gemstones and pearls, he created the blossoms' natural visitors: bee, wasp, dragonfly, beetle, and fly. If you listen closely in a quiet moment, you can almost hear the whirring and buzzing, up and down – just like in a daydream.

The Sardonyx of Schaffhausen

In the Swiss city of Schaffhausen, the All Saints Museum is home to one of the most precious cameos of antiquity. This jewel is an oval cameo carved from three layers of sardonyx and depicts a woman. This unique piece of work was created by the gem cutter Hyllos (a son of Dioscourides) and dates from the time of Caesar Augustus. On the back of the cameo, an engraved silver relief depicts the likeness of a falconer. On the basis of the marginal inscription "Comitis Ludiwici de Vroburg," the jewel is identified as being owned by or being a gift given to a Froburg count of this name (cf., Walter Ulrich Guyan, *Schaffhausen–Schätze der Region*, 1987).

The cameo framework (78 mm by 95 mm) dates from the late Middle Ages. It is a gold mount richly set with gemstones and pearls. This magnificent framework was created in the area of the Upper Rhine, sometime between 1230 and 1240. The work of art is 15 centimeters high and 12.5 centimeters wide and is embossed, engraved, punched, and cast from gold. Embossed, engraved niello silver foil was also used.

This antique cameo is one of the most superb testimonies to the art of gem cutting. It shows a young woman in a standing position, leaning on a pillar and, in three-quarter view, turning to the right. In her left hand, the woman is holding a horn of plenty (containing pomegranates, grapes, and a lotus blossom) decorated with a delicate tendril and, in her left hand, she is holding the divine staff of Mercury with the sacred ribbons. The necklace (a capsule, or "bulla" as it was called), a garland of corn ears and olive leaves show that it is not a goddess portrayed

This uniquely beautiful gemstone bouquet (height 49 cm) was presented by Empress Maria Theresa in 1760 to her bridegroom and later husband Franz Stephan of Lorraine as a betrothal gift. As a surprise, the bejeweled bouquet appeared one morning in the imperial mineral collection. Approximately 1,500 diamonds and 1,300 color gems (among these, rubies, sapphires, emeralds, topazes, peridots, hyacinths, garnets, opals, and turquoises) were incorporated into a magical flowery work of art by goldsmith Johann Michael Grosser. Secular Treasury, Vienna.

here, but a member of the imperial Augustan house who is being honored by her depiction as the "goddess of peace" (according to Albert Knöpfli). Various researchers suspect that this woman was Livia, the wife of Caesar Augustus who died in the year 29 A.D. or perhaps his granddaughter Livilla (who died in 43 A.D.), the wife of Drusus, who is depicted as the bringer of good luck (Felicitas) after the birth of their twins.

The cameo cutter used the color layers in the sardonyx in exemplary fashion for this work – the velvet brown uppermost layer for the cloak, the horn of plenty, and the garland. However, the face, the upper body clad in a *chiton* (working garment made of linen or wool) as well as the fabric pooling around the feet "are in the bluish white of chalcedony" (W. U. Guyan). A third, black-reddish layer serves as a background for the female figure. From inside to outside, the oval frame is comprised of a bluish-white, a red-brown, and a brown-black layer.

This valuable antique gem has a setting that corresponds to its importance in a unique way. The cameo is contained in a wreath of leaves that is surrounded by a triple wreath of high set gemstones and pearls. The inner wreath is made up of sixteen sapphires and sixteen turquoises and the middle one of sixteen garnets between sixteen golden eagles (the bodies of the birds are individually embossed and punched, whereas the heads are cast). The outermost wreath is decorated with four large gemstones – a garnet at the top, a sapphire to left and right. The lower gem has been added. In addition, four large pearls (in settings) that are surrounded by small leaves as well as eight blue labradorites form the framework to the sardonyx. Between the gemstones and pearls, sixteen gold lions appear in the outer wreath with their heads turned, like those of the eagles, to face outward.

"The contrast between the virtuoso goldsmith work and the natural products, i. e., between the gleaming gold and the colorful gems is typical of the fashion jewelry in the Middle Ages" (W. U. Guyan).

The lions and eagles strengthen the assumption that a Froburg count was the patron of this work of art. Among the counts of Froburg in the thirteenth century, there were two with the name of Ludwig. Ludwig III is documented between 1201 and 1259. Together with his brother Hermann, he appears several times in the retinue of Emperor Frederick II in Italy. Ludwig IV appears in documents from 1240 onward; he died in 1279. Both counts in the Froburg family could have been the owners of this jeweled work of art. The relief on the reverse, however, points more to the time of Ludwig III in terms of style. According to Walter Ulrich Guyan: "The former director of the Germanic Museum in Nuremberg has determined that the setting of the gemstones dates from the same period as the plate portraying a knight–Count Ludwig IV himself." The lions that appear in the surrounding frame indicate the coat of arms of the Froburg counts, which was decorated with a lion. The eagles, however, could be reminiscent of the House of Hapsburg, whose coat of arms bears an eagle. These indications strengthen the assumption that Ludwig IV of the Froburg family was the owner and patron of the work of art; his mother was a member of the Hapsburg family.

One of the most precious cameos of antiquity is the *Sardonyx of Schaffhausen*. This gemstone is a cameo cut from a three-layer sardonyx and depicts a woman. The emperor's wife, Livia, who died in 29 A.D.), was probably the model for this work by the famous Roman gem cutter Hyllos (he worked in Rome at the time of Caesar Augustus). She is represented as the "Goddess of Peace." All Saints Museum, Schaffhausen (cf., illustration on page 217).

Until the middle of the nineteenth century, people were of the opinion that the precious sardonyx was from the Burgundy spoils. The Lucerne historian Theodor von Liebenau pointed out in a contribution to the *Allgemeine Schweizerzeitung* in 1881 that this jewel originated from the Paradies convent (on the left bank of the River Rhine). When the convent of nuns was closed down during the Reformation, the ruling, mostly Catholic "eight old places" claimed the right to Thurgau's ownership of the convent. The city of Schaffhausen, however, had already taken over the convent treasure. The "onyx" thus appears on the city's 1619 list of possessions and income and also in the treasury book of 1660 as *Unichel* (German version of the word "onyx"). The original owner, however, was Count Ludwig II of Froburg and the jewel was handed down to his successor Ludwig IV. The star of the Froburg family, once an influential and powerful line of counts, was already sinking. The only daughter of Ludwig IV entered the Paradies convent as a widow in 1279 where she died in 1281. She had probably received the "onyx" in its magnificent setting from her father as a gift and had taken it with her into the convent. W. U. Guyan (as above) assumes that the superb piece served as a brooch "to decorate the ceremonial robe of the abbess."

The Diamond Clasp with the *Dresden Green*

The *Dresden Green* is the largest green diamond in the world. It forms part of the crown jewels of Saxony and is housed in the *"Grünes Gewölbe"* (Green Vault) in Dresden.

The radiant apple-green, pear-shaped diamond weighs 40.7 carats and has an almost surrealistic history. It came into the possession of Frederick Augustus II, Elector of Saxony (as king of Poland: Augustus III) in 1742. He was the only legitimate son of Augustus the Strong.

The sale to the ruler of Saxony was made during the Leipzig fair. A gemstone trader from the Netherlands showed Frederick Augustus the unparalleled diamond. A gem in that color and of that size was completely unknown at that time. The Elector of Saxony reached an agreement with the Dutchman and paid 200,000 talers for the green diamond – an enormous sum at the time.

Diamonds were first found in Brazil at the start of the eighteenth century. By then, Amsterdam had been a center of diamond cutting and diamond trading for over a century. After the discovery of diamonds in Brazil, a large number of Brazilian raw diamonds found their way to the Netherlands for cutting; possibly the *Dresden Green* was among them. Since the seller of the jewel was Dutch – not an Oriental or a Turk, who, as diamond traders, also did business at the Leipzig fair – this assumption would appear to be correct (cf., *Edelsteine*, Friedrich Sommer and Dr. Werner Böttger, 1992).

After Elector Frederick Augustus II acquired the green gem, it took a further quarter of a century before his heir and successor had the large green diamond, together with selected and precious white diamonds, turned into a clasp in 1768.

The largest green diamond in the world is the *Green Dresden* (40.7 carats). It shines out from a wealth of diamonds cut in a variety of styles. The gemstones are grouped as a clasp of brilliant-cut diamonds. This forms part of the crown jewels of Saxony. The *Green Dresden* was first examined scientifically by gemologists G. Bosshart (then at the SSEF gemstone laboratory in

Zurich) and R. Kane (at that time, at the GIA, Santa Monica, California, USA), whereby the authenticity of the very rare green color was confirmed. *Grünes Gewölbe* (Green Vault), Dresden.

199

The Dagger, the Moor, and the Throne of the Czars

Green is the color of the prophet. The Turkish sultans therefore had a predilection for green gems, particularly emeralds. The treasury of the Topkapi Palace Museum in Istanbul houses an enormous number of deep green emeralds: raw gems, step-cut emeralds, numerous cut emeralds, as well as many treasures set with the green gems.

One superb work of jeweled art is the 35-centimeter long world famous dagger. The handle of the Topkapi dagger is adorned with three large, convex emeralds from Colombia. They stand out and thus make for a firm grip. The fact that these richest beryls do not originate from India but from South America demonstrates how much the sultans set great store by acquiring the finest of green gemstones.

The precious dagger was intended as a gift. It was commissioned in 1747 by Sultan Mahmud I. A clock is contained under a flip-top lid formed by a large emerald at the top of the handle. The gold sheath of the dagger is adorned with numerous diamonds and painted enamel work of exceptional precision. This unique gift was intended for a friend of the sultan's, the ruler of Persia, Nadir Shah who, after plundering Delhi, had given the sultan the gift of one of the seven precious thrones, or "throne of pearls," from his spoils. (This throne is still in the Topkapi Museum.)

On their way to deliver the dagger in Persia, the sultan's emissaries learned of the sudden death of the shah. The latter was murdered by his bodyguards in 1747. The sultan's men retraced their steps and brought the dagger back to Constantinople.

The *Grünes Gewölbe* (Green Vault) in Dresden houses the *Moor with the Emerald Druse*, as it is known. Colombian emeralds rest in their original rock and are carried in a dish by an African. The gemstones and the parent rock are apparently heavy since the "Moor is bending his head and upper body backwards in order to counterbalance the load." The precious druse with sixteen large emeralds came to Dresden in 1581 as a gift from Emperor Rudolph II to Elector Augustus of Saxony (Augustus the Strong). Despite the heavy load, the Moor is smiling, presenting the precious gems in an exquisite tortoiseshell dish. What a lucky find! A tree stump, covered in tortoiseshell, supports the dish. The Moor's jewelry (gilded silver with a large number of gemstones) originates from the workshop of Johann Melchior Dinglinger (1664–1731) from Biberach on the River Riss (Germany). The tortoiseshell dish and the tortoiseshell covering were the work of the "court ivory and amber worker," Wilhelm Krüger. The wooden statuette itself (height: 63.8 cm) is ascribed to Balthasar Permoser.

The collection of old czar thrones in the armory of the Kremlin also contains the gold throne of Czar Boris Godunov (around 1550–1551). It has a wooden core covered with gold leaf. Countless gemstones, mainly turquoises, decorate the sovereign's chair. Documents from the seventeenth century confirm (cf., K. W. Donava and L. W. Pissarskaya, *Die Rüstkammer des Kreml in Moskau*) that the throne was given to Czar Boris Godunov by the Persian ruler, Shah Abbas I.

Above: The *Moor with the Emerald Druse* owes its existence to a gift: the "philosopher on the German Empire throne," Rudolph II (he reigned from 1576 until 1612) honored the Elector of Saxony in 1581 with a mineral specimen containing sixteen large emeralds. In 1724, the king of Saxony at that time commissioned the figure of a Moor to support the emerald druse (height of the statuette 63.8 cm). *Grünes Gewölbe* (Green Vault), Dresden.

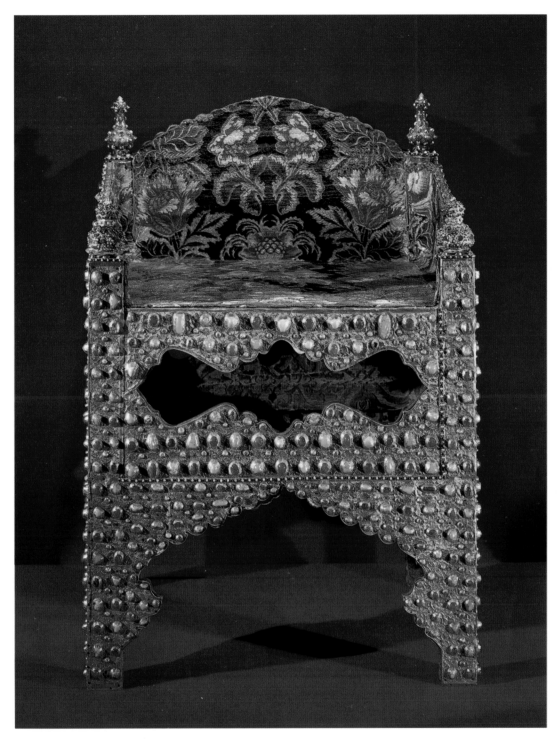

Below: Three large emeralds from Colombia are the prominent jeweled features of an extremely valuable dagger sheath and its handle, which is also decorated with diamonds and enamel decoration. The 35 centimeter long *Topkapi dagger* was intended as a gift: Sultan Mahmud I commissioned it to honor the Persian ruler, Nadir Shah, as a reciprocal gift for the magnificent "throne of pearls." For tragic reasons, the gift was never delivered. Topkapi Palace Museum, Istanbul.

Above: The golden throne of Czar Boris Godunov (around 1552 until 1605) is made of a wooden core covered with gold leaf. Countless gemstones (mainly turquoises) decorate the costly chair, which was given to the czar as a gift by the Persian ruler, Shah Abbas I, in 1604. The throne is Persian work from the period before the end of the sixteenth century. Kremlin Treasury, Moscow.

Three rings from ancient Egypt capture the development of the signet ring.
Top: Cut signet stone on thin gold wire.
Center: The wire has been replaced by a solid band.
Bottom: This ring was cast and only differs from a present-day signet ring in the signature on the signet plate.

OF SEALS, AMULETS, AND TALISMANS

Who has ever counted the magnificent works? Who has ever counted the admiring and covetous glances drawn by timeless jewels? Humans have always admired and coveted famous jeweled works of art even if there was little chance of ever owning them. Just as are people, jewels are "children of Mother Earth." And if you think of the primary matter, of atoms and molecules, then they are all creations of the universe: humans and gemstones, each in their own way, are the highlights of phases in creation.

One's "own gemstone" has been a reality since time immemorial. It is often the most precious part of a ring. Rings were known in the Neolithic period – made of bones, still without decoration, but probably a token of rank. In the Stone Age, there were rings of stone, amber, and metal (gold, silver, copper) and, in the Bronze Age, bronze was the most important material. Precious metals were also the objects of artistic endeavor.

The Seal: Older Than the Art of Writing

The seal is considered to be "older than the art of writing." Seals were already in use at the end of the fourth century B.C. in the ancient Orient for the acknowledgment and confirmation of an agreement or for proof of ownership. The seal had the position of a personal signature. The seal stamp was an important utensil that its owner always had to carry on his person so that it did not fall into the unauthorized hands of others. The best way to ensure such security was for the owner of a seal to wear it on his finger as a signet ring.

Prometheus, the Mythical Ring Wearer

According to Greek mythology, Prometheus was the first mythological wearer of a ring. As an enemy of the gods and a friend of humans (he stole the fire from Mount Olympus for them), he earned the wrath of Zeus, the king of the gods. Zeus had him chained to a rock face on the highest peak in the Caucasus Mountains by Hephaestus. Every morning, an eagle ripped open the stomach of the chained god and fed on his liver. The wounds were always healed by the next morning and the liver restored. The torture would begin again. One day, however, Hercules appeared in the area on his way to secure the golden apples. He espied the eagle sitting on Prometheus's knees and killed him with an unfailing arrow. Zeus pardoned the chained Prometheus because his own son, Hercules, had delivered him from his terrible fate. However, the father of the gods ordered Prometheus "to wear for the rest of his life a ring forged out of iron" on his finger, with a stone from that rock face in the Caucasus. In this way, the act of being chained would continue, albeit symbolically. Prometheus had brought fire to earth, the old Roman god of fire Vulcan (a "colleague" of Hephaestus) "forged" the first diamonds in his legendary, blazing smith's hearth!

The Shiny Egyptian Beetle

In ancient Egypt, the wearing of rings during the Middle Kingdom (after 1990 B.C., start of the twelfth dynasty) and in the New Kingdom, starting with Tuthmosis I, (1515–1493 B.C., eighteenth dynasty) has been proved, particularly in the shape of a signet ring. Under the pharaohs, the "shiny Egyptian beetles," set in gold, appeared on the rings. A "beetle" with the name of scarab was still an important decorative stone in men's rings in ancient Greece. The scarab is a dung beetle, the female of which species lays her eggs in the pill-shaped balls of dung that the male makes. The mysterious birth of this beetle from balls of dung made it well respected among the ancient Egyptians; it was considered to be an "original being." They saw in it a form of the sun god. Since the Middle Kingdom, the seal stones took the shape of this holy

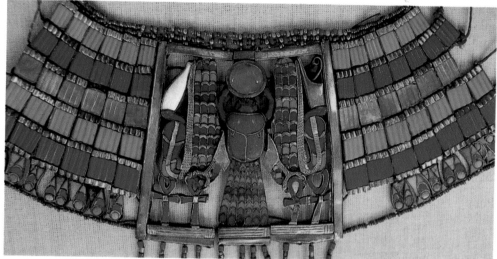

beetle – the scarab. The ancient Egyptian seal stamp was composed of glazed stone, precious metal, or gemstones. The base bore the names of rulers or important persons, but sometimes only the figures of gods, symbols, or ornaments. The scarabs were not just set into rings, however, but also into other items of jewelry. Their function as a seal increasingly became of secondary importance as the scarabs took on a new meaning as amulets to ward off harm (evil spirits!). Gemstones at that time, as at all times, awoke magic notions. The scarab motif frequently appears in olivines (particularly in peridots) processed by gem cutters. One scarab fashioned in lapis lazuli became famous. On his Egyptian campaign, Napoleon carried one of these decorative stones, which he had had removed from a pharaoh's tomb. Napoleon later gave the ring with this stone on a festive occasion to the wife of Prince Schwarzenberg, the Austrian envoy in Paris. The valuable jewel is still in the possession of the Schwarzenberg family.

Egyptian papyruses mention many gemstones. Along with unknown names, there are repeat mentions of lapis lazuli, malachite, and jasper. In a hymn to the god Osiris, the words say: "You are the one with limbs of gold, a head of lapis lazuli and a crown of malachite." Since the New Kingdom, signet rings with an engraved plate were also known in Egypt.

Ancient Egyptian jewelry with scarabs.
Top right: A splendid ring-shaped bracelet. An onyx cabochon is surrounded by garnets and amethysts.
Left: A signet ring from the time of Tutankhamen (eighteenth dynasty, 1387–1346 B.C.). The gold signet ring bears a cartouche of a name. Rockefeller Museum, Jerusalem.
Above: Neck adornment with scarab (Tutankhamen Museum, Cairo). Photo: Oskar Baumli, Meggen, Switzerland.

Above: Signet ring of the Roman Emperor Augustus (63 B.C.–14 A.D.). It is a black onyx cameo with a sphinx.

The Gemma Augustea

The art of gem cutting in Greece was influenced by the Egyptians for a long time. As the Greek writer and historian Herodotus (490 B.C., died around 425–420 B.C.) reports, cameos and seal cylinders were also known in Babylon: every distinguished man wore a signet ring there.

In the meantime, Greek gem cutters took their artistry into the Roman Empire. The center of their creative work was first the port of Alexandria, where a large colony of Greek artists existed. Around the year 12 A.D., the famous gem cutter Dioscourides created the *Gemma Augustea* with the likeness of Caesar Augustus there. According to Hermann Hild, "The Roman Octavian, when Caesar had the name 'Augustus,' the sublime, accepted and used as a seal a cameo portraying a sphinx as long as he still fought for power and he had to give the appearance of a Republican. When he had subjugated Cleopatra's Egypt and the Near East, he sealed with the likeness of Alexander the Great, with whom he could be ranked .... Afterward, as the unchallenged ruler over the world as it was known at that time, he used his own likeness as a seal with the cameo of Dioscourides."

The Emperor Nero (37–68 A.D., emperor 54–68 A.D.) was a great enthusiast of gemstones. It is said that, since he was short-sighted, as well as not to be dazzled, he viewed gladiator fights in the arena through a monocle made from an emerald.

The Romans' greed for gemstones produced some odd quirks, as is demonstrated by the story of Senator Nonius. He was put on a list of enemies to be disposed of (proscription list) by Antonius (who, together with Octavian, later known as Augustus, and Lepidus was a triumvir) simply because of the fact that Nonius owned a magnificent opal. According to another version, more favorable to Antonius, an opal the size of a hazelnut that belonged to Senator Nonius, was to have been the pledge of his love for Cleopatra. Nonius took the gem into exile with him for fear of possible consequences. The opal has been considered as the bringer of bad luck until more recent times. Perhaps the fate of Senator Nonius was the trigger for this idea. However, opals mostly brought "bad luck" to the gem cutters and ring setters. They had to replace the value of the fragile gemstones if they broke during processing.

The fact that demand for precious minerals was high in Rome is documented by Pliny the Elder, the great naturalist, who summarized the natural history of his time in his work *Naturalis Historia*, and who was killed in 79 A.D. when Vesuvius erupted. Pliny criticized the fact that fake gemstones were being produced by putting foils under them and substituting normal glass.

In the time of popular migration as well as in the early Middle Ages, the goldsmiths continued the antique shapes. The ring had great importance as a love token: in the thirteenth century rings with words of love were in existence. The bands of the rings sometimes closed with two interlinked hands. Convex gems served as ring decoration until the end of the Middle Ages. High gemstone settings became the fashion. The rings became more solid and heavier in design. In the upper middle

classes, signet rings with cameos were very popular. The rings of worldly and religious dignitaries were of great value. The papal rings from the fifteenth and sixteenth centuries count among the rings of honor and status, made of gilded bronze, with gemstone decoration and portrayals of the papal insignia (key of St. Peter and tiara) and symbols of the Evangelists. However, it is unclear whether these were actually the rings of the popes as a symbol of their honor and investiture or mementos for pilgrims to Rome. One papal ring is the pope's signet ring, the so-called fisherman's ring. According to church law, the bishops also wear a ring on their blessing hand.

The Magic Power of the Circle

The importance of rings in popular beliefs and religion is said to be based on the "binding magical power of the circle" (protective function). For example, engagement and wedding rings are a symbol of this binding or bond. From a very early date, rings were considered to be symbols of special power. In fairy tales and legends, they master demons and, as rings with gemstones, they have defensive powers. For example, they ward off the evil eye. The ring also serves its wearer as an amulet, and, with particular gems, it protects against physical and mental suffering. Gemstones in rings also had the function of talismans. They became strength-giving, active bringers of good luck. In the case of Johann Wolfgang von Goethe (*Westöstlicher Diwan*; "West-Eastern Divan"), "cut gems" were considered to be talismans. The term *talisman* has been in use in the English-speaking world since the seventeenth century. Talismans, particularly precious, radiant gems, however, are also considered to be "accumulators of extraterrestrial radiation powers."

The Talisman of Charlemagne

The two sapphires of Charlemagne form a famous talisman, but not set in a ring. Two convex, blue corundums with flat undersides are put together. Between the two gemstones is a small piece of wood "from the true Cross of Christ." This jewel can be seen in Reims.

Rings are also a symbol of authority. Abbots, bishops, cardinals, and popes wear gold rings decorated with gemstones on the fourth finger of their blessing hand. In the case of bishops, the gems are frequently dark purple amethysts, whereas cardinals have sapphires. Church law also permits the wearing of rings for Doctors of Theology. Pope John XXIII wore a particularly beautiful ring on his right hand. It had a large round opal surrounded by diamonds.

The Duke's Ring and the Ring of Paracelsus

Let us now look at two rings from the Middle Ages that are connected with high-ranking or famous persons. The first ring is the oldest verifiable item preserved in the Vienna Secular Treasury. It is a ring cut out of sapphire. The owner of this precious jewel was the Hapsburg Duke Ernst the Iron (1377–1424), the son of Duke Leopold of Austria who fell at the battle of Sempach (1386) and the father of Emperor Frederick III (1415–1493).

The ring of a great scholar, Philippus Theophrastus von Hohenheim, named Paracelsus (born 1493 in Einsiedeln, Switzerland, died in 1541 in Salzburg, Austria), still puzzles his adherents. When Paracelsus (by nationality, a Swiss) died in the fall of 1541 in Salzburg, the city compiled an inventory of his estate. This was of little importance; the most valuable item was "a silver goblet with lion's feet," which the abbot's envoy from the Einsiedeln convent took as a "death matter" back to Einsiedeln, since the master of a serf had the right to the best of his

The talisman of Charlemagne (who reigned from 800 to 814) originally contained a relic consisting of hair of the Mother of God held between two sapphire cabochons. In 1804, the Virgin Mary relic was exchanged for "a piece of the true Cross of Christ." A lighter, blue glass flow replaced the front sapphire cabochon. The relic of the Cross was supposed to be more visible that way. Garnets, Baroque pearls, and emeralds decorate the gold frame of the relic jewel front and back. Emperor Charles was wearing the hair relic (height 7.3 cm; width 6.5 cm) on a chain around his neck when his tomb was opened (1166). Treasury of Reims Cathedral.

estate. (Paracelsus had been a serf, a bondsman, of the Einsiedeln convent since his mother had been a "woman of the house of God" and, in the Middle Ages, the child always followed the distaff side.)

However, the inventory also mentioned two rings: a gold one (gilded?) with a topaz (more likely to be brownish quartz) and a second one with a molten blue stone. According to a comment (footnote) by Prof. Dr. Ildefons Betschart, Benedictine father from Einsiedeln and Professor at the Theological Faculty in Salzburg (vgl. P. Ildefons Betschart, *Theophrastus Paracelsus*, 1942), the actor Johannes Steiner (St. Gallen civic theater) acquired an iron ring that showed traces of former gilding from a Dresden antique dealer before the Second World War. A coat of arms was cut into the brownish gem: three balls in a rising bar – the coat of arms of the counts of Hohenheim. The somewhat baroque frame of the coat of arms bore the Maltese cross as decoration. Did a relative of Paracelsus, Count Georg von Hohenheim have the family coat of arms engraved in the stone? This question remains unsolved to this day.

However, we mainly owe a debt of gratitude to Paracelsus for his philosophical insight into the nature of gemstones. In his theory of principles, he contrasted the maternal principle – this lives in the elements – with another principle, namely that which "grows" within the mother: the fruit of the elements. Basic substances are sal, sulfur, and mercury, not simply "salt," "brimstone," and "quicksilver," however, but what these elements symbolize. "So many types of fruit of the elements," according to Paracelsus, "so many types of sulfur, sal and also mercury. A different sulfur is in gold, another one in silver, another in iron, another in lead … as is another in the sapphire, another in the emerald, another in the ruby, cryolites, amethysts, etc. And not just so many different types of sulfur, but also so many different types of sal. The same is true for the mercuries." (quoted according to Hermann Hild, as above). From the lap of the "four mothers"–the elements of fire, water, light, and earth – sal, sulfur, and mercury emerge as the *ultima materia*. Whatever lives in the stones is a *quinta essentia* – a final reality – the *arcanum*, which humans should take care of and use.

In every age, humans have also endeavored to gain happiness from gemstones and the possibility of alleviating his or her frequently unhappy lot in life with the help of these precious stones. The powers that gemstones are thought to hold are the products of popular imagination and desires that originate in the major needs and hardships of many. Gemstones are the pledge of helpful powers. Paracelsus also wished to alleviate people's lot in life – by putting the focus on the creative powers of nature. His theory of minerals perceives a symbol of the original creative power of nature in minerals and precious stones. Whoever went "under the stone," "received the protection of the one who had created him."

Does this explain the development of pomp and splendor in emperors' crowns, popes' crowns, scepters and sovereigns' robes? Covered with superb precious minerals, they were intended to guarantee good fortune, health, and well-being.

Below: Bishop's ring from the first third of the twelfth century. The gold ring with a sapphire was found in the tomb of the archbishop of Trier, Albero Montreuil (held office from 1131 until 1152). Albero managed to have Conrad III von Staufen elected as the German king in 1138. Trier Cathedral treasury.

Above: Bishop's ring with beryl and diamonds (red gold, 585). The oval, faceted beryl (variety: heliodor) weighs 3.5 carats. The gem is surrounded by sixteen diamond roses (total weight 1.0 carat). Each side of the ring mounting has a cross featuring a diamond rose. Privately owned.

Stones of the month – Birthstones

Gemstones are the "tears of heaven," or "supernatural drops of blood" if the flowery formulations of older poets are to be believed. Gemstones are also "gentle promises," "promises and temptations from the world of fairies and fairy tales" as sagas and traditions handed down through many centuries and many different cultures repeatedly report. One of

Capricorn–January: GARNET

Aquarius–February: AMETHYST

Pisces–March: AQUAMARINE

Cancer–July: RUBY

Leo–August: PERIDOT

Virgo–September: SAPPHIRE

these definitely applies to gemstones, however: unparalleled, irrefutable proofs and reminders of the glowing prehistoric times of our Mother Earth, of the "magma of creation," whose formative power and richness of life they seem to forever encapsulate in their highly faceted sparkle and glow.

Gemstones are a magnificent testimony to our own existence and misdemeanors, our human fate. They gleam and sparkle now just as they did millions of years ago – human gem-cutting skills have only creatively released this gleam and fire and made it available to us all.

Evidence of Eternal Change

The ancient peoples of Mesopotamia drew parallels between the many colors of gemstones on earth with the wondrous celestial lights and therefore assigned specific jewels to the individual planets of the sun. To them earthly existence and misdemeanors were indivisibly linked with the passage of the stars and the magic reflection of the heavenly gleam in their decorative objects and jewels. Our present-day "stones of the month" are said to date from these early times, and, although they no longer reflect any earth-shaking forces, they still provide evi-

Aries–April: DIAMOND

Taurus–May: EMERALD

Gemini–June: MOONSTONE

Libra–October: TOURMALINE

Scorpio–November: TOPAZ

Sagittarius–December: TURQUOISE

dence of the eternal change in time and the dumb persistence of the world within it. Nowadays, this is no longer in the sense of a universal good or evil, but only as individual memories of the wholly personal existence and growth of a specific person. "Birthstones" are what the stones of the month have now become. They make select and beautiful gifts, which suggest no other intention than giving pleasure. However, a gemstone can belong to a person to the extent that a magic relationship develops. The gem becomes a healing stone, because its wearer wants it to be so.

Garnet
January's Gem, Zodiac Sign: Capricorn

The garnet, the gemstone for the month of January (zodiac sign: Capricorn), is not considered to be particularly valuable because it is so widespread. People who hold this opinion, however, are apparently not so well acquainted with the varied world of garnets. The fact is that there is hardly any other family of gemstones that unites such a broad spectrum both in terms of luster and color, as well as rarity and size of widely varying gemstones, for example, the red garnets rhodolite, almandine, and pyrope, but also the precious green uvarovite from the Urals, which is an almost priceless gemstone due to the fact that it only forms fairly large crystals.

Aquamarine
March's Gem, Zodiac Sign: Pisces

Those born in the month of March, under the zodiac sign of Pisces, can choose between two birthstones, since the spring moon has both the magical, sea-blue aquamarine and the heliotrope, much admired by the Babylonians, Arabs, and Egyptians. The heliotrope, this dark green chalcedony with blood-red sprinkles, is the "men's stone" for March since it mostly decorates men's hands. Because of its composition, it is frequently used as a gem for rings bearing coats of arms or signet rings.
The "ladies' stone" of this spring month, however – the aquamarine (the "green of the sea") – has several world-famous brothers such as the wonderful green emerald and the delicate peach blossom or cyclamen-colored morganite.

Emerald
May's Gem, Zodiac Sign: Taurus

The emerald is the gemstone for those born in May (zodiac sign: Taurus) and was undoubtedly held in great respect in ancient Rome. Pliny the Elder, the Roman naturalist (23–79 A.D.), studied the "green gemstone." In his opinion, the green of the emerald was the most beneficial of all green color shades. It was also Pliny who assigned the emerald to the beryls, while others of his time tended to think of emerald as a family of its own. The fact that Pliny was correct was only established in the nineteenth century. Julius Caesar collected rare emeralds as remedies. A particularly valuable emerald weighing 225 carats and bearing the engraved portrait of the Julius Caesar is now in the United States.

Amethyst
February's Gem, Zodiac Sign: Aquarius

The amethyst is February's gemstone (zodiac sign: Aquarius). It owes its name to its wine-red color: "amethyst" comes from the Greek verb *amethyein*, which means "not being drunken." The Greeks' idea that the stone can protect its owner from insobriety is associated with the belief that by wearing the gemstone of the god Bacchus, one would also have the power of this god over the wine and thus be immune to drunkenness. Greater importance was later attached to protection against passion: people hoped that by wearing an amethyst ring, they would be able to control their own boiling blood.

Diamond
April's Gem, Zodiac Sign: Aries

The Indians call April's stone (zodiac sign: Aries) a "fragment of eternity." When looking at a sparkling diamond, radiating its luster like a miniature sun, we rarely recall how much suffering and pain has been linked with this enchanting jewel over the course of history. The lustrous beauty of diamonds banishes many a dark moment and its preciousness causes a lot of shadows to be forgotten. When linked with the diamond, precious and superb gemstones become even more beautiful and valuable. Beauty and value are also the two characteristics that have caused this gemstone to be considered the finest of all jewels in popular opinion.

Moonstone
June's Gem, Zodiac Sign: Gemini

June (zodiac sign: Gemini) has two birthstones: the moonstone and alexandrite. In addition, it has the pearl, which is not a gemstone. The pearl is our oldest jewel: It was formerly found on beaches by hunter-gatherers when searching for food. A small, inconspicuous little ball that was thrown away or kept for pleasure. Even today, a glance at an exquisite pearl either creates enchantment or rejection, which does not necessarily mean the lack of a sense of beauty.
According to reports, the famous "moonstone temple," Anuradhapura, dating from around 1100 B.C. is said to have had altar steps that were decorated with magnificent moonstone mosaics. Moonstones vary in color from dull gray to clear as spring water, silvery shimmering white.

Ruby
July's Gem, Zodiac Sign: Cancer

Ruby (from the Latin *ruber* [red]) is the birthstone for July (zodiac sign: Cancer). Its sparkling shades of red, under a shiny, lacquerlike surface, make it the quintessential color gem. It is difficult to think of any color gem to rival the ruby's supremacy. Edward Streeter, the great gemstone connoisseur, awarded the ruby second place, after the pearl, and ranked it higher than a diamond. Queen Alexandra, the daughter-in-law of Queen Victoria, was a famous devotee of rubies. She had Victoria's precious opal jewelry reworked with the iridescent opals replaced by fiery red rubies.

Sapphire
September's Gem, Zodiac Sign: Virgo

The gemstone for those born under the sign of Virgo is sapphire. "Sapphire blue," however, is not a designation that can even begin to describe the color character of this superb mineral with any precision. A sapphire is not simply "blue" if it is blue at all (since there are also red, green, yellow, brown, violet, white, and orange-colored sapphires!). It has such a wealth of blue shades and color tints that it is impossible to pin it down to one specific blue or "sapphire blue." In his *Anatomy of Melancholy* (1621), Robert Burton wrote as follows about the sapphire: "It is the most cheerful of all gemstones. It frees the spirit and creates well-being."

Topaz, Citrine
November's Gem, Zodiac Sign: Scorpio

The topaz, "red-gold like the autumnal leaves," is the birthstone for the month of November (zodiac sign: Scorpio). Even if is not as valuable as some of its equally colored cousins, in its most exquisite versions it is still a thoroughly valuable and elegant "drop of heavenly gold" and has repeatedly inspired belletrists and poets to make flowery comparisons: "I compare its gold to cut topazes" was how a student in bacchanalian mood praised the golden yellow wine of the Rhinegau.
And, as literature and saga report, also the "heavenly honey," the nectar of the blessed, is said to be contained in the color of the topaz. This was also the reason for such confusing designations as "golden topaz" or "honey topaz" being used.

Peridot, Chrysoprase
August's Gem, Zodiac Sign: Leo

It shimmers "like damp moss," the green gemstone of August: peridot – the gem for those born under the sign of Leo. The island of Zabargad (St. John) in the Red Sea, where the ancient Egyptians first carved it out of the rock, is also green. They knew it only by the name of "topazion." This name is attributable to the fact that the island of Zabargad was frequently enveloped in fog and people were lucky if they were able to "guess" the island's location (Greek *topazein* [to guess, assume]).
Peridot was also given the name of "seaman's emerald" since seafarers had brought it as a valuable gift to Europe.

Tourmaline, Opal
October's Gem, Zodiac Sign: Libra

Tourmaline, the birthstone for October, has been documented in the Netherlands since 1703: the Dutch seafarers called it *Aschentrekker* (ash-pullers) because they could draw out the ash in their clay pipes with the electrostatically charged gemstone.
One famous owner of a tourmaline was the inventor of the lightning conductor, Benjamin Franklin (1706–1790). Intensely interested in electrostatic phenomena, he thought the tourmaline was an exceptionally interesting gem. The poles of this jewel can actually be charged electrically just by warming it to human body temperature. In order to study this property, Franklin had a tourmaline set freely movable in a ring so that he could turn the negative or positive uppermost at will.

Turquoise
December's Gem, Zodiac Sign: Sagittarius

The birthstone for those born in December (zodiac sign: Sagittarius) is called "pierre turquoise" in France. This designation could lead one to assume that the turquoise has something to do with Turkey or the Turks. This assumption is incorrect: The turquoise originates from Persia. The blue gem is called *ferozah* in the language of its country of origin. In France, however, it has kept its erroneous designation up to the present day. The opaque turquoise is the only ornamental stone beside angel's skin coral to assure itself a place, cut in cabochon form, in goldsmith work along with sapphires, rubies, and diamonds. Mab Wilson, the eminent gemstone connoisseur, praised the turquoise as the "gem of the archaic smile" (cf., Hermann Hild, *Glanz und Geheimnis edler Steine*, Saarbrücken 1963).

Above: The breastplate of the high priest of the Jews. Twelve gemstones symbolize the twelve tribes of Israel.

Increasing Individuality

The age-old question of which gems suit which people, or which gemstone above all others corresponds to a particular character has lost none of its importance over the last seven thousand years. (In Rudolf Steiner's anthroposophy, attempts were repeatedly made to answer this ancient question and to find individual answers to it.) Although magic has lost its power for many people, the increasing individuality has rediscovered and reevaluated the special nature of the small treasures from ancient times. Thus, the blue turquoise has become the "young girl's gem," and the deep red-violet amethyst has become the "stone of the spirit and superiority" (bishops' rings!). Random gemstone categorizations of this type have always made it difficult for jewelers to provide their customers with ornamental gems "which suited them." The result was a wealth and confusion of equally valid birthstone charts that a specially convened world conference of jewelers was called upon to decide which gem should be assigned to which month. However, the 1913 jewelers' convention in Kansas City (USA) was also unable to reach a decision. They allowed the different rulings to remain in place. The ancient order of the Babylonians – this was when the signs of the zodiac and birthstones first emerged – was only retained for a few gemstones. Nevertheless, some jewels such as topaz, garnet, sapphire, amethyst, and beryl, had already been assigned to specific signs of the zodiac with a certain amount of regularity for centuries. For example, along with emerald, jasper, onyx, and so forth, they had also already decorated the breastplate of the high priest of Memphis (Egypt) and the high priest of the Jews. This breastplate was decorated with twelve gems. Since the Jewish religion was monotheistic, which thus forbade planet cult, the twelve could hardly refer to the twelve signs of the zodiac. Instead, they symbolized the twelve tribes of Israel. (In Christianity, the ancient twelve gemstones were mostly associated with Christ's twelve apostles.) The following gems are assigned to the months January through December (or the relevant zodiac signs for these months):

Capricorn	December 22 – January 20	= garnet
Aquarius	January 21 – February 19	= amethyst
Pisces	February 20 – March 20	= aquamarine, blood stone (heliotrope)
Aries	March 21 – April 20	= diamond
Taurus	April 21 – May 21	= emerald
Gemini	May 21 – June 21	= pearl, alexandrite, moonstone
Cancer	June 22 – July 22	= ruby
Leo	July 23 – August 23	= peridot
Virgo	August 24 – September 23	= sapphire
Libra	September 24 – October 23	= opal, tourmaline
Scorpio	October 24 – November 22	= topaz, citrine
Sagittarius	November 23 – December 21	= turquoise, zircon

212

213

Gemstone Medicine

Ancient medicinal scientific facts were collected by Pliny the Elder and set forth in his work *Naturalis Historia*. The strange-sounding names of several gemstones indicate that foreign nations and their experiences have made their contributions to a knowledge of the healing powers of precious minerals. What the Roman natural history researcher Pliny wrote down was adopted by the Arabs. Antique knowledge, enriched with Arabian and Indian elements, was perpetuated throughout the western world of the Middle Ages. The Spanish Moors in particular acted as go-betweens.

In the Revelation to John (chapter 21, verses 19 and 20), there is mention of the heavenly Jerusalem: "The foundations of the wall of the city were adorned with every jewel; the first was jasper, the second sapphire, the third agate, the fourth emerald, the fifth sardonyx, the sixth carnelian, the seventh chrysolite, the eighth beryl, the ninth topaz, the tenth chrysoprase, the eleventh hyacinth, the twelfth amethyst." The Zurich (Switzerland) polyhistorian, doctor, natural historian, and theologian Conrad Gesner (1516–1565) was of the opinion that each of the gems mentioned in the revelation had a special *arcanum* (secret).

Jasper protects against all enemies, banishes illnesses, and renews the blood.

Sapphire provides faith and God's mercy. It protects against malevolence, envy, deceit, and sadness and renews the strength of heart and eyes. It causes resistance to "poison, pestilence and acute abscesses."

Chalcedony protects against demons and "attacks of black bile" (melancholy). It protects against melancholy and black magic.

Emerald is the safest remedy against all poisons.

Sardonyx helps against plant-based and animal poisons and melancholy is also relieved.

Carnelian provides "bold courage" and protects against evil people and poisoners. It also stills the blood.

Chrysolite helps against asthma and melancholy. It banishes demons and guards against nightmares.

Beryl strengthens the eyes and protects against unjust suspicions (the gem to counteract "mobbing").

Topaz helps when the danger of bleeding to death threatens. It also protects against sudden death.

Chrysoprase protects "against the accursed thirst for gold" (*"Vires eius tribuunt contra sacram auri situm,"* as Gesner puts it). This is reminiscent of the "accursed hunger for gold," the *auri sacra fames* of the Roman poet Ovid. Chrysoprase renews the powers of the heart and refreshes tired eyes.

Hyacinth ensures blissful sleep. It guards against the plague, assures wealth, and provides protection against lightning.

Amethyst prevents drunkenness when drinking wine. It is the gem of love and liberates the spirit.

Even in ancient times, popular medicine recommended the use of

Above: The most important natural scientist of ancient Rome, Pliny the Elder (23/24–79 A.D., killed when Vesuvius erupted), combined the natural scientific and medical knowledge of his time in his work *Naturalis Historia* (thirty-seven books) and made it accessible to all. The depiction of the scholar reproduced here dates from the Middle Ages.

gemstones, among other things as amulets. The gems were also placed on wounds and bound onto aching parts of the body. Precious minerals were pulverized and the powder was taken as a remedy. For example, in 1534, Pope Clement VII took such a powder for his fatal illness. Unfortunately, deaths repeatedly occurred after taking gemstone powder: powdered diamonds also served as recipes for suicide or the murder of unpopular persons when the diamond powder was mixed into meals. This was reported, for example, by the famous goldsmith and sculptor, Benvenuto Cellini.

Hildegard von Bingen and the Healing Gems

Hildegard von Bingen dispensed almost exclusively with gemstone powder in her gemstone remedies. The sole exception was beryl powder – as an antidote. Hildegard always used whole gemstones. They were either placed in the mouth for a while or steeped in wine, which was then consumed –naturally without the gemstone! In the case of high fever, an onyx is steeped for five days in vinegar and then removed: all the sick person's food is then spiced with this vinegar. It was believed that the power of the healing onyx is transferred to the vinegar and this would banish the "harmful juices" that caused the fever.

Gemstone medicine is currently enjoying a renaissance. St. Hildegard (she was never canonized by Rome, however) was born in 1098 in Bermersheim (now part of the district of Alzey, Germany) and died in 1179 in the Rupertsberg convent she founded near Bingen. As a young girl, she entered the convent of Disibodenberg (which ceased to exist centuries ago) and was trained there by the nun Jutta, who has been beatified in the meantime. Hildegard became the abbess in 1136 and subsequently founded the Benedictine convent in Bingen (1147/1150). She had already had visions as a child and became the first major mystic in the German-speaking area. In descriptions of her travels and extended exchanges of letters, she proved to be a sharp observer of her times. With her theological writings, particularly her books *Physica* and *Causae et Curae*, she presents descriptions of nature and mentions numerous popular remedies and methods of treatment. Her work *Scivias (Know the Ways)* is still popular today.

The important book of remedies *(Physica)* describes "the healing powers of all natural things in the sequence of the six original days of Creation" (cf., G. Hertzka and W. Strehlow: *Die Edelsteinmedizin der heiligen Hildegard*, 1985). According to Divine Creation, gemstones were created on the fourth day as "creations of light," following the creation of plants and trees on the third day of Creation. Hildegard's gemstone medicine also provides "solid instructions for medical practice," although the author describes many of the gemstones as the embodiments of cosmic moments (hour of the day, sun, halo round the sun, eclipse of the moon). The source of Hildegard's work is thought to be Bishop Marbod of Rennes (1035–1123), who had compiled a book about gemstones sixty years previously.

Above: Hildegard of Bingen Dictates H\er Visions. This miniature dates from the thirteenth century. Codex Scivias. State Library of Hessen, Wiesbaden, Germany.

"Waves" and "Rays" as Active Substances?

Hildegard's work was therefore assumed to be of visionary origin. Certain arguments would definitely corroborate this assumption. Doctors involved in gemstone medicine discovered that in the case of treatment with gemstones, it was not the slightest traces of substances that were effective, as is the case in homeopathy, but there were no substances! It was more likely "waves" and "rays" that were thought to be the effective sources. (For example, "the rhythmic effect of jasper on the heart stream.") So it is not a question of magic but something like early, natural scientific medicine.

Hildegard does not offer any "blessing" of gemstones. These are "by their very nature" hostile toward evil. In her foreword to the fourth book of the *Physica (About Gemstones)*, Hildegard writes: "Each gem has fire and dampness within it. But the Devil shuns and hates and despises gemstones because he remembers that their beauty appeared in them before he fell from the grace accorded to him by God and also because certain gemstones are created by fire in which he receives his punishment. Since, by the will of God, he was conquered by fire ...."

The Unknown "Prase"

Hildegard names the twelve stones of the secret Revelation to John in her gemstone book, but she does not make "any connection with the biblical sequence" (cf., Hertzka, Strehlow, page 12, as above). Hildegard the mystic describes the following sixteen gems: hyacinth, onyx, beryl, sardonyx, sapphire, carnelian, topaz, chrysolite, jasper, prase, chalcedony, chrysoprase, ruby, amethyst, agate, and diamond.

"Prase" has now almost disappeared totally from the gemstone trade. It is the "leek-green" gem (from the Greek *prason* [leek]) – a green variety of quartz and is related to the amethyst. The great scientist of the Middle Ages, Albertus Magnus, does not mention prase in his book on minerals. He also pays no attention to Hildegard's observations. She fails to be mentioned in his five books about minerals, although these were written a hundred years after Hildegard's book (Albertus Magnus, *De mineralibus libri V*).

The fact that the gemstone medicine of St. Hildegard could influence not only physical illnesses but also psychosomatic ones is revealed in this extract about sardonyx: "If a person carries sardonyx on his bare skin and also (still) puts it in his mouth frequently, so that his breath flows over it, takes it out and puts it in again, then his intellect and knowledge and all sensations in his body will be strengthened. Thus, great anger and stupidity and lack of discipline will be removed from this person. Because of such purity, the Devil hates and flees the sardonyx."

Gemstones convey purity and beauty; they cheer the spirit and bring happiness. "The greatest joy comes from looking at beautiful works," said the Greek philosopher Democritus (born around 460 B.C.) Friedrich von Logau (1604–1655: *Sinngedichte*) wrote: "Joy, moderation and rest/Close the door to the doctor."

Opposite: Please refer to pages 197–198 for a more detailed description.

THE FASCINATION OF INTERNAL LIFE

Sphere like web and divergent rays of silli-manite needles decorate the interior of an andalusite from Santa Teresa, Brazil, also indicating that it is of metamorphic origin. Inclusions characterize the individuality of every gemstone and bear witness to their natural provenance.
It is not necessary to understand much of the geologic development of a gemstone but some knowledge of its mysterious origin gives the jewel a special interest and a special value.

Microphotos (pages 218–221): Eduard Gübelin, Lucerne.

The world of human concepts is mainly influenced by the eyes and thus by light, color, and shapes, all three of which are phenomenological methods of expression for gemstone inclusions. Anyone who loves gemstones and enjoys their lustrous, colorful, and captivating beauty cannot help but want to see into their mysterious depths. The hidden inner charms are not easily revealed to the questing eye. Even a magnifying glass is frequently insufficient. It is only through the lens of a microscope that the jewels reveal iconographic scenes that are often even more fascinating than their external beauty. A wealth of unique variety is expressed in an inexhaustible treasure trove of the most superb forms and shapes. Minute crystals hover in the unreal red, green, or yellow light of a seemingly limitless space. Petrified microphytes stand in the imaginary glow of light reflexes. Algae woods and bamboo groves waft in the deep-green shimmer of marine depths. Hollows harbor enigmatic essences preserved from prehistoric times. Small bubbles, which quiver at the slightest movement, are sometimes present in these gemstone juices. Due to their elegance, all these artistic still lifes inside the gemstones are not only a cause for admiration and renewed delight, but their variety is also a testimony to nature's creative pleasure. Just as fossils in rocks give paleontologists information about past geological periods in the earth's history, the inclusions in precious jewels bear witness to formation and growth conditions as well as to the gemstones' place of origin. Although the science of gemstones has paid due systematic attention to inclusions from its very start, mineralogy has only fairly recently become involved with this informative field of knowledge. Initially, the inclusions served only to differentiate between natural gemstones and synthetic products. Now, however, they also play an important role in gemstone identification. Pliny the Elder (23–79 A.D.) reported in his work on natural history about the knowledge of gemstone inclusions in his day: "*Carbunculi* (ancient general term for transparent red gemstones such as ruby, spinel, and garnet) can be recognized by the fact that they have minute inclusions, bubbles, or blisters which look like silver. *Smaragdi* (this undoubtedly refers mainly to green stones such as emeralds) reveal damage. Thus each gem has its own features dependent on the country which it comes from." Mineralogists recognized the important significance of inclusion research only when alerted by the results of analyses during the course of gemstone research. During the past twenty years, mineralogists have placed increasing emphasis on systematic investigations into inclusions. As a result, both sectors can now benefit from this fruitful cooperation. The astonishing results that science can achieve can be demonstrated by the example of quartz, for which research has identified over 135 different mineral inclusions up to the present day.

The term *inclusion* is used very broadly by gemologists. It covers the entire range of a mineral's inherent and foreign inhomogeneities. These include cavities and visible structural flaws or features, traces of growth such as twinning and color zoning, gaseous, fluid, and solid inclusions as well as subsequent damage such as a fracture crack or a cleavage crack. Gaseous inclusions are very rarely found in natural minerals.

They mostly occur in combination with liquid, which can either be water combined with water vapor, carbon dioxide (CO_2) in gaseous or liquid form, methane (CH_4) or other hydrocarbons, alone or intermingled. Inclusions that unite gas and liquid within them are called fluid inclusions. They are caused by the liquid condensing as the crystallizing gemstone cools, thereby prompting the liquid to shrink. As a result, the residual liquid is unable to fill the hollow completely. Subsequent heating of the solution to the critical temperature leads to further homogenization of the two phases. Solid inclusions, as the name suggests, mean the presence of solid substances, generally in the form of foreign minerals (accompanying minerals). They grew before or at the same time as the host gem or entered it through cleavages or fracture cracks.

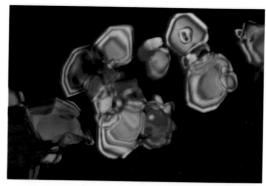

The formation of inclusions and their presence in gemstones is closely linked with the geologic-tectonic processes described in the chapter "The Exquisite Rarity." The mineral inclusions actually provide eloquent messages about rock formations (parent rock), place of formation, and growth, that is, the origin and provenance of the gemstones. The mineral inclusions are either precursors, contemporaries, or latecomers of the host gem. They are therefore either formed before the gemstone (protogenetic inclusions) and then later incorporated by the latter or created at the same as the gemstone (syngenetic inclusions), or they were exsolved as minority components from a mixed crystal (separation) and formed (epigenetic inclusions) an independent mineral inside the host gem (e.g., rutile in rubies and sapphires) at a subsequent time. However, there is the additional possibility that the inclusions entered the already-formed host gems through cleavage or fracture surfaces, as is the case with the decorative images called dendrites found in dendritic and tree agate.

Until the late 1970s, gemology was forced to rely on variable and uncertain factors such as crystal form, color, and geologic relationship with the host gem when defining mineral inclusions. As a result, the naming of mineral inclusions was frequently dubious. One of the few reliable conclusions, that the so-called "silk" in rubies and sapphires was composed of rutile needles, was based on the observation that the chemical analyses indicated an excess of titanium.

Since then, several elaborate apparatuses for electronic analysis have been developed (electron microprobe, scanning electron microscope, energy-dispersive x-ray fluorescence spectroscopy, Raman laser spectroscopy, etc.) and used for gemological research. For the identification of mineral inclusions with the first three instruments, the mineral inclusions must be cut flush with the surface of the gemstone, whereas the laser beam in the Raman method can penetrate several millimeters into the gemstone, which allows the gemstone to be analyzed without harming it. In x-ray diffraction analysis, a minute amount of powder must be scraped off the mineral inclusion, which means that it has to be exposed on the surface of the gemstone.

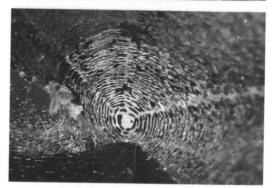

Although liquid inclusions contribute a substantial amount to the striking internal life of gemstones, they are of less importance to gemol-

From top to bottom:
1. Heavily rounded, corroded grains of quartz as protogenetic mineral inclusions in an emerald from Maji moto, Lake Manyara, Tanzania (25x).
2. The nest of black, metallically gleaming stibnite needles grew syngenetically with the host quartz (32x).
3. A syngenetic secondary "fingerprint" of nature has spread out into a partly healed crack. Sapphire from Pailin, Cambodia (20x).
4. Epigenetic fracture filled by brown iron ore dendrites in a colorless beryl (goshenite) from Brazil (20x).

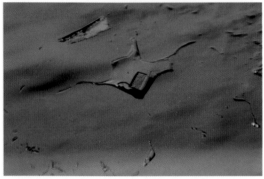

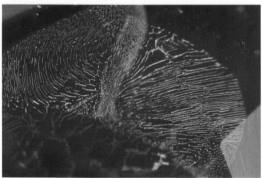

From top to bottom:
1. Large, two-phase inclusion of an aqueous solution and its vapor bubble in rock crystal, Swiss Alps (50x).
2. Three-phase inclusion comprised of an aqueous solution, its gas bubble and a cubic salt crystal (NaCl) in a hydrothermally formed emerald from the Muzo Mine, Colombia (100x).
3. Multiple-phase inclusion with several tiny daughter inclusions and a gas bubble in an aqueous solution. Beryl, Brazil (64x).
4. Liquid lining of a partly healed fracture in a sapphire from Kyaukpyatthat, Myanmar (Burma) (32x).

ogists than mineral inclusions. During the formation of numerous gemstones, foreign trace elements were washed in by hot solutions, the so-called fluids that circulate in many rocks. The fluids were incorporated as the crystals grew just as were the mineral inclusions. Just as with the mineral inclusions, liquid inclusions offer clear information on the condition of the fluids and the growth conditions of the host gem. It is therefore in the interests of gemological research to gain more profound knowledge of the geologic processes during the gemstones' period of formation by analyzing the liquid inclusions. Formerly, this was done by determining the critical properties of the fluid, for example, the homogenization temperature (critical temperature of carbon dioxide at around 31°C), of the melting and liquefaction point as well as the critical pressure. More detailed and more reliable results are obtained by using microthermometry and, more recently, spectrometric procedures such as proton-induced x-ray emission and Raman laser technology. An even further advanced method of analysis is the ablation method whereby microthermometry, ultraviolet laser, and an ICP mass spectrometer are used one after the other. This permits the determination of the concentration conditions or the absolute contents not only of the fluids but also of the salts in the liquid inclusions. From this data, interesting conclusions can be drawn about the gemstones' formation conditions, and the so-called "daughter crystals," which were precipitated in the fluid medium during cooling of the growing crystal, can be identified.

There is a never-ending variety of inclusion images in gemstones and the internal life of one gem never resembles that of another. These varied inclusions are not, however, random products by any means, but the results of a development in accordance with petrological and chemico-physical laws. For this reason, they are distributed throughout the wealth of the gemstone world in a regular pattern and are in no way arbitrary. Each gemstone grows in a rock space from which it incorporates existing minerals into itself or surrounds simultaneously crystallizing accessory minerals, or obtains chemical elements from it that produce new inclusions. In accordance with the physical laws of its own crystal growth it "processes" substances from its environment within itself and forms growth features in its interior that again appear as inclusions. An individual microscopic inclusion can provide considerable information about the paragenetic formation of a gemstone, for example about the chemico-physical condition of a gemstone's place of formation at the time of its crystallization. Such knowledge in turn yields information as to the particular type of deposit from which the corresponding gemstone originated. A differentiation between natural gems and synthetic stones can mostly be made on the basis of their characteristic inclusions. Many contain inclusions that are only found in specific gems. Providing that such inclusions are determined, the authenticity and even, in many cases, the location can be confirmed. Whether the gem is an artificial imitation can also be determined.

Since the appearance of synthetic materials on the gemstone market, inclusions play a primary role in gemstone identification. The importance of inclusions is increasing in proportion to the increasing number of new and better synthetic stones (imitations, syntheses, and artificial products) and artificial methods of treatment that are discovered, commercially developed, and marketed. Despite the outstanding importance of inclusions, they are regrettably still scorned by many gemstone devotees as being unwanted *flaws*, without recognizing and appreciating their bewitching beauty or their fascinating eloquence. Synthetic stones are laboratory products that are reproducible in terms of quantity, size, and uniformity, but a gemstone is, in contrast, a unique and unmistakable natural masterpiece with individual characteristics. If inclusions do not optically cloud or mechanically weaken a gemstone, the highest tribute must be paid to them as infallible signs of authenticity for their natural origin and absolute originality.

Typical inclusions in diamonds processed for jewelry applications tend, above all, to be small and are visible as individual points, turbidity, clouds, growth lines, twinning lamellae, tension fractures, or inclusions of other minerals.

Diamonds with large inclusions are rarely traded. In the case of diamonds, the cubic "zirconia" imitations are more important than synthetics. These have an even more sparkling fire than diamonds. In color gemstones, practically inclusion-free examples are no rarity. As a rule of thumb, it can be stated that the likelihood of encountering an inclusion-free gem is all the greater the more frequently it occurs in nature. Extremely rare gemstones such as rubies or emeralds are, admittedly, rarely ever seen without the accompanying characteristic inclusions. In rubies, the structural inclusions are foreign guest minerals and wisps of reticulated irregular design, growth zones, and twin lamellae. The most common inclusion material is rutile, which appears as hair-fine silky fibers. Rubies originating from Myanmar typically contain rutile needles limited to nests and calcite crystals. The fine rutile hairs are as delicate as a spider's web and arranged trigonally. In contrast, rubies from Thailand very rarely contain rutile silk, but have the distinctive feature of liquid films along healed cracks as well as areas of stress created around other mineral inclusions such as apatite, garnet, and magnetite. In the case of Sri Lanka, its mainly lighter-colored rubies have loose silk gratings throughout the gems, accompanied by biotite, magnetite or pyrite, and zircon. African rubies also have a specialty. They do not contain rutile silk but fibrous segregations of boehmite that stretch out vertically from the twin lamellae. They contain apatite and magnetite as accessory minerals. The synthetic production of rubies has achieved such high a level of perfection in the past few decades that gemology is obliged to employ numerous diagnostic criteria in order to identify the surrogates.

A clear identification of whether a gem has been formed naturally or only in imitation of nature, or even from which deposit the natural gem has originated has decisive financial repercussions in the world of gemstones. For this reason, an in-depth knowledge of inclusions in natural gemstones and in their synthetic counterparts is imperative in today's gemstone trade and jewelry branch.

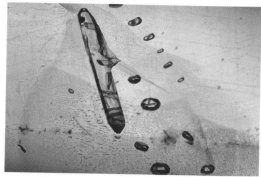

From top to bottom:
1. Partially broken diamond octahedron in a brilliant-cut diamond (15x).
2. Image of a locally specific inclusion in a lilac-colored sapphire from Sri Lanka: negative crystals in an aqueous solution, small, light-colored diaspore crystals, and a small black tablet of hematite (66x).
3. Inclusion image in a ruby from Mogok, Myanmar with some "silk" made up of rutile fibers, a cloud of TiO_2 substance, and a group of small calcite crystals (66x).
4. Mineral assembly of calcite (light crystal) and parisite (brown rods) in an emerald from the Muzo Mine, Colombia (66x).

A
PASSION
FOR
COLLECTING

Above: Thanks to its fascinating blue and its extreme rarity, benitoite is one of the most prized and magnificent of collectors' gems. The enlarged photograph shows some select benitoites in different shades of blue, with weights ranging from 1.10 carats to 4.77 carats. Collection: M. Scott, USA. Photo: Erica and Harald Van Pelt, Los Angeles.

Collecting things is a human trait and is done either out of necessity, as it was initially, or out of joyful enthusiasm for the special qualities of a specific item. Collecting minerals as well as gemstones has developed into a popular hobby. Gemstones are mostly collected for the beauty inherent in their luster and color. It is worthwhile to assemble *rare* gemstones into collections, *rare* as distinct from the gemstones widely available in the trade. If these collector's items are truly first-class in nature and of fine quality, they will maintain their value and represent a mobile capital safeguard that can be redeemed at any time. Gemstones that can be categorized as rare are those found in only one location on earth, for example, benitoite (Benito County, California) and ekanite (Sri Lanka), or gemstones whose deposits were exhausted following on the heels of their discovery as was the case with brazilianite (Brazil) as well as jerejemevite and cuprite (both from Namibia).

Amblygonite was only acknowledged as a gemstone in its own right a few decades ago after the German mineralogist Schröder came across a nameless gem in a drawer in the mineral collection at the Mineralogical Institute in Hamburg in 1953. Until then, it had sailed under the flag of spodumene due to its almost identical features. It is yellow in color and originates from Brazil, Myanmar, and Sri Lanka. The historic landscape of Andalusia in southern Spain, where it was first found, was godfather to andalusite. It is distinctive for its strong and attractive pleochroism. The colors of sherry yellow, mint green, and bordeaux red shine out in three vertically superimposed directions. *Andalusite* is so to say a link between commercial gemstones and the less well-known collectors' gems since it is fairly frequently encountered in some countries, including Brazil, Myanmar, and Sri Lanka. *Apatite*, also called the asparagus stone due to its yellow coloring, nevertheless spans the entire color spectrum. Its special feature is that it is a renegade mineral. Irrespective of its low level of hardness (H = 5), it is fairly durable. Although formed in prehistoric times geologically speaking and repeatedly crystallized later, it is present in all types of rocks and has safely survived most geologic transformations. It is therefore a widespread guest mineral in a large number of gemstones. It is found in almost all gem-producing countries. *Axinite* owes its name to its axelike crystal shape. Its color can best be compared to the rust brown of cloves. It is the optical mixture of the pleochroic colors of olive green, plum red, and cinnamon brown. It is found in Brazil, Switzerland, and Sri Lanka. *Benitoite* is one of the few gemstones that can claim a genuine designation of origin for itself since it is found solely in Benito County, California (USA). Its color ranges from colorless to all shades of blue to the most magnificent sapphire blue, which occasionally used to lead to its being confused with the sapphire. The marked dichroism of benitoite facilitates its distinction from sapphire. Its twin colors are colorless and blue, whereas those of sapphire are greenish-blue and blue. Since benitoite can appear colorless or blue depending on the line of vision, the cut must be correctly aligned with the emergence of the blue color. Large examples are rare. The largest ever discovered weighs a mere 9 carats. No new gems have been marketed for decades due to the exhaustion of the mine. However, new seams have recently been opened in the immediate vicinity of the former deposit. With its three pleochroic colors – blue, gray-blue, and brown – *cordierite* served the Vikings as a navigation stone that told them the position of the sun. Among its more remarkable locations are Brazil, Madagascar, Myanmar, Switzerland, and Sri Lanka. *Danburite* is one of the finest yellow gemstones. Until 1990, it was mined exclusively in Myanmar. Since then, Madagascar and Sri Lanka also have been supplying collectors' markets. The colorless variety originates from Japan and Mexico. The only green danburite discovered so far and weighing 22 carats also originates from Myanmar. *Ekanite* only gained the position of a new gemstone in the mid-twentieth century. It was discovered on Sri Lanka by the gemologist F. L. D. Ekanayake. Its color themes are reminiscent of greenish and brownish tea. Originally, it crystallized as a tetragonal crystal, but then collapsed over the course of 550 million years to an amorphous, glassy stone due to its thorium and uranium content. Together with obsidian and desert-glass, it is one of the few natural glass substances on earth. Ekanite remains constantly radioactive, thus making it unsuitable for jewelry. *Euclase* is derived from the Greek and indicates its easy cleavage with *eu* (good) and *klasein* (cleave). It cloaks itself in many different colors such as light blue, sapphire blue, rose red, and green, all of which vary in intensity. Euclase is a typical epigone of beryl. It originates from mostly younger, gem-rich pegmatites and therefore is mainly found in the former beryl deposits in Brazil, on Sri Lanka, and in Zimbabwe. *Fluorite* and *fluorspar* are used as equal aliases. Its German name of *Fluss* indicates its use as flux in the metal industry and *spat* to its ease of cleavage. This rarely completely clear gemstone is composed of calcium and fluorine. With a hardness of 4, it is among the softest of gemstones. Its low refraction of light gives it a glassy appearance. It competes in every imaginable color and can truly be described as the most frequent collectors' gemstone found in Switzerland, where colorless, yellow, green, and, in particular, superb pink fluorites abound. They have recently also been mined in Pakistan. Of all the fluorites in the world, only the rose-red Swiss fluorite contains tetrahedral cavities filled with an aqueous solution and a gas bubble, which is visible using a microscope. The fluorite mined in England has the individual name of *Blue John*, and its processing into decorative objects gives it an original identity. The fluorite in the state of Illinois (USA) is largely marked by its oil inclusions that fluoresce under ultraviolet light. Opaque *hematite* is also known under the name of bloodstone since it turns the water used during cutting blood red. When it occurs as very thin lamellar crystals, it is colored red; it turns from red to black the thicker it becomes in fractions of a millimeter. Its strong metallic luster is attributable to its high refractive indices. Its main countries of origin are Brazil and Switzerland, where the so-called iron rose of hematite is available as a much sought-after singularity. Externally, steel can resemble hematite. It is very easy to differentiate between the two: If hematite is drawn across a rough porcelain surface, it leaves behind a cherry-red streak; steel does not.

Top: Top left: an andalusite of 9.04 carats from Sri Lanka. Center: three apatites in different colors, from left to right, from Mexico, Myanmar, and Canada. Bottom right: an axinite of 8.71 carats from Mexico.

Center: Top left: a danburite of 30.37 carats from Madagascar. From left to right: a blue-green euclase of 7.65 carats, a yellow euclase of 6.21 carats, and a green kyanite of 8.37 carats, all from Brazil, and a blue kyanite of 4.56 carats from Alpe Spondo, Ticino, Switzerland. Bottom right: green danburite of 21.50 carats from Myanmar.

Bottom: All fluorites: the greenish and rose-red ones from Switzerland, the blue and violet ones from Belgium, and the yellow one is from Illinois (USA).

Photos: James G. Perret, Lucerne.

223

Top: Two sillimanites: the blue, round silli-manite of 18.86 carats originates from Sri Lanka, the steel blue one of 11.79 carats from Myanmar.

Center: All the kornerupines shown here are from Sri Lanka and represent the commonest colors encountered.

Bottom: The sinhalite limits its color range from brown-yellow to yellow-brown. This sinhalite weighs 45.69 carats and comes from Sri Lanka.

Photos: James G. Perret, Lucerne.

The outstanding Danish mineralogist Kornerup lent his name to *kornerupine*. The color palette mixes all the shades of green from yellow-green, green-yellow, yellow-brown, to brown. It is one of the more familiar rare gemstones on Sri Lanka. Other deposits are found in Brazil, Madagascar, and Myanmar. With its Greek-derived name, *kyanite* indicates the characteristic that sets it apart from others, since it has two different degrees of hardness of 5 and 7, respectively, in two different directions. Its color ranges from light blue to deep royal blue. A famous location for it is Pizo Forno in Switzerland. *Obsidian* embodies the most macabre of all gemstones: Mayan and Aztec priests armed themselves with it to remove the hearts from the living bodies of their human sacrifices. It occurs in all colors but mostly in darker shades. A popular variety is the so-called "snowflake obsidian" with white flakes on a black background. Obsidian is volcanic glass found in Mexico and Peru and was used at a very early stage by peoples in Central and South America. *Scapolite* is a characteristic collectors' item with the roots of its family tree in many countries. Brazil provides it in colorless, white, and yellow varieties; Madagascar, Namibia, and Tanzania have mainly yellow versions. Because of Myanmar's soil, its scappolite comes in a purely colorless version as well as differing shades of yellow, rose red and blue. In Sri Lanka, the colors range from colorless, rose red, and gray through to black. For a long time, the rose-red variety was found only in Myanmar. Sri Lanka unexpectedly followed in the 1980s, and for a few years Pakistan has also been supplying the market. The interesting aspect of these three locations is the fact that the scapolites from these deposits have different properties. Scapolites have one feature in common with feldspars and garnets. Like them, they comprise an isomorphic series (solid solution) by the fact that between the end members marialite ($Na_3[Al_3Si_9O_{24}]$.-$NaCl$) and meionite ($Ca_3[Al_6Si_6O_{24}]$.$CaCO_3$) sodium and potassium can be exchanged at will and in infinitely variable quantities. Characteristics vary depending on the percentile content of one or the other cation. The name betrays it all in the case of *sillimanite* (fibrolite). In spite of its fibrous composition, it is a transparent gemstone with a colorless or steel blue or sapphire blue appearance. It is found in Myanmar and Sri Lanka. Connoisseurs appreciate its lively luster. It is exceptionally rare and extremely difficult to cut. Only skilled lapidaries with an exceptional gift for delicate work should attempt to do so, if the result is not to be an embarrassment of countless minute splinters. *Sinhalite* is a gift of the twentieth century, just as are benitoite and brazilianite, ekanite and painite, serendibite and taaffeite. Since it had gemological properties similar to those of the peridot, it was praised as a brown peridot until 1952 when it was identified as a gemstone in its own right. The cause of this reorientation was the arrival of a major batch of brown stones at a London Gemstone Testing Laboratory and the accompanying challenge of a precise mineralogical identification. The new mineral received the suggestive name of sinhalite in honor of its sole place of origin on Sri Lanka. This was borrowed from Sinhala or lion island as Sri Lanka was called at one time. The largest example facetted so far weighs an impressive 252 carats. *Sphene* (titanite) is a rare Swiss example on the gemstone scene. As a crevice mineral it is found in different locations in the Alps. Those of gemstone quality are very few and far between. It features a very high refractive index and strong dispersion, which is the reason for flashes of other spectral colors alongside its body colors of green, yellow, and brown. In accordance with its high birefringence, it hardly ever reveals its interior clearly to the human eye. The Smithsonian Institution in Washington, D.C. (USA) houses a collection of yellow sphenes arranged in a necklace that are allegedly of Swiss origin. In

addition to Switzerland, sphene is also found in some typical gemstone countries. The identification of *taaffeite* was also happened by chance. In 1946, Edward C. R. Count Taaffe picked up an unattractive stone from the workshop waste of a colleague and sent it to the London Gemstone Testing Laboratory as he had no opportunity to investigate it himself. After thorough analysis, it proved to be an unclassified mineral and was included in the nomenclature under the name of its discoverer. Taaffeite possesses an astonishing wealth of colors ranging from rose red to violet, mellow colors, gray-blue to pure blue and chestnut. Sri Lanka has been more or less the main supplier since the middle of the 1970s, although stones from Myanmar occasionally crop up. For approximately thirty years, only two taaffeites were in circulation worldwide. At that time, it was considered to be one of the rarest minerals ever. The heaviest cut taaffeite is a gem of 12.5 carats.

The price of diamonds is determined by the selling organization of De Beers and is strictly controlled on all continents. The price of commercial gemstones depends on quality, rarity, supply, and demand, but fashion trends also can have a temporary influence. The rarity of commercial gems tends to be relative. In the case of collectors' gems, however, rarity is the backbone and is the distinctive, predominating characteristic. Teamed with bewitching beauty, rare gems guarantee collectors, firstly, the satisfaction afforded by a varied, fascinating hobby and, secondly, protection against an erosion in value.

Left: The green sphene weighing 13.00 carats comes from Madagascar, the yellow-brown one weighing 6.12 carats is from Mexico, and the yellow one weighing 3.03 carats is from Switzerland.

Center: The mellow-colored taaffeite on the right is the largest polished example in the world, 13.32 carats. The rose-red one weighs 2.97 carats, and the blue, heart-shaped one is 3.23 carats. All of them originate from Sri Lanka.

Right: Scapolites in a variety of colors. The yellow one weighs 13.68 carats, the violet one 6.41 carats, and the colorless one 4.71 carats. They all come from Tanzania. The rose-red, heart-shaped scapolite weighs 8.08 carats and originates from Myanmar.

Photos: James G. Perret, Lucerne.

NATURAL OR NOT?

SYNTHETICS, COMPOSITES, IMITATIONS

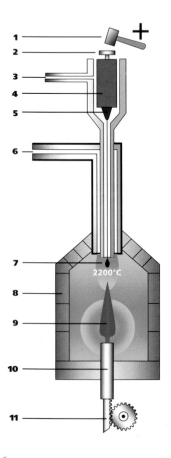

At an early stage in human history attempts were made to imitate gemstones. The precursors were the Egyptians, who imitated nature with colorful glasses and porcelains. Nature, at that time, only gave up her precious treasures grudgingly, and their sources were only accessible within close geographic confines. The reason for these imitations was not the wish to commit fraud, but an effort to reproduce the natural beauty of gemstones and to eradicate the problem of their rarity. Glass and porcelain remained the only bases for gemstone imitation over a long period of time, in fact, until the end of the nineteenth century. With the advancement of technology, the substitute materials changed, but once again it was not an intention to defraud but the necessity to smooth the way for cheaper and better industrial products. As a result, it was not the gemstone trade that originally provided the impetus for the manufacture of synthetics but the watchmaking industry. Correspondingly, the discoverer of the synthetic process was recruited from a peripheral professional environment, of which A. Verneuil, a French chemist, is an example.

According to common acceptance, manufactured artificial stones that come close to natural gemstones in appearance, but whose chemical composition and characteristics do not correspond to them, are imitations. Imitations made of glass – used for centuries for jewelry, cult, and ornamental objects – can hardly be differentiated from natural gemstones with the naked eye. The file, the instrument used since time immemorial for testing for authenticity or fake, as it attacks the softer glass, led to the development of composite stones. For the upper parts, mostly natural, hard gemstones were used, even those with inclusions, solely for false pretenses, since they would resist the file. However, as a result of a lack of knowledge of the chemical elements that constitute gemstones and their physical properties, this type of imitation process did not extend much beyond its unsatisfactory beginnings.

Only with the discovery of chemical elements at the end of the Middle Ages and the development of analytical chemistry in the eighteenth century did more reliable possibilities open up for a more real reproduction of gemstones. In chemistry, the breaking down of a substance into its components is called an analysis and the composition of a substance from its basic substances is known as synthesis. This is the basic definition of synthesis. Irrespective of their manufacturing process, synthetic stones are composed of the same chemical elements and possess analogous crystallographic and physical characteristics as do their precious counterparts in nature.

During the course of the twentieth century, a range of different processes for the production of synthetic stones reached production stage. In the long term, those of Verneuil for synthetic rubies (1902) and IG Dye Trust in Germany for synthetic emeralds (1935) were successful since they united the required technical and commercial advantages. Both methods pursued the manufacture of crystals by fusion: Verneuil according to the flame fusion method and IG-Farben by using R. Nacken's method of a so-called diffusion melt, which is used by Chatham (USA), Gilson (France), Zerfass (Germany) and several others. A successful further development is the flux fusion method, which is the one now mainly used by most manufacturers of synthetic stones. Syntheses made from melts require the use of fluxes that very frequently deposit a variety of natural-looking inclusions in the synthetic stones.

The purely artificial products include all the crystalline stones produced by any artificial process that have no natural counterpart, for example, moissanite, strontium titanate, YAG, GGG, and, most recently, zirconia (cubic zirconium oxide), which mainly serve as dia-

mond imitations. Except for their characteristic inclusions, these artificial products possess crystallographic and physical properties that deviate unequivocally from the imitated gemstones.

Composite stones (doublets and triplets) are, as their name states, assembled out of two, three, and occasionally more layers with the intention of either protecting a soft or fragile gem or to simulate a compact, natural gemstone. A shining example of this is sometimes the opal, which often appears in such thin layers that it requires the support of an underlay and/or surface protection. As a whole and compact gemstone, it is of course incomparably expensive.

If it can be proved that a synthetic stone has, as a laboratory product, the identical chemical and physical properties as a natural gemstone, there are still unmistakable features to recognize it. The different formation and growth processes leave behind, both in the natural gemstone and in the artificial manufacturing process of the synthetic, diagnostically conclusive and typical characteristics. They are primarily attributable to a circumstance that cannot be implemented for any commercial purpose, that is, the fact that nature took several hundreds to thousands of years for the crystallization of gemstones, whereas the synthetics are created in a few hours to a few weeks. The nonetheless impressive progress made in synthesizing technology is fortunately always accompanied by intensive scientific research and improvements in equipment so that, for all synthetic stones, their identifying features are always available to differentiate them from natural gems. As has always been the case, the most superior and reliable investigation results can undoubtedly be obtained by microscopic research into the inclusions.

The fact that color as the most immediately impressive element in gemstones can gain in beauty as a result of human intervention is well known from antiquity. Of all the methods used to influence color in the past, three methods have proved their worth until the present day: "burning" or heating and irradiating in the case of color gemstones

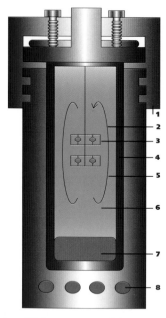

Right: The flux fusion method:
1. Feed tube
2. Quartz (SiO_2 glass) or silica placed above a platinum screen
3. Growing crystals (emeralds)
4. Flux of lithium molybdate
5. Feed of beryllium oxide (BeO)
6. Feed of alumina (Al_2O_3)

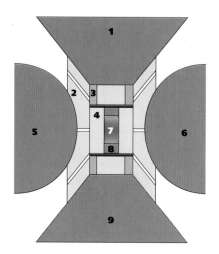

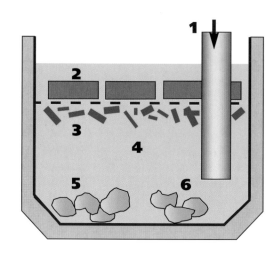

Center: High-pressure, high-temperature "bell" apparatus for the production of synthetic diamonds:
1. Top piston
2. Gasket assembly
3. Nickel ring
4. Internal chamber wall
5./6. Pressure cylinders
7. Reaction zone with graphite (melt and crystallization zone)
8. Insulation pin
9. Lower piston

Left: Autoclave for the manufacture of hydrothermal, synthetic gems (internal pressure up to 1,000 bar):
1. Collar
2. Overheated water
3. Seed crystals
4. Platinum or silver lining
5. Convectional flow
6. Baffle
7. Nutrients
8. Heating coils

Microphotos (page 229): Eduard Gübelin, Luzern

and dyeing or "impregnation" in the case of mainly porous gems such as agates or turquoises. Normally, the heat applied is carried out at a temperature of several hundred degrees. The desired color change always aligns itself as far as possible with the ideal color of the gemstone. In the case of aquamarine, which often has a green tinge, this is a radiant sky blue. Amethyst, morganite, pink topaz, sapphire, tanzanite, tourmaline, and zircon are normally heat-treated. The proof of thermal treatment cannot always be provided, which is hardly surprising since all these gemstones could have been exposed to higher temperatures just as much during their natural growth. All humans are doing is completing what nature did not quite finish. At times, the treatment of gemstones can be highly complex, as is the case with pink topaz. After initial heating, the gem is treated with gamma rays, followed by a second heating, to give permanence to the color change caused. Rubies and sapphires are subjected to temperatures of up to 1,900 degrees to improve their color. There are consequences: The high temperatures leave molten, rounded mineral inclusions and areas of tension in the interior. Such "atoll" inclusions permit the identification of artificial color changes. In the case of diamonds, color changes are effected by means of radiation or bombardment with atomic elementary particles. The uncommon rarity of strongly colored diamonds is the impetus for artificial coloration.

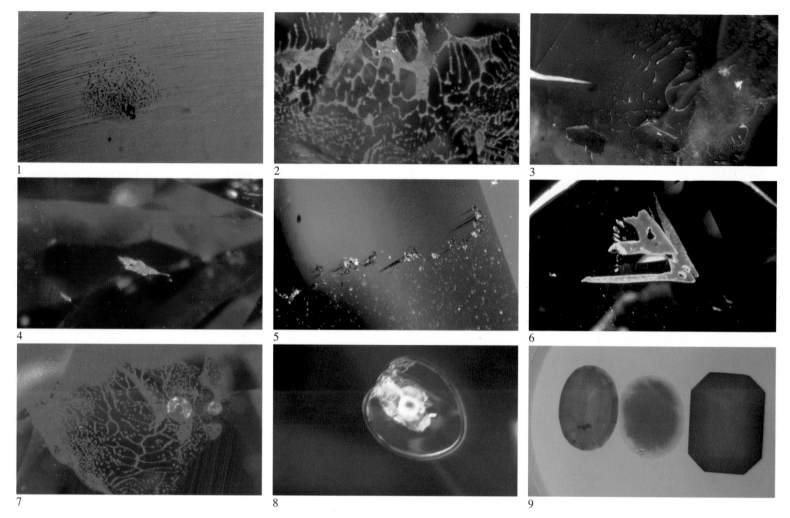

In order to prevent unfair competition and deception, the international professional associations American Gem Trade Association (AGTA), Confédération Internationale de la Bijouterie, Joaillerie, Orfèvrerie (CIBJO), and International Color Gemstone Association (ICA) demand that synthetics, artificial products, imitations, and treatments must be explicitly and unmistakably designated as such in sales discussions and in all written declarations. The ICA issued a declaration in the sense of a worldwide compulsory language regulation for its members for the purpose of the uniform designation of alterations to gemstones. The *N.E.T.* chart, as the codex is called, subdivides the possible effects into three main sectors: N = not enhanced, E = enhanced, or T = treated. An increase in purity or lack of color by means of oiling or the filling of cracks with synthetic resin as well as heating all come under the E heading of enhanced. The following processes come under the T heading of treated: coated, diffusion treated, dyed, glass-filled, irradiated, and laser-treated. Interested parties thus have the right to the mention during a sales discussion of any additional treatment of a gemstone. On written documentation such as an invoice or certificate that accompanies the gemstone, it is sufficient if it contains one of the three letters N, E or T as information on which type of treatment the gemstone has undergone. The aim of this type of disclosure is primarily to increase customers' confidence in the jewel trade.

1. Diagnostic inclusion image in a synthetic Verneuil ruby: tiny gas bubbles and curved growth striations (25x).

2. Flux residue cause a typical inclusion image in a synthetic ruby by T. Chatham (25x).

3. The platinum tablets as well as the traces of flux residue indicate synthetic manufacture by T. Chatham (25x).

4. Flux inclusion in a synthetic, so-called "Ramaura" ruby by J. Osmer (32x).

5. Hydrothermal, synthetic emerald. Black, wedge-shaped two-phase inclusions radiate from the seed plate (light triangle at the right edge). The inclusions are intended to simulate a natural emerald. Russian origin (50x).

6. Evident flux residue in a green artificial product (YAG) (25x).

7. Characteristic, netlike wisp and melted crystals of a thermally treated Thai ruby (50x).

8. So-called "Atoll" inclusions are features of thermally treated sapphires (50x).

9. Of the three sapphires put into methylene iodide (n = 1.75), only the middle one has a natural color. The two others betray diffusion treatment because of their sharper and darker girdle and distinct facet edges (10x).

GLOSSARY

The following abbreviations are used when describing minerals:
Density (specific gravity) = D
Hardness = H
Refractive index (R.I.) = n

Adamantine Designation for the specific high luster of diamonds (derived from the Greek name for diamond *adamas.*

Adularescence The appearance of a bluish-white, cloudy shimmer on the surface in moonstone, caused by interference on alternate lamellae of sodium and potassium feldspar.

Allochromatic This term means "foreign-colored" and refers to minerals whose coloration is due to the integration of transition elements (which do not belong to the chemical composition).

Amethyst almond Almond-shaped druse lined with amethyst crystals.

Amorphous This term means "shapeless" and refers to minerals that have no specific shape of their own or fixed arrangement of their inner structure. These are noncrystallized minerals as opposed to crystals.

Anion A negatively charged ion. It is usually nonmetallic in character and consists of one or more atoms carrying a definite number of negative electric charges (F, O, Cl, etc.).

Asterism The optical appearance of star-shaped rays of light on convex-cut gemstones caused by the reflection of incident light on incorporated inclusions.

Baguette Slim rectangular, stick-shaped cut (used for preference on diamonds).

Brecciated Brecciated rock is a sedimentary rock composed of generally angular debris that has been consolidated.

Brilliancy The term brilliancy covers all optical effects caused on a cut gemstone by incident light.

Bruting The is the raw processing of a gemstone. The first raw shape given during cutting of a previously sawed gemstone or ornamental stone by cutting with a vertical grindstone.

Cameo Comes from the Italian *cammeo;* cut ornamental stone (gem) with pictorial depictions in relief.

Carnelian Red-brown, brown, or brown-red chalcedony, which was used for preference in ancient times for the production of cameos.

Cation A positively charged ion consisting of either a single atom or of a group of atoms and bearing a specific number of unit positive charges equal to its electrovalence.

Cat's eye Convex-cut ornamental stone over the surface of which a light-colored stripe of light wanders when the stone is moved. This unusual play of light develops in a variety of gemstones, in particular among the chrysoberyls, as well as in quartz, tourmaline, aquamarine, and so forth.

Chalcedony group Coarse, cryptocrystalline, that is, microscopically finely fibrous crystalline quartz in different colors and color intensities. Translucent to opaque SiO_2. D = 2.6, H = 7, n = 1.53.

Chatoyancy Derived from *chat*, the French word for cat, it means the appearance of a light shimmer that moves over the bead-shaped or convex surface of a gemstone as a narrow line of light and resembles the slit-eye of a cat. The effect is caused by reflection of the incident light on fine parallel fibers inside the gemstone.

Chromophore, chromophoric This term from Greek *chromo* (color) and *phorein* (to carry) means coloring agent, pigment, responsible for color.

Cobalt Chemical element; symbol Co; steel gray, bright, magnetic metal that is frequently used as a colorant to give a blue color to synthetic stones and glass.

Cohesion The inner force (adhesive force) that holds together the molecules of a body.

Colloidal A substance in exceptionally fine distribution dissolved in another substance, for example, in this case, particle substances in liquid = colloidal solution.

Color gems An often used but unofficial classification for gemstones that are appreciated for their characteristic colors, for example, ruby, sapphire, emerald, aquamarine, garnet, peridot, topaz, tourmaline, and zircon. The exception is diamond.

Conglomerate A sediment rock is rounded rock debris (rubble) cemented together.

Contact metamorphism This means the alteration of rocks after they have come into contact with the rising molten masses.

Contact minerals The minerals that resulted from the process of contact metamorphism.

Contact rock Rock that was either involved in the process of contact metamorphism or is the product of contact metamorphism.

Cryptocrystalline From Greek *kryptos* (hidden), meaning a rock or aggregate consisting of crystals too small to be recognized under the ordinary microscope (contrary to phonerocrystalline).

Culet The name of the small facet that hich often flattens the lower point of a brilliant cut (or other cuts such as navette, marquise, baguette, and drop).

Cymophane Another term for cat's-eye chrysoberyl.

Danburite An unusual gemstone (collector's gem); light to wine yellow from Myanmar, colorless from Japan, and rose red from Mexico. D = 3, H = 7, n = 1.633.

Dendritic Derived from *dendrou*, the Greek word for tree, it means the treelike or mosslike interwoven formations of iron oxide or manganese oxide in minerals or the joints of layers.

Density (or specific gravity) of a substance is its weight compared with the weight of the same volume of pure water at a temperature of 4°C.

In other words, the density (or specific gravity) of a substance in g/cm^3 states how many times heavier or lighter it is than the same volume of pure water at 4°C.

Derived This term means "formed from," in this case the result of a geochemical process, for example, Jura limestone that was the result of sedimentation.

Desilification Removal of silica (silicic oxide) as can happen during the metamorphosis (transformation) of rocks.

Diorite Grainy, mostly greenish-black deep rock that is somewhere in the middle of the transition series from alkali rocks (granite) to basic rocks (gabbro).

Dopstick A device to which a gemstone is cemented or clamped during the cutting process and on which it is applied to the grindstone.

Druse (crystal druse) hollow lined with crystals (e. g., rock crystal, amethyst, calcite) in rocks with central residual cavity.

Dullam (Ceylonese) Residue of heavy minerals in the washing basket.

Emerald cut The so-called step cut of rectangular shape with truncated corners ("coupiert") used mainly for emeralds as well as for diamonds ("taille émeraude"), aquamarines, morganite, topaz, tourmaline, and many other gemstones.

Enstatite Unusual gemstone (collector's gem) in the pyroxene mineral group of green, brown-green or brown color. $Mg_2Si_2O_6$. D = 3.27, H = 5.5, n = 1.667.

Falcon's eye/Hawk's eye Cryptocrystalline quartz with finely fibrous inclusions of the blue mineral crocidolite (version of serpentine). It is blue and is notable for its cat's-eye effect (chatoyancy). Closely connected with tiger's eye.

Forsterite Mixed member of olivine, low in iron and rich in magnesium. Mg_2SiO_4.

Gabbro Rich in magnesium, low in silica, thus a basic deep rock, black-green in color with a grainy structure (or grainy texture).

Gem Engraved ornamental stone with relief (cameo) or incised (intaglio, used as a seal) pictorial depictions. Derived from *gemma*, the Latin word for gemstone, it also gives gemology its name.

Gemologist Derived from the Latin word *gemma* (gemstone), gemologist describes a person who is involved in the science of gemstones (gemology).

Gemology Science of gemstones derived from the Latin *gemma* (gemstone) and the Greek *logos* (word.).

Glyptography The art of working on stone or metal with chisel or stylus is the art of stone cutting (gem glyptography is the art of cutting gems).

Gneiss Widespread metamorphic rock in the group of crystalline schist group. The main mineral components are the same as those of granite: quartz, feldspar, and mica. The structure is mostly schistous.

Hauyne A mainly rich blue mineral and a component of lapis lazuli.

Hexagonal Six-sided: summarizes those crystal systems marked by a system of coordinates with a six-figure vertical main axis and three horizontal axes of equal length in one plane at an angle of less than 120° with each other.

Hydrothermal phase The final stage in the deposits formed directly by magma and their minerals that are deposited in this phase from the hot aqueous solutions.

Idiochromatic Single color, that is, by nature self-colored gemstones and ornamental stones as a result of their chemical composition, whereby the color of the chemical substance (pigment) is their own, that is, the constitutional component of the chemical composition.

Idiomorphous Refers to a crystal whose faces are characteristic of the mineral species to which it belongs (e.g., hexagonal prism of beryl).

Illam (Ceylonese) The layers of alluvial deposits rich in gemstones on the island of Sri Lanka.

Imperial jade The designation for the finest jadeite qualities colored emerald green as a result of chromium.

Inclusions Accumulation of foreign matter (foreign minerals, liquids, or cracks) in gemstones that have been incorporated during growth or have crystallized out of the enclosed supersaturated solutions or have formed due to mechanical pressure or expansion. Inclusions influence the purity as well as the transparency of gemstones, but they also serve as important indicators of authenticity and origin.

Inherent Intrinsic, the inseparability of object and property.

Interference The effect of the mutual influence and superpositioning of two homogeneous waves of light of the same frequency and approximately the same direction whereby they converge to form a light movement, the condition and type of which results from the individual components.

Isometric Synonymous with the cubic crystal system.

Ion Electrically positive or negative charged atom (atomic ion) or molecule (molecular ion).

Isomorphism, isomorphous Crystals whose chemical composition may vary although their crystal forms belong to the same crystal class.

Isomorphous series Minerals with equal crystal forms but different chemical formulae though belonging to the same mineral species (e.g., feldspars, garnets, olivines).

Isotropic Refers to minerals whose properties are the same in all directions, for example, refractive index, lattice structure, hardness. Cubic and amorphous substances.

Kimberlite Brecciated, diamond-containing, serpentinelike, blue-green variety of peridot ("blue ground"), a basic deep rock composed of olivine. Kimberlite forms the infill of the "pipe mines" (volcanic vents) that are well known as primary deposits of diamonds.

Labradorescence The colorful iridescence of labradorite and spectrolite.

Lazurite Also called lazure rock, it is usually a mixture of other blue minerals, mainly hauyne, nosean, sodalite, and so forth. It is considered to be one of the components of lapis lazuli.

Leucosapphire Fantasy name for colorless sapphire (no longer very common).

Limonite Also called brown ironstone or brown iron ore, an aqueous iron oxide that forms a crust. It is often the parent rock (matrix) for turquoise, which it also simultaneously penetrates in the form of branched veins.

Liquid magmatic Liquid magmatic formations are the rocks (e. g., granite) and deposits (e. g., those of labradorite, peridot, and zircon) created from the slow-evaporating parts of magma.

Magma Liquid molten mass of silicates (slow-evaporating components) saturated with gases (highly volatile components) enclosed within the earth's core that can break out in volcanic processes (eruptions) on the earth's surface.

Magmatic Composed of magma. Magmatic reaction is the formation of all rocks and minerals that have crystallized out of the molten liquid parts (the magma) deep in the earth's crust.

Manganese Chemical element; symbol Mn; silver gray, hard, very brittle metal; constituting component of some gemstones and ornamental stones (rhodochrosite, rhodonite, spessartine).

Marbles Metamorphic, that is, later transformed, grainy limestones (in the technical sense, of every calcite and dolomite that is capable of taking a polish).

Marquise Elongated cut in the shape of a small boat with pointed ends, mostly used for diamonds.

Matrix The natural rock in which minerals occur (parent rock).

Metamorphic Transformed, from metamorphism, which means transformed. The transformation of mineral parageneses after being deposited due to external effects such as contact with magmatic rocks, by regional pressure and temperature changes (e. g., contact metamorphic limestone, crystalline schist).

Methylene iodide test (D = 3.33) An application of the so-called flotation method. The principle is based on the fact that specifically heavier substances sink in a liquid, whereas specifically lighter substances float to the surface, for example, moonstone, citrine. To determine the density of gemstones and ornamental stones, a gemologist frequently uses so-called "heavy liquids." One of these liquids is methylene iodide with a density of 3.33. Specifically heavier gemstones, for example, topaz (D = 3.53–3.56), sink in it; specifically lighter ones, for example, citrine (D = 2.65) float.

Mica Group of important rock-forming minerals with mostly leaflike, scaly aggregates. The best known are the colorless, silvery muscovite, brown biotite, and green fuchsite. Chemically, the micas are complex silicates of aluminum.

Mica schist Collective term for a group of metamorphic rocks in the crystalline schist family characterized by their high quartz and mica mineral content and low proportion of feldspar.

Monoclinic Inclined simply. Monoclinic crystal system: the composition of those crystal categories that features a system of coordinates with three axes of different lengths of which two (a and c) cross at a sharp angle, while the third (b) is vertical to both.

Morion (Smoky quartz) Dark, smoky brown to almost black smoky quartz. D = 2.65, H = 7, n = 1.548.

Morphology This term from Greek *He morphé* (form, shape) strictly refers to the study of crystal forms; in general, the external shape of a crystal.

Navette Elongated, boat-shaped cut, oval at the tips, mainly used for diamonds.

Octahedron Crystal form in the cubic crystal system delineated by eight equal-sided triangles, that is, two four-sided pyramids placed base to base.

Ornamental stones In the widest sense, all minerals that are suitable for jewelry or ornamental purposes. In a narrower sense, all opaque, nontransparent minerals, such as agate, jade, lapis lazuli, malachite, rhodochrosite, rhodonite, and turquoise.

Paragenesis The joint occurrence (association) of minerals as an expression of the set pattern of being created alongside each other and in succession.

Parent rock Designation for rock in which the gemstones and ornamental stones have formed at the same time as the rock or after its solidification.

Pegmatite Liquid magmatic or pneumatolytic rocks that were formed intrusively by granitic molten residues. Generally, they form very coarse-grained veins or lenses in granitic to syenitic rocks. Pegmatites are notable for their minerals of rarer elements, particularly such elements as lithium, caesium, boron, and beryllium, as well as for rare earths such as thorium and uranium. Numerous gemstones such as beryl, topaz, and tourmaline are found in pegmatites. The main components of pegmatite are quartz and feldspar.

Pegmatite mineral Mineral that is the result of pegmatitic rock or mineral formation.

Pegmatitic Denotes creation during pegmatite formation and in veins of pegmatite or in the immediate vicinity.

Pegmatitic phase One of the highly important stages in gemstone formation in the magmatic area of deposit and mineral formation.

Phenacite Unusual, always colorless gemstone (collector's stone). Chemically, a beryllium silicate: $Be_2(SiO_4)$. D = 2.96, H = 7.5–8, n = 1.662.

Phenomenon gems Gemstones that have unusual light effects (phenomenon), for example, adularescence, asterism, and chatoyancy.

Phonerocrystalline Crystals that are individually visible to the naked eye.

Pincoid A crystal form that is parallel to two of the crystal axes (e. g., basal plane).

Placers Loose, mostly washed together sands, clays, and rubble as well as gravel deposits in which minerals and gemstones (placers) and precious metals resistant to weathering and mechanical transport accumulate and therefore are frequently in exploitable concentrations.

Pleochroism The characteristic of anisotropic (i. e., birefringent) crystals, to show different colors in different directions by means of the unequal (i. e., selective) absorption of light, for example, alexandrite, cordierite, kunzite, and tourmaline.

Pneumatolytic The term given to mineral formations in which the highly thermal and highly volatile components released from the consolidating magma were particularly involved. A range of gemstones owe their existence to pneumatolysis, for example, emerald, topaz, and tourmaline.

Pneumatolytic deposits Deposits that are the result of pneumatolytic mineral formation.

Prism Columnar crystal form whose faces cross two axes of the system of coordinates but run parallel to the third (vertical) one. In optical terms, a three-sided body cut from glass.

Pyrope Fire- to blood-red magnesium-rich variety of garnet, it is therefore a magnesium silicate garnet. $Mg_3Al_2(SiO_4)_3$. D = 3.7–3.9, H = 7.25, n = 1.73–1.76.

Quetzal Aztec name for a fruit-eating, tropical bird with long covering tail feathers found in the damp mountain forests stretching from southern Mexico to Panama.

Raw gems Raw, that is, uncut, minerals or gemstones.

Rhombic dodecahedron A crystal form delineated by twelve congruent lozenge shapes that crystallizes in the cubic crystal system, for example, diamond and garnet.

Rhombic or *orthorhombic* All crystals whose faces refer to a system of coordinates with three axes of unequal length that are vertical to each other. They have a rectangular or rhombic-shaped base.

Rich placers Exploitable concentration (or accumulation) of usable minerals or gemstones in deposits on the earth's surface that have formed by the effects of water (rain, rivers) in the geologic location (gravel, sand, valley floors, river sediment, etc.).

Rutile (fine rutile needles) Dark reddish-brown to black, tetragonally crystallizing mineral of titanium oxide. Often forms inclusions in garnet, corundum, and quartz and in its finest version as fine needles it is responsible for asterism. D = 4.25, H = 6, n = 2.62–2.90.

Scheelite Calcium wolframite ($CaWO_4$). Unusual gemstone of yellowish-white, golden yellow, brown to orange-yellow color with an adamantine luster. D = 6, H = 4.5, n = 1.925.

Secondary embankments Secondary deposits (placers, as they are known), mineral parageneses that have been transported from their place of formation and are now in a second location, for example, river rubble, river deposits, and valley floor embankments.

Sedimentary Caused by sedimentation, that is, deposits created from water. Sedimentary reaction means all the processes of rock and mineral destruction and redeposition by the transformation and reforming of the rocks and minerals on the earth's surface, in lakes and in the upper layer of the earth's crust.

Sedimentary rock Layered and deposited rock caused by sedimentation (e. g., dolomite, limestone, conglomerate, and sandstone).

Sedimentation The deposition and formation of deposit and layered rock by erosion forces such as wind, water, and ice and by precipitation from sources such as rivers, seas, and lakes.

Segregation Separation of the components of a mixed crystal.

Serpentine Serpentine rocks are weathering products that have been formed mainly by transformation from olivine rocks and are popular for ornamental purposes. Serpentine minerals, for example, bonamite, are used as jewelry stones particularly because of their similarity to jade. $Mg_6(OH)_8Si_4O_{10}$. D = 2.5–2.6, H = 2–4, n = 1.56.

Shelf banks Sandbanks in flat lake areas up to a depth of 200 meters of water. The shelf is considered to be a land shoal surrounding the land in a narrower or wider belt.

Silicates Compounds of the silicic acids (generally silicon dioxide SiO_2) with bases of which potassium, sodium, calcium, magnesium, iron, and aluminum are the most common.

Solid-solution series Minerals with different chemical compositions yet equal morphology and belonging to the same mineral species (synonym of isomorphous series).

Spectroscopic Refers to spectrum or spectroscopy. The spectrum is a range of colors that spreads out the colors contained in white light (spectral colors) side by side after refraction or diffraction (red, orange, yellow, green, blue, indigo, violet). Each of these colors corresponds to a specific wavelength. When white light passes through a colored substance, certain wavelengths are destroyed (absorbed), with the result that their loss in the spectrum leaves

behind black lines or bands (absorption spectrum) that serve to identify the coloring element (spectroscopy, absorption spectroscopy).

Sphalerite Uncommon gemstone (collector's gem) with the mineralogical name of zinc blende, yellow, orange, green, transparent with a semimetallic luster. ZnS. D = 4.09, H = 3.5, n = 2.37.

Spherulite Ball-shaped, radiating mineral aggregate.

Stalagmite Pillar-shaped formation of calcite (limestone) growing upward from the ground formed by drips from the roof of a cave.

Star gem Generally, gemstones with asterism, that is, with a star-shaped light effect.

Step cut Rectangular cut, mainly used for color gems (occasionally also for diamonds) in which the long edges of the facets are parallel to the edges of the rectangular table. The number of steps is generally higher than those of the top.

Syenite Granitelike, intermediate deep rock. Differentiated from granite by its low quartz content. Used as a building or paving stone as well as for ornamentation.

Synthetic Gems artificially produced by technical chemical processes by human hand and having the same chemical, structural, and physical characteristics as their natural counterparts (e. g., synthetic ruby). They differ from authentic gemstones in their inclusions.

Tetragonal Polygonal. The tetragonal crystal system in which all the forms are referred to two axes of equal length as the horizontal axes while the four-figure main vertical axis is either longer or shorter than these.

Tetrahedron Crystal form in the cubic crystal system delineated by four triangles with identical sides. The tetrahedron corresponds to the basic structural form (uniform cell) of the diamond.

Thorium Radioactive element; symbol Th; silver-gray luster, soft, ductile metal. Half-life of the isotope Th232: 1.39×10^{10} years.

Tiger's eye Yellow to yellow-brown, with silky luster, a gemstone variety of cryptocrystalline quartzes with cat's-eye effect (chatoyancy), caused by fine, parallel hornblende fibers pseudomorphed by quartz. D = 2.6, H = 7, n = 1.53.

Titanium Chemical element; symbol T; silver-white, easily malleable metal; trace element that determines the color shade in blue sapphires.

Transparency The degree to which a medium allows light to pass through it, often a degree of light transmittance.

Triclinic Triple angle. The crystal system with the lowest degree of symmetry. The three axes are of unequal length and are not at right angles to each other.

Trigonal Three-edged. The trigonal crystal system has a principal axis of threefold symmetry

BIBLIOGRAPHY

and three equal axes in a plane below 120° and crossing each other.

Uranium Radioactive element; symbol U; silver-white heavy metal. The basis for different disintegration series that serve in the science of mineralogy and geology to determine the age of rocks and deposits.

Vanadium Chemical element; symbol V; hard, brittle, lead-gray lustrous metal. Frequently a trace element that determines the color shade or is even a colorant in specific gemstones (ruby, emerald, tourmaline).

Variety Designation of the gemological system for deviating chemical and/or color types of a sort (e. g., aquamarine, morganite, and emerald are all varieties of beryl):

The gemological part

Austin, R. L., *Gems and Jewels, London,* Evans Bros. Ltd. (1979)

Bancroft, P., *Gems and Crystal Treasures,* Fallbrook, CA, Western Enterprises/Mineralogical Record (1984)

Gübelin, Eduard, *Inclusions as a means of gemstone identification,* Los Angeles, Gemological Institute of America (1953)
Gemstones, Berne, Hallwag Verlag (1963)
Die Edelsteine der Insel Ceylon, Scriptar-Verlag, Lausanne (1968)
Edelsteine, Silva Verlag, Zurich (1969)
Internal World of Gemstones, ABC-Verlag, Zurich (1974)
The Color Treasury of Gemstones, New York, Thomas Y. Crowell Company (1975)
Die Eigenschaften der undurchsichtigen Schmucksteine und deren gemmologische Bestimmung, Zt. Deutsche Gemmologische Gesellschaft, Idar Oberstein (1981)
Photoatlas of Inclusions in Gemstones, ABC-Verlag, Zurich (1986)

Heiniger, E. A. and Heiniger, J., *The Great Book of Jewels,* Edita SA, Lausanne, [»The Origin of Gemstones«, by E. J. Gübelin] (1974)

Kazmi, A. H. and Snee, L. W., *Emeralds of Pakistan: Geology, Gemology and Genesis,* Geological Survey of Pakistan and Van Nostrand Reinhold, New York (1989)

Kazmi, A. H. and O'Donoghue, M., *Gemstones of Pakistan: Geology and Gemmology,* Gemstone Corp. of Pakistan, Peshawar(1990)

Keller, P. C., *Gemstones and their Origins,* Van Nostrand Reinhold, New York (1990)

Keller, P. C., *Gemstones of East Africa, Phoenix,* Geoscience Press, Tucson (1992)

Legrand, J., *Diamonds: Myth, Magic, and Reality,* Crown Publishers, New York [»Clarity and Color«, by E. J. Gübelin] (1980)

O'Donoghue, M., *A Guide to Man-made Gemstones,* released in 1984 as *Identifying Man made Gemstones,* Van Nostrand Reinhold, New York (1983)

The historical part:

Abeler, Jürgen, *Kronen – Herrschaftszeichen der Welt,* Econ-Verlag GmbH, Dusseldorf and Vienna (1972)

Betschart, Pater Ildefons OSB, *Theophrastus Paracelsus,* Verlag Benziger, Einsiedeln/Cologne (1942)

Blakemore, Kenneth and Andrews, Gordon, *Collecting Gems and Ornamental Stones,* W. & G. Foyle Ltd., London (1966)

Biehn, Heinz, *Die Kronen Europas,* Wiesbaden (1957)

Bloch, Peter, *Köln und die Heiligen Drei Könige,* article in the »Neue Zürcher Zeitung«, edition no. 3188, July 28, 1964

Bulgak, L. W., Godovikov, A. A., Niedermayr, G.,

Smirnova, M.A., Tschistyakova, M.B., *Zarenschätze,* catalog to an exhibition at the Museum of Natural History, Vienna

Busch, Harald and Lohse, Bernd (editor) *Wunderwelt der Schreine,* UmschauVerlag, Frankfurt a. M. (1959)

Causey, Andrew, *Aachen relives glorious empire of Charlemagne,* The Illustrated London News, July 10, 1965

Coche de la Ferté, Etienne, *Antiker Schmuck,* Hallwag, Berne/Stuttgart

Edle Steine, *annual calendar for jewelers;* 1983, 1986, 1989, 1991, 1992, 1993, 1994 and 1996 editions

Feldman, L., *L'histoire fabuleuse des bijoux: c'est plus passionnant qu'un roman …* (article)

Frolow, A., *Les reliquaires de la Vraie Croix,* Paris (1965)

Gauthier, Marie-Madeleine, *Strassen des Glaubens, Relics and reliquaries of the Occident,* Office du Livre (1983)

Goreva, Olga W., Polynina, Irina F., Raimann, Alfons, *Die Schatzkammer der Sowjetunion,* Hirmer-Verlag, Munich (1990)

Guyan, Walter Ulrich, Schaffhausen, *Schätze der Region,* Union Bank of Switzerland Schaffhausen branch, Schaffhausen (1987)

Herm, Gerhard, *Der Aufstieg des Hauses Habsburg, Glanz und Niedergang des Hauses Habsburg,* Econ-Verlag, Dusseldorf (1993)

Hertzka, Gottfried and Strehlow, Wighard, *Die Edelsteinmedizin der Heiligen Hildegard,* Freiburg i. Br. (1985)

Hild, Hermann, *Glanz und Geheimnis edler Steine,* Universitätsverlag Saarbrücken (1963)

Hildegard von Bingen, *Causae et Curae (The art of healing),* published by H. Schipperges, Salzburg, 3rd printing

Hildegard von Bingen, *Sci Vias,* Maura Böckeler (1963)

Holzhausen, Walter and Kestin, Edmund, *Prachtgefässe – Geschmeide – Kabinettstücke (Goldsmiths' art in Dresden),* Verlag Ernst Wasmuth, Tübingen (1966)

Loubier, Hans, *Der Bucheinband* (1904)

Meen, V. B. and Tusingham, A. D., *Crown Jewels of Iran,* University Press of Toronto (1968)

Michel, W. M., *Die Inschriften der Limburger Staurothek,* Archive for ecclesiastical history of the central Rhineland (1976)

Morel, Bernard, *Un essay sur la grande couronne de Charles V,* Bulletin a.f.g., issue no. 41 (December 1974)

Oman, Charles, *Goldschätze aus Europas Kirchen,* Goldschmiede-Zeitung, (12/1983)

Rauch, I., Schenk zu Schweinsberg, E., Wilm, J. M., *Die Limburger Staurothek,* in »Das Münster 8« (1955)

Reger, Karl Heinz, *Hildegard-Medizin,* Munich (1984)

Schnitzler, H., *Zur Regensburger Goldschmiedekunst,* in »Forschungen zur Kunstgeschichte

PICTURE CREDITS

und christlicher Archäologie«, Baden-Baden (1953)

Steenbock, Frauke, *Der kirchliche Prachteinband im frühen Mittelalter,* Deutscher Verlag für Kunstwissenschaft (1966)

Steingräber, Erich (Editor), *Schatzkammern Europas,* (Authors: Pierre Verlet, Hermann Fillitz, Herbert Brunner, Joachim Menzhausen, K. W. Donava, Ljudmila W. Pissarskaya), Hirmer-Verlag, Munich (1968)

Vacha, Brigitte (Editor), *Die Habsburger* (Authors: Walter Pohl, Karl Vocelka), Verlag Styria, Graz/Vienna/Cologne (1992)

Wandruszka, Adam, *Das Haus Habsburg,* Herder, Vienna/Freiburg/Basle (1978)

Wilson, Mab, *Strahlende Steine*

Abeler Jürgen, Wuppertal: 153, 171, 172 (left)

Amt für kirchliche Denkmalpflege, Trier: 182, 207 (top)

National Archeological Museum, Madrid: 188

Archiv für Kunst und Geschichte, Berlin: 203 (left), 204

Argyle Diamonds, West Perth: 25

Baumli Othmar, Meggen: 201 (right), 203 (bottom right)

Carrieri, Mario, Milan: 190, 191

Christies (International) SA, Geneva: 55 (top)

Christie's Images, Long Island City: 192, 193

De beers London: 49 (6, 7, 13)

Dombauverwaltung, Cologne: 187

Cathedral Museum, Monza: 173 (bottom)

EMb-Service, Lucerne: 22, 23, 28 (1, 2), 29 (3), 30/31, 34, 88 (top right), 155 (right), 157 (right), 184, 185, 202, 203 (top), 207 (bottom), 214, 215, 226, 228

Germanisches Nationalmuseum, Nuremberg: 156

Giraudon, Paris: 49 (8)

Gübelin, Eduard J., Lucerne: 3, 6, 9, 10, 11 (center), 12 (top, bottom), 13 (top, bottom), 14, 17, 18, 21, 26, 27 (right), 28, 29, 33 (right, bottom), 35, 36, 37 (left), 38 (bottom), 44 (bottom), 45, 49 (9), 50, 52, 53, 54, 57, 58, 59 (right), 63, 64, 65 (right), 66, 67 (right), 69 (top, right), 70, 73 (right), 74, 80, 81, 84, 85, 87, 88 (center left, bottom right), 96 (right), 98, 99, 102, 110 (right), 111 (left), 115 (right), 116, 120 (right), 121 (top, center), 124 (3, 6), 128, 129 (top right), 131, 132, 135 (right), 136, 140, 141, 144, 145, 147 (right), 208, 209, 218, 219, 220, 221, 223, 224, 225, 227, 229

Hansmann, Liselotte and Claus, Munich: 65 (left), 92 (center), 162, 163, 174, 181, 195, 200

Her Majesty's Stationery Office, Norwich: 109 (right), 164, 165, 166

Hermitage, St. Petersburg: 68

Kunsthistorisches Museum, Vienna: 78, 157 (left), 158, 159, 160, 161, 175, 176, 183, 205

Museum zu Allerheiligen, Schaffhausen: 198, 217

Monuments Historiques et des Sites, Paris: 206

Naturhistorisches Museum, Vienna: 197

Peretti, Adolf, Adligenswil: 12 (center), 92 (top left, top right)

Preussischer Kulturbesitz, Berlin: 189

Rachmanov, Nicolaj, Moscow: 42, 60, 69 (bottom), 76, 93, 103, 106 (left), 110 (bottom), 111 (right), 125 (left), 167 (top, bottom), 168, 169 (left), 170, 172 (top right), 177, 178, 179, 201 (left)

RMN, Paris: 48 (1, 4), 155 (left), 173 (top), 196

Royal Collection 1998, Her Majesty Queen Elizabeth II: 166 (bottom)

Sachs, Traudel, Sobernheim: 11 (bottom), 19, 32, 71, 74 (top left), 75 (top), 88 (top left), 92 (top), 99 (left), 105, 106 (right), 107 (bottom left, right), 110 (bottom left), 117, 124 (2, 4), 125 (right), 129 (left), 213

Sevdermish, Menahem, Ramat Gan: 212

Sotheby's, Geneva: 51, 65 (right), 79 (right)

Steffens, Ralph Rainer, Mainz: 186

St. Peter Erzabtei, Salzburg: 154
Photo: Carl Pospesch, Salzburg

Tower of London: 49 (5, 10, 11)

Van Pelt, Erica and Harold, Los Angeles: 2, 4, 8, 11 (top), 15, 16, 27, 33 (top left), 37 (right), 38 (top), 39, 41, 43, 47, 48 (2, 3), 55 (bottom left), 59 (left, center), 61, 62, 67 (left), 73 (left), 75 (top left, right), 77, 79 (left), 83, 89, 90, 91, 95, 96 (left), 97, 101, 109 (left), 112, 113, 114, 115 (left), 119, 120 (left), 121 (bottom), 123, 124 (1, 5) 127, 129 (bottom right), 133, 135 (left), 137, 139, 143, 147 (left), 148, 149, 151, 199, 222

Victoria and Albert Museum, London: 55 (right)

Weibel, Max, Pfaffhausen: 13 (center), 44 (top), 107 (top)

INDEX

Aachen Cathedral 186
Abdurreza mine (Iran) 151
Abeler, Jürgen (goldsmith and jeweler) 173
Abu Said (Ruler of Granada) 166
Achates River (Sicily) 134
Achmed I, Sultan 161, 200, 201
Adula (Swiss Alps) 87
Adularescence 18, 19, 86, 87
Afghanistan 12, 13, 62, 81, 142, 166
Africa 12, 14, 24, 25, 48, 51, 86, 90, 146, 148, 165
Agate 130, 134, 216,
  Color change 228
  Decorative objects 135
  Deposits 135
  Formation 134, 135
  Inclusions 134
  Polishing 36
  Staining 135
Agilulf crown 109
Aichal mines (Russia) 51
Alabanda (Asia Minor) 90
Albero Montreuil 207
Albertus Magnus 157
Albite 44, 86
Alexander, Czar 84
Alexandrite 8, 10, 11, 12, 82, 84, 212
  Deposits 85
  Formation 85
  Mining 85
Alfred the Great, crown 163
Allochromatic coloration 17, 18
Alluvial placers 13
Almandine 17, 93
  Deposits 90
  Formation 90
Almandine garnet 18
Amblygonite 222
Amethyst 12, 17, 19, 22, 38, 104, 105–107, 206, 208, 210, 212, 214, 216
  Color change 228
  Deposits 105
Ametrine 38, 106
Amsterdam (Netherlands) 198
Amulet 206
Anakie (Australia) 58
Anay (Bolivia) 106
Ancient twelve gemstones 212
Andalusite 10, 222, 223
  Inclusions 218
Andamooka (Australia) 97
Andradite, deposits 93
Andranondambo (Madagascar) 12, 68, 70
Angola 51
Angushtary (turquoise) 150
Anna (Empress), Crown 169
Anthroposophy 212

Anyolite 114
Apatite 11, 13, 20, 22, 222, 223
April, see Stones of the Month
Aquamarine 11, 17, 21, 73, 74, 75, 208, 210 212
  Color change 228
Aquarius, see Zodiac signs
Arab (turquoise) 150
Arendahl (Norway) 103
Argyle diamond mine (Australia) 25, 51
Aries, see Zodiac signs
Arizona 90
Ärmland (Sweden) 146
Arpel, Pierre, Parisian jeweler 171
Artificial stones, see Synthetic stones
Aschentrekker 125
Asscher, Joseph, gem cutter 165
Asterism 19, 44, 57
Atahualpa (emerald) 192
Atahualpa, Inca prince 192
Athemstett, Andres, master goldsmith 194
Atherstone, Dr. W. Guybon 48
August, see Stones of the Month
Augustus the Strong, Elector of Saxony and King of Poland 176, 200
Augustus, Roman emperor 204
  Signet ring 204
Australia 10, 14, 25, 26, 27, 48, 51, 58, 68, 70, 71, 97, 98, 146
Austria 78, 81, 93, 117, 161
Aventurine (sun stone) 19, 86, 104
Avisavella (Sri Lanka) 110
Axinite 222
Aztecs 78
Azurite 10, 13, 145
  Blue azurite 13
Baboon mine near Karoi (Zimbabwe) 74
Baguette 35
Bahia (Brazil) 73
Baja California 91
Balas rubies (spinels) 108, 154, 155
Bamberg Cathedral 162
Banded stones 135
Barbosa, Heitor Dimas 125
Barite 10
Barkhaneh (turquoise) 150
Barmen 167, 169
Basileios Proedros 184
Belo Horizonte mine (Brazil) 81
Benito County (California) 222
Benitoite 8, 20, 222, 223
Berengar I, King 173
Beryl 8, 10, 11, 12, 18, 20, 24, 35, 74–75, 214, 216
  Beryl powder 215
  Deposits 73, 75

Formation 72, 73
Gold beryl 17, 74
Green beryl 17
Inclusions 219, 220
Mining 75
Star beryl 57
Biennais, Martin-Guillaume, Parisian goldsmith 163
Birthstones 208, 209, 210
Bishop Godehard's Codex, lid 182
Bishop Godehard's Gospels 182
Bishop's ring 205, 207
Bishop's ring with beryl and diamonds 207
Black opal, see Opal
Black Prince, Duke of Aquitaine 166
Black Prince's Ruby 108, 163, 165, 166
Blood stone 212
Bo Phloi (Thailand) 58
Bobrovka River (Russia) 92
Bocskay, Istvan, Prince of Transylvania, crown 161
Bohemia 90, 93
Boris Godunov, czar's throne 200, 201
Bosshart, G., gemologist 198
Botha, L., General 165
Boulder opal 97
Bow brooch 111
Bowl-cutting 36
Braganza diamond (topaz) 118
Brahamani group 46
Brasilianite 114, 222
Bratina (brotherhood dish) 176
Brazil 12, 14, 25, 46, 48, 73, 74, 81, 85, 86, 91, 93, 97, 105, 112, 120, 124, 198, 219, 220, 222, 223, 224
Breast decoration with a likeness of Czar Peter I 179
Breastplate of the high priest 212
Brilliance 32, 35, 40
Brilliant 163
Brilliant cut 32
Brittleness 20
Broken Hill (Australia) 146
Buddha statue 138
Bulfontein mines 48
Burbar (Colombia) 81
Burgundian court beaker 175
Burma ruby 64
Cabochons 36
Caesar 78
California 73, 94, 146
Cambodia 10, 64, 68, 71, 126, 129, 219
Cameo 37, 38
Cameo, antique 197
Campolungo (Switzerland) 62
Canada 89, 93, 140, 223
Cancer, see Zodiac signs

Cap of Kazan 167
Cap, Doge of Venice 152
Capital safeguard 222
Carnelian 135
Cassiterite 10
Cat's-eye 44, 82, 84
  Effect 19, 44
  Mining 85
Catalan (Uruguay) 105, 135
Catherine I, Empress of Russia 169
Catherine II; Empress of Russia 125, 169
Cavities 11
Centenary (diamond) 49
Central Selling Organization (CSO) 48
Certificate 229
Chalcedony 20, 38, 134, 214, 216
Chalchihuitl (green stone), see Jade
Champasak (Cambodia) 129
Chantaburi (Thailand) 58
Chara River (Siberia) 136
Charlemagne 154, 156, 159
  Bust reliquary 186
  Imperial crown 78, 154, 155, 156
  Talisman 206
Charles II, coronation crown (Edward's crown) 165
Charles IV, Emperor 186
Charles the Bold, Duke of Burgundy 174
Charles V, Emperor 173, 175
Charles V, King of France 155
Charles VI, Emperor 196
Charoite 136
Chatoyancy 19, 44, 82, 84
Chile 12
China 144
Chivor mine (Colombia) 80, 81
Chrysoberyl 8, 10, 11, 20, 84, 112
  Cat's eye 44
  Formation 82
  Mining 85
Chrysocolla 10
Chrysolite 214, 216
Chrysoprase 13, 14, 211, 214, 216
Citrine 12, 13, 17, 18, 21, 22, 38, 105, 107, 211, 212
  Color change 105
  Heat treatment 105
Clarity grading 50
Cleavage 20, 22
Clement VII, Pope 215
Cleopatra 204
Cleopatra mine on the Red Sea 78
Cobalt spinel 108
Codex of Bishop Godehard 182
Coins coupés 35
Collecting gemstones, see Gemstones
Cologne Cathedral 186

Colombia 8, 27, 79, 80, 81, 191, 192, 220, 221
Color 23
  Optical 19
  Physical 18
Color change 228
  Agate 135
  Citrine 105
  Tanzanite 117
  Zircon 126
Color creation, chemical 16
Color gems 42
Color scattering 18, 19
Composite stones 227
Condé diamond 49
Conrad II; Emperor 157
Consecration crowns 188, 191
Constantine Monomachus, Emperor of Byzantium 167
Constantine the Great, Emperor 154
Coober Pedy (Australia) 97
Cordierite 19, 223
Cordilleras, Peruvian 14
Coronation cloak 159
Coronation crown of Charles II, "Edward's crown", see Charles II
Coronation ring of Edward the Confessor, see Edward the Confessor
Cortez, Spanish conquistador 78
Corundum 8, 18, 20, 21, 56–57, 59, 67
Corundum Deposits 58
Corundum Formation 59
Cosquez (Colombia) 81
Côte de Bretagne (spinel) 154
County, Alexander 112
Cromwell, Oliver 163
Cross of Saint Andrew 179
Cross relic 206
Cross reliquary 184
Crown 152
  Alfred the Great, see Alfred the Great
  Andes, of the 79, 191, 192
  Bavarian royal crown 163
  Charlemagne, see Charlemagne
  Edward the Confessor, see Edward the Confessor
  Empress Anna, see Anna
  Empress Farah Diba, see Farah Diba
  French royal crown 154, 155
  Istvan Bocskay, see Bocskay Istvan
  King Reccesvinth, see Reccesvinth
  King Svinthila, see Svinthila
  Kunigunde, see Kunigunde
  Monomachus 167
  Queen Mary, see Mary

Crown insignia 163
Crown jewels, English 163
Crown of the Andes, see Crown
Crown of the Mother of God with the crystal grotto 191
Crystal lattice 23
Crystal structure 23
Crystal system 22
Cullinan (diamond) 49, 53, 165
Cullinan I (Star of Africa) 165, 166
Cullinan II 163, 165
Cullinan III 165
Cullinan IV 165
Cuprite 222
Cushion cut 35
Cutting shapes 33, 34, 35
Cutting style 34
d'Souza, Manuel 117
Danburite 223
Dandolo, Doge of Venice 191
Darya-i-Nur (diamond) 172
Dat Taw mine, Mogok, see Myanmar
De Beers Consolidated Mines Ltd. 48
de Boot, Boetius, Bohemian court jeweler 125
De Souza Mine, Merelani, Arusha (Tanzania) 116
Deccan plateau (India) 46
December, see Stone of the Month
Delong ruby 65
Demantoid 17, 18
Denmark 97
Diadem from Csorna (Hungary) 93
Diamond 8, 10, 18, 20–21, 22, 24, 29, 32–33, 40, 46, 48, 50, 51, 52, 53, 209, 210, 212, 216, 225
  Brown diamond 18
  Clarity 54
  Color 54
  Cut 32
  Deposits 51, 53
  Formation 51
  Green diamond 8, 18
  Imitations 227
  Inclusions 54, 221
  Pink diamond 19, 49, 51
  Raw diamond 53
  Synthetic diamonds
Diamond clasp with the Dresden Green 198
Diamond deposits of CDM (Consolidated Diamond Mines) near Oranjemund (Namibia) 26
Diamond powder 215
Diamond syndicate 48
Diffraction coloration 18, 19
Dinglinger, Johann Melchior, goldsmith 200
Diorite 11
Dioscourides, gem cutter 204

Don Pedro the Cruel, King of Castile 166
Drausch, Valentin, gem cutter 194
Dullam 27
Dürer, Albrecht 156, 174
Dutoitspan mine 48
Duval brothers 169
Eagle's Crown 173
East Africa 90
Eberhard of Friuli 173
Ediger, Czar of Kazan 167
Edward the Confessor
  Coronation ring 163
  Crown 163
Edward VII, King of England 165
Edward's crown, see Charles II
Egg of Naples (spinels) 154, 155
Egypt 38, 78, 142, 150
  Jewelry with scarabs 203
  Rings 202, 203
  Signet rings 202, 203
Eifel Mountains (Germany) 86
Eisenhower, General 71
Ekanite 114, 223
Elahera (Sri Lanka) 70
Elizabeth ("Queen Mum") 166
Elizabeth I, Queen of England 163
Elizabeth II, Queen of England 165
Emerald 8, 10, 12, 13, 17, 18, 20, 22, 24, 27, 42, 76, 79, 81, 163, 192, 200, 201, 204, 209, 210, 214
  Colombian 192
  Cut 35
  Deposits 79, 80, 81
  Formation 76, 78, 80, 81
  History 78
  Inclusions 76, 78, 219, 220
  Mining 80, 81
  Synthetic 226, 229
Empress crown, small 167, 169
Enhancement 229
Enstatite 10
Ernst the Iron (Duke), ring of 206
Espirito Santo (Brazil) 73
Ethiopia 97
Euclase 10, 11, 22, 223
Eugénie Blue (diamond) 48
Eugénie, Empress of France 173
Facet-cutting 32, 35
Fancy corundum 58
Fancy cut 35
Fancy form 34
Farah Diba 171
  Crown 171, 172
  Wedding diadem 172
Farida, Princess 171
February, see Stones of the Month
Feldspar 10, 11, 13, 20, 24, 88
  Formation 86
Felix, martyr 186
Ferdinand I, Emperor of Aus-

tria 173
  Emerald vessel 78
Figurine 38
Filabusi (Zimbabwe) 85
Finland 86
Finsch mine 48, 53
Fire 40
Fire agate 134
Fire opal 94, 96, 97, 98
Fire spinel 110
Firgamu (Afghanistan) 142
Firmness 20
First Star of Africa, see Cullinan I
Flame fusion method 227
Fluorapatite 10
Fluorite 10, 12, 22, 223,
Francis I, Emperor of Austria 161
Francis II, Emperor of Austria 161
Franklin (USA) 146
Franz Stephan, Duke of Lorraine 196, 197
Frederick August II, Elector of Saxony 199
Frederick II, Emperor 159
French royal crown, see Crown
Fuente de Guarrazar (Toledo, Spain) 188
Gabbro 10, 11
Gachala (Colombia) 81
Garnet 10, 20, 24, 35, 90, 208, 210 212
  Deposits 90
  Formation 90
  Star garnet 44, 57
Garnet-lherzolite 8
Gemini, see Zodiac signs
Gemma Augustea 204
Gems 37, 38, 197, 204
Gemstone cut 34, 35
Gemstone polishing 35, 36, 58
Gemstone washer 27
Gemstones
  Character 212
  Collecting 222, 223, 224, 225
  Color change 228
  Identification 218
  Imitations 226
  Importance 212
  Inclusions 218, 219, 220, 221
  Jewel trade 229
  Medicine 215, 216
  Mining 24, 25, 27, 58, 59
  Research 218, 219, 220, 221
  Synthetics 226, 227
Geological formation 10
George III, King of England 165
George V, King of England 165
George VI, King of England 165
German emperor's crown 90, 156
Gesner, Conrad (doctor, natural historian and theologian) 214
Gessler's hat 152

Ghundao mine (Pakistan) 120
Gisela, daughter of Louis the Pious 173
Glyptography 37, 38
Goethe, Johann Wolfgang von 206
Golconda (India) 46
Gold beryl, see Beryl
Gold crown of King Reccesvinth, see Reccesvinth
Golden Fleece, 174, 175
Golovin, F. A., Field Marshal 176
Gondwanaland 14
Gothic treasure 188
Granites 11
Graphite 23
Great Table (diamond) 172
Green Dresden (diamond) 49, 198
Grinding 36
Grinding hardness 20, 23
Grosser, Johann Michael, court jeweler 196, 197
Grossular, deposits 93
Guiding star (gemstone in the imperial crown) 157, 159
Gustav III, King of Sweden 125
Habachtal (Austria) 78, 81
Hair ornament "aigrette" 69
Hanati hills (Tanzania) 14
Handling system 24, 25
Hardness 20, 22
Harlequin opal 99
Hawaii 103
Hawk's-eye 44
Healing power of gemstones 214, 215, 216
Heat treatment 228
    Citrine 105
    Tanzanite 117
    Zircon 126
Heinrich von Uelmen 184
Heliotrope 210
Hematite 20, 23, 223, 224
Henry II, Emperor 162
Henry II, King of the Irish, emerald ring of 78
Henry IV, King of England 166
Henry VIII, King of England 163
Hephaestus 202
Hercules 202
Hermitage, malachite room 144
Hermocillo (Mexico) 93
Herodotus 204
Hessonite 93
Hidden, W. E. 112, 113
Hiddenite 113
    Deposits 112
Hildegard von Bingen 215, 216
Honduras 94, 97
Hong Kong 140
Hope diamond 49
Humbert I, King of Italy 173
Hunza valley (Pakistan) 13, 62, 111

Hutton, Barbara 138, 140
Hyacinth 214, 216
Hyllos, gem cutter 197
Idar (Rhineland Palatinate, Germany) 135
Idar-Oberstein 36
Idiochromatic coloration 18
Ikonostases Saint Isaac's Cathedral, St. Petersburg (Russia) 144
Illam 85
Imitations 226, 229
Imperial cross 156, 159
Imperial crown 154, 156, 157, 159, 169
    Austrian 161
    Charlemagne, see Charlemagne
    Roman-German 157
Imperial Gospels 185
Imperial insignia 156
Imperial orb 159
Imperial State Crown 110, 163, 165
Imperial sword 157, 159
Imperial treasures 159
Incas 78, 79
Inclusions, also see Gemstones, Agate, Diamond, Emerald, Ornamental Gems, Quartz, Ruby, Spinel
    Identification 219, 220, 221
India 14, 23, 36, 46, 48, 66, 68, 71, 73, 86, 166
Indicolite 122, 124
Indonesia 97
Industrial diamonds 51
Inkyauk ruby mine, Mogok, see Myanmar
Intaglio 38
Interference colors 18, 19
International professional associations 229
Inverell (Australia) 70
Iran 14, 109, 150, 151, 160, 171, 172
Iris quartz, see Quartz
Iron crown of Lombardy 78, 173
Irradiation 107
Irradiation coloration 18, 19
Itabira (Brazil) 81
Italy 93, 134
Itrongay (Madagascar) 89
Ivan III, Grand Prince of Russia 167
Ivan IV, Czar of Russia 167
Jacobs, Erasmus Stephanus 48
Jade 20, 138, 141
    Carving 140
    Cutting 141
    Deposits 140
    Imperial jade 138
    Mining 140
    Trade 140
Jadeite 13, 14, 138

Deposits 140
Formation 138
Jade necklace (Mdivani necklace) 138
Jagdalek (Afghanistan) 13, 62
January, see Stones of the Month
Japan 148, 223
Jasper 10, 134, 214, 216
Jean de Berry, Duke 175
Jerejemevite 222
Jewel of the Order of St. Catherine 178
Jewel sets of the Electors of Saxony 175, 176
Jewelry set "Spring" 42
John XXIII, Pope 206
July, see Stones of the Month
Kafubu Feld (Zambia) 81
Kallait, Kallelith 150
Kalu-Ganga River (Sri Lanka) 25, 59
Kane, R., gemologist 199
Karawanken (Kärnten, Austria) 117
Karoi (Zimbabwe) 74
Kashmir (India) 23, 68, 71
Katlang (Pakistan) 118
Kazakhstan 97
Kelani-Ganga River (Sri Lanka) 25, 59
Kenya 64, 58, 91
Kesselstatt, Christoph, Graf von 182
Kimberley glossion (Australia) 48, 51
King of Lahore 166
Kioo hills (Kenya) 86
Kirschweiler (Germany) 99
Kistna River 46
Koh-i-Noor (diamond) 48, 166
Kornerup, mineralogist 224
Kornerupine 224
Krüger, Wilhelm, court ivory and amber worker 200
Kunene (Namibia) 91, 93
Kunigunde (Empress)
    Crown 162
    Head-shaped reliquary 162
Kunz, George Frederick 112, 113
Kunzite 11, 22, 113
    Deposits 112
Kyanite 223
Kyaukpyatthat, see Myanmar
La couronne royale – dite de Charlemagne, see Crown, French royal crown
Labrador 86
Labrador coast (Canada) 89
Labradorescence 89
Labradorite 11, 18, 19, 21, 44, 86, 87, 88
    Deposits 89
Lacroix, Alfred, mineralogist 89

Laitakari, mineralogist 89
Lammenpää (Finland) 88
Lapis lazuli 12, 23, 142, 144, 203
    Deposits 142
    Mining 142
    Paint 142
Lazulite 20, 23
Leipzig fair 198
Leo VI (Byzantine emperor), votive crown 191
Leo, see Zodiac signs
Leucosapphire 57
Leydsdorp, Transvaal 81
Libra, see Zodiac signs
Liddicoatite-tourmaline 124
Liebmann, Ivan 169
Light 40
Light of the eye, see Nur Ul-Ain
Lightning Ridge (Australia) 97, 98
Limburg, St. George's Cathedral 184
Lincoln, Abraham 71
Lodwar on Lake Turkana (Kenya) 58
Longido volcano (Tanzania) 64
Lotter, Abraham, enameler 194
Louis VI, King of France 154
Louis XIV, King of France 196
Louis XV, royal crown 155
Luc Yen, Vietnam 13, 64
Ludwig III, Count of Froburg 198
Ludwig IV, Count of Froburg 198
Luster 23
Maaden (Iran) 14, 150
Madagascar 12, 14, 68, 70, 71, 73, 81, 86, 88, 89, 91, 93, 105, 112, 223, 224
Magic 206
Mahanadi group 46
Main growth forms 22
Maine (USA) 112
Maji moto (Tanzania) 81, 219
Maji moto mine (Tanzania) 80
Malacacheta, see Minas Gerais
Malachite 10, 13, 17, 23, 132, 144, 145
    Cat's-eyes 144
    Deposits 144
    Formation 144
    Green malachite 13
Mali 97
Mananjary (Madagascar) 81
Mandarine-spessartite 91
Marcasite 23
March, see Stones of the Month
Maria de Médicis, mirror 196
Maria Theresa, Empress 196
    Gemstone bouquet of the Empress 196, 197
Mary of Burgundy 174
Mary, Queen 165
    Crown 166

Mary, Queen of Scots 163
Maw-sit-sit 138, 140
Max III Joseph, Elector 176
Maximilian I, Elector of Bavaria 194
Maximilian, Duke of Burgundy 174, 175
May, see Stones of the Month
Mdivani necklace (jade) 140, 141
Mdivani, Nina, Princess 140
Medicine 214
Mednorudyansky near Nizhny-Tagil (Siberia) 144
Meetiyagoda (Sri Lanka) 88
Meionite 224
Merelani Hills (Kilimanjaro) 117
Meteor Stone of Krasnojarsk (peridot) 103
Mexico 91, 93, 94, 96, 97, 223, 224
Mica 11
Microcline (amazonite) 86
Minas Gerais (Brazil) 73, 105, 120
    Golconda mine 124
    Malacacheta 85
    Palmital mine 74
Minas Novas (Brazil) 112
Mineral assembly of calcite and parisite 221
Mingora mine (Pakistan) 26, 80, 81
Mining 25
Mining, ways of 28
Mir mine (Russia) 51
Mirror of Maria de Médicis 196
Miserono, Dionysio, gem cutter, Prague 78
Miter (bishop's hat) 159
Miter of Abbot Rupert of the Benedictine Abbey of St. Peter, Salzburg 154
Mogaung, see Myanmar
Mogok, see Myanmar
Moldavite 20
Mong Hsu, see Myanmar
Monocle 204
Monomachus cap 167
Montana (USA) 68
Moonstone 11, 18, 18–21, 22, 44, 86, 87, 88, 89, 209, 210, 212
Moor with the emerald druse 200
Morganite 11, 73, 228
Morogoro (Tanzania) 58
Muhammad Reza Shah, Emperor of Iran 171, 172
Müller, Johannes von, Swiss historian 152
Muso (Colombia) 221
Muso mine (Colombia) 8, 27, 79, 81, 220
Mwadui (Tanzania) 48
Myanmar (Burma) 12–14, 25, 66, 68, 73, 86, 103, 126, 140, 222–225
    Dat Taw mine 65

Inkyauk ruby mine 62
Kyaukpyatthat 71, 220
Mogaung 14, 140
Mogok 12, 57, 58, 60, 62, 63, 65, 71, 111, 221
Mong Hsu 64, 66
Myanmar rubies 62
Pyaunggaung 102
Yadana Kadè, sapphire mine near Kyaukpyatthat 70
Nabor, martyr 186
Nadir Shah, ruler of Persia 200
Naipa mine (Alto Ligonha, Mozambique) 74
Namibia 26, 91, 93, 222
Napoleon 173
Napoleon III, Emperor 173
Naturalis Historia, see Pliny
Nephrite 20, 138
Nero, Roman Emperor 204
New South Wales (Australia) 97
New York 90
New Zealand 140
Nicholas II, Czar 167, 169
Nonius, Senator 204
Novello (Zimbabwe) 85
November, see Stones of the Month
Nur Ul-Ain ("light of the eye", pink diamond) 172
Nuremberg 157
Obsidian 20, 224
October, see Stones of the Month
Old Egyptian jewelry with scarabs, see Egypt
Old Russian emerald jewelry "Spring" 76
Oligoclase (sunstone) 89
Oligoclase-feldspar 19
Olivine 10, 11
Onyx 216
Onyx cameo 204
Opal 13, 18, 19–20, 24, 44, 96, 99, 159, 204, 206, 211, 212, 227
    Black opal 97, 98
    Deposits 94, 97, 99
    Formation 94, 96, 97, 99
    Mine at Lightning Ridge (Australia) 26
    Mining 97, 98
Order chain (Collane) 175
Order of Saint Andrew Pervosvanny 176, 179
    Star 178
Order of St. Anna 178, 179
Order of St. Catherine 179
Order of the Golden Fleece 174–176, 178, 179
    Oath of allegiance cross 176
Order pendant 176
Orloff diamond 167, 169
Ornamental gem 23, 130, 132
    Inclusions 132

Orphanus, gemstone in the imperial crown 157
Orthoclase 21, 44, 86
Otto I, Emperor 90, 156, 157
Otto III, Emperor 159
Ötztal (Austria) 93
Padparadscha 21, 57, 59
Pahlevi crown 171
Pailin (Cambodia) 64, 71, 219
Painite 114
Pakistan 11, 13, 26, 62, 80, 81, 103, 111, 118, 120, 223
Palmital mine, see Minas Gerais
Panel reliquary 184
Panjsher valley (Afghanistan) 81
Panna group 46
Papal ring 205
Paracelsus, ring 206, 207
Paragenesis 12
Parsunen (miniature portraits of the Russian sovereign) 179
Pauzié, Jérémie, court jeweler 169
Peace Ruby 65
Pearl 212
Pegmatites 11
Peltzer, Zacharias, gem cutter 194
Pennar River 46
Peridot 11, 13, 17, 18, 20, 35, 103, 208, 211, 212
    Deposits 100, 103
    Formation 100, 103
    Mining 102
Peridotite 10
Permoser, Balthasar 200
Persia 166
Peru 14, 97, 224
Peter the Great, Czar of Russia 169, 176, 179
Pfisterer, Leopold 111
Phanerocrystalline quartz, see Quartz
Phenomenon gem 44
Philip I, King of France 154
Philip the Good, Duke of Burgundy 174
Pierre Turquoise (turquoise) 150
Pink diamonds, see Diamond
Pink quartz, see Quartz
Pink topaz, see Topaz
Pisces, see Zodiac signs
Pius XII (Eugenio Pacelli), papal tiara 152
Pizo Forno (Switzerland) 223
Pizzaro, Spanish conquistador 78, 192
Placer deposits 14
Placers 24
Plagioclase 86
Plaque crown 155
Platen, August Graf von 174
Pliny the Elder, natural scientist 90,

142, 150, 204, 214, 218
Naturalis Historia 214
Plush (USA) 86, 89
Pneumatolytic deposits 12
Po Lin Monastery, Lantau Island near Hong Kong 138
Polishing 32, 34, 35
Polycarp, martyr 183
Ponderosa (USA) 86
Popayán (Colombia) 79, 191, 192
Portuguese (diamond) 48
Prase 216
Prase-opal 97
Prasiolite 104
Precious color gems 42
Precious opal 94, 99
Premier mine 51, 53
Primary birthplace of gemstones 13
Primary gemstone deposits 11, 14, 24
Primary origin 25
Profile stones 36
Prometheus 202
Pushkin (Zarskoje Selo) 142
Pyaunggaung, see Myanmar
Pyrite 20, 23
Pyrope 10, 17
    Formation 90
Pyrope garnet 93
Quarrying 27
Quartz 10, 11, 20, 22, 24, 35, 134
    Crystalline 20
    Formation 104
    Inclusions 104, 219
    Iris quartz 18
    Phanero crystalline 107
    Rose 21, 107
    Smoky 12, 18, 19, 105, 107
    White 11
Quebec (Canada) 93
Queen mine (USA) 11
Queensland (Australia) 97
Querétaro (Mexico) 97, 98
Quetzal-itzlipyollitli (bird of paradise stone) 94
Quy Chao (Vietnam) 64
Ratnapura (Sri Lanka) 58
Raw diamond, see Diamond
Raw gem 34
Real, Felix, Liechtenstein gastronome 172
Reccesvinth, King of the Western Goths 188
    Crown 188, 189
    Gold cross 189
Recovery plant 28
Reflection of light 40
Refraction of light 40
Régent (diamond) 48, 155
Reidler, Joh. Jos. Anton, goldsmith 153

Reimer, Hans, enameler 194
Reliquary 183
Revelation to John 214
Reza Khan 171
Rhodes, Cecil John 48
Rhodochrosite 13, 14, 18, 130,
   146, 147
   Deposits 146
   Formation 146
Rhodolite 93
   Deposits 91
   Formation 91
Rhodonite 18, 146, 147
   Deposits 146
   Formation 146
Richard II 166
Richard of Cornwallis, King 186
Ring 202, 204, 205, 206
   Duke Ernst the Iron, see Ernst
   the Iron
   Paracelsus, see Paracelsus
   Prometheus, see Prometheus,
   also see Egypt
   Symbol of authority 206
Rio Grande do Sul (Brazil) 105, 135
Rock Creek, Montana (USA) 58
Rock crystal 12, 14, 17, 19, 21, 38,
   104, 107
   Inclusions 220
Rome 154
Rondé, L. and C. 155
Rosser Reeves ruby 65
Rubellite 122, 125
Ruby 8, 10, 12, 13, 17, 18, 20, 21,
   22, 27, 35, 38, 45, 56, 60, 63,
   65, 66, 163, 166, 208, 211, 212,
   216
   Color 60
   Dat Taw mine, Mogok 65
   Deposits 64
   Formation 60, 62
   Inclusions 64, 221
   Mining 63
   Queen Theresa's jewelry 65
   Siam rubies 64
   Star ruby 44
   Synthetic ruby 226, 229
   Thai rubies 62
Rudolph crown 161
Rudolph II, Emperor 161, 200, 204
Russia 12, 51, 76, 92, 93, 118, 125,
   167, 169, 176, 179
Russian czars' crowns 167
Saas (Switzerland) 90
Sabaragamuva (Sri Lanka) 58
Sagittarius, see Zodiac signs
Saint-Denis, Abbey of 154
Saint Isaac's Cathedral (iconos-
   tases), St. Petersburg 144
Saint Vladimir, Russian Grand
   Prince 167
San Carlos (USA) 103

San Diego county, California
   (USA) 112
San José mine (Brazil) 124
San Luis (Argentina) 13, 146
Sanarka River (Russia) 118
Sancy (diamond) 48, 155
Sandawana (Zimbabwe) 81, 85
Sanidine 86
Santa Teresa (Brazil) 218
Santa Terezinha (Brazil) 81
Sapphire 10, 11, 12, 13, 19, 20–21,
   22, 23, 27, 35, 42, 56, 57, 59, 66,
   67, 71, 163, 206, 208, 211, 212,
   214, 216
   "Astroline" set 67
   Color change 228
   Cutting workshop 70
   Deposits 68
   Formation 68
   Heads of Presidents George Wa-
   shington, Abraham Lincoln and
   General Eisenhower 71
   Heat treatment 227
   Inclusions 219, 220, 221
   Mining 70, 71
   Star sapphire 44, 57
   Yadana Kadè mine near Kyauk-
   pyatthat, see Myanmar
Sapphirine 10
Sard 135, 214, 216
Sardonyx 214, 216
Sardonyx of Schaffhausen 197,
   198
Saxony 97
Scale of hardness 20, 22
Scapolite 224, 225
Scarab 38, 203
Scepter, English 165
   Russian 171
Schleich, Hans, master gold-
   smith 194
Schneckenstein, Vogtland 120, 121
Schröder, mineralogist 222
Schwanenburg, Hans, master gold-
   smith 194
Schwegler, Ulrich, master gold-
   smith 194
Scorpio, see Zodiac signs
Scratch hardness 20, 23
Seal 202
Seal cylinder 204
Second Star of Africa, see Cullinan
   II
Secondary deposits 13, 14, 24, 25
Self-colored 17
Separation process 29
September, see Stones of the
   Month
Set of insignia for a Madonna group,
   Augsburg (Germany) 153
Shah Abbas I, Persian ruler 200,
   201

Shah diamond 172
Siam rubies, see Ruby
Siberia 73, 136, 144
Sierra Leone 51
Sigismund, Emperor 157
Signet ring 202, 205, see also Au-
   gustus, Egypt
Sillimanite 224
Sinai 150
Sinhalite 103, 114, 224
Skardu (Pakistan) 11
Slovakia 94
Smoky quartz, see Quartz
Smuts, J. C., South African states-
   man 165
Sodalite 23
Sogdianite 148
Songea (Tanzania) 129
Soraya Esfandiari 171
South Africa 14, 48, 51, 86, 90, 146
South America 14, 106
Sovereign hats 152
Spectrolite 11, 18, 21, 44, 86, 88
Spessartite 21
Spessartite garnet 90
Spessartite Deposits 91
Spessartite Formation 91
Sphalerite 18
Spinel 10, 11, 13, 17, 18, 20, 21,
   35, 108, 110, 111, 166
   Deposits 111
   Formation 109, 111
   Inclusions 111
   Mining 110
   Star 44, 57
Spodumene 20, 112
Sri Lanka 12, 13, 14, 23, 25, 27,
   57–59, 64, 68, 70, 71, 73, 85, 86,
   88, 91, 93, 108, 110, 126, 129,
   221, 222, 223, 224, 225
St. Dionysius 154
St. George, the "Dragon-
   slayer" 194
Staff, Johann, jeweler 17
Staining 135, 228
Star beryl, see Beryl
Star formation 19, 44
Star garnet, see Garnet
Star of Africa, see Cullinan I and II
Star of the Order of Saint Andrew
   Pervosvanny 178
Star ruby, see Ruby
Star sapphire, see Sapphire
Star spinel, see Spinel
Star stones 44
State crown, English, see Imperial
   state crown
State insignia of czarist Russia 167
Staurothek (Limburg) 184
Steiner, Rudolf 212
Step cut 35
Stephansbursa 159

Stone engraving 37
Stones of the Month 208–211
   January 208, 210
   February 208, 210
   March 208, 210
   April 209, 210
   May 209, 210
   June 209, 210
   July 208, 211
   August 208, 211
   September 208, 211
   October 209, 211
   November 209, 211
   December 209, 211
Stony Point (USA) 112
Streak color 23
Streak test 22
Stuart sapphire 163, 165
Sugi, Japanese professor 148
Sugilite 148, 151
   Deposits 148
Suppatt (Pakistan) 103
Svinthila, King of the Western
   Goths 188
   Crown 189
Swan Brook mine, near Inverell
   (Australia) 27
Switzerland 62, 90, 152, 223–225
Switzerland Alps 12, 87, 220, 222
Symbols of authority 152
Synthesis 226, 227
Synthetic stones 226, 227, 228,
   see also Diamond, Ruby, Emer-
   ald
Taaffe, Count Edward C. R. 225
Taaffeite 21, 114, 225
Talisman 206
Tamerlaine 166
Tanzania 12, 14, 48, 58, 64, 68, 70,
   71, 80, 81, 91, 93, 97 114, 116,
   129, 225
Tanzanite 24, 35, 114, 115, 117
   Blue 8
   Color change 117, 228
   Heat treatment 117
   Mining 116
Taurus, see Zodiac signs
Thai rubies, see Ruby
Thailand 10, 25, 58, 59, 68, 71,
   126
Theodelinde, Queen of the Lom-
   bards 189
   Crown 189
Theory of principles 207
Three Magi
   Relics 186
   Reliquary 186, 187
Thulite 114
Tiara 152
Tiffany (diamond) 48
Tiger's-eye 44
Timur ruby (spinel) 108, 109, 166

Timur, ruler of Eastern Iran 109, 166
Titanite 18, 225
Tolkovsky, Marcel 32
Topaz 10, 11, 12, 18, 19, 20, 21, 22, 24, 35, 118, 120, 121, 209, 211, 212, 214, 216
   Blue 118
   Deposits 120
   Formation 120
   Mining 120
   Pink 118, 120, 121, 228
Topkapi dagger 200, 201
Toughness 20
Tourmaline 10, 11, 12, 18, 19, 20, 21, 24, 35, 38, 40, 74, 122, 124, 125, 209, 211, 212
   Bi-color 11
   Color change 228
   Deposits 125
   Formation 125
   Mining 124
Trans-Siberian Railroad 136
Transvaal 12
Treasure of Guarrazar 188
Tsavolite 17, 93, 114
Tsavolite Green 8
Tunduru River (Tanzania) 58, 70, 129

Turkey 97
Turquoise 10, 13, 14, 20, 23, 150, 151, 209, 211, 212
   Color change 228
   Deposits 150
   Formation 150
Twelve, the number 212
Udacznaya mine (Russia) 51
Ukraine 97
Umba River (Tanzania) 64
Umba valley (Tanzania) 58, 70, 71
Umbalite 114
Underground mining 25, 28
United States of America, see USA
Urals 11, 73, 81, 84, 132, 144, 146
Uri (Switzerland) 152
USA 11, 12, 58, 68, 71, 75, 86, 89, 91, 103, 112, 135, 146
Uta book box 180, 182
Uta Gospels 180
Uyu River 14
Val Malenco (Italy) 93
Variscite 23
Vatican 154
Victor Emanuel II, King of Italy 173
Victoria, Queen of England 90, 163, 165, 166
Vietnam 10, 12, 71, 126, 129

Virginia (USA) 91
Virgo, see Zodiac signs
Vitzitziltecpatl (hummingbird stone) 94
Vladimir Monomachus, Prince of Kiev 167
Volcanic pipes 28
von der Vogelweide, Walther 159
Votive crowns 188, 191
Wadi Sikait (Egypt) 78
Wah-Wah Mountains (USA) 12, 75
Washing pit (Sri Lanka) 27
Washington, George 71
Water polishing 36
Wenzel, King of Bohemia 90
   Crown 71
Wessels mine (South Africa) 148
Wesselton mines 48
Winston, Harry, jeweler 172
Wittelsbacher (diamond) 48
Yekaterinburg (Russia) 93
Yevstifeyev, Ivan (goldsmith) 169
Ylämaa (Finland) 11
Yogo Gulch, Dry Cottonwood Creek (USA) 58, 71
Zabargad, Red Sea island 100, 102, 103
Zaire 48, 51
Zambia 12, 81, 91, 105

Zanskar Mountains (Kashmir) 66
Zermatt (Switzerland) 90
Zeus 202
Zimbabwe 74, 81, 85, 223
Zimelien (treasures) 159
Zircon 10, 11, 14, 18, 20, 21, 35, 126, 212
   Color change 126, 228
   Cutting 129
   Deposits 126, 129
   Formation 126
   Heat treatment 126
   Mining 129
Zodiac signs 208, 209, 210, 212
   Aquarius 208, 210, 212
   Aries 209, 210, 212
   Cancer 208, 211, 212
   Capricorn 208, 210, 212
   Gemini 209, 210, 212
   Leo 208, 211, 212
   Libra 209, 211, 212
   Pisces 208, 210, 212
   Sagittarius 209, 211, 212
   Scorpio 209, 211, 212
   Taurus 209, 210, 212
   Virgo 208, 211, 212
Zois von Edelstein, Freiherr Siegmund 117
Zoisite 114, 117